Civil Obedience

Critical Human Rights

Series Editors
Steve J. Stern ❧ Scott Straus

Books in the series **Critical Human Rights** emphasize research that opens new ways to think about and understand human rights. The series values in particular empirically grounded and intellectually open research that eschews simplified accounts of human rights events and processes.

When a human rights disaster unfolds under military dictatorship, such as the ruthless regime of General Augusto Pinochet in Chile between 1973 and 1990, the military perpetrators and their secret police agents are a key focus of human rights scholarship and activism. The victims of atrocity—including extrajudicial murder, mystery disappearances, torture, and sexual violation—are another legitimate focus. Yet the disaster and its legacy after democratic transition extend far beyond perpetrators and victims. In a work of extraordinary nuance and clear writing, Michael J. Lazzara exposes the interplay of civilian complicity with a dictatorship built on massive human rights violations, and complacency with socioeconomic continuities and lack of accountability carried forward into the postdictatorial period. The dance of complicity and complacency crossed a wide spectrum of civilian actors, including former leftists as well as conservatives who accommodated the new postdictatorial order and developed narratives of "mastery" that pushed aside ethical self-examination. This sobering reinterpretation of the Pinochet legacy in Chile challenges us all to consider how readily civilians slide into arrangements of consent and self-interest that turn the unacceptable into the acceptable, the outrageous into the normal.

Civil Obedience

*Complicity and Complacency
in Chile since Pinochet*

Michael J. Lazzara

The University of Wisconsin Press

Publication of this book has been made possible, in part, through support from the Anonymous Fund of the College of Letters and Science at the University of Wisconsin–Madison.

The University of Wisconsin Press
728 State Street, Suite 443
Madison, Wisconsin 53706
uwpress.wisc.edu

Gray's Inn House, 127 Clerkenwell Road
London EC1R 5DB, United Kingdom
eurospanbookstore.com

Library of Congress Cataloging-in-Publication Data

Names: Lazzara, Michael J., 1975- author.
Title: Civil obedience: complicity and complacency in Chile since Pinochet / Michael J. Lazzara.
Other titles: Critical human rights.
Description: Madison, Wisconsin: The University of Wisconsin Press, [2018] |
Series: Critical human rights | Includes bibliographical references and index.
Identifiers: LCCN 2017046340 | ISBN 9780299317201 (cloth: alk. paper)
Subjects: LCSH: Chile—History—1973-1988. | Chile—History—1988- | Dictatorship—Chile—
    History—20th century. | Human rights—Chile—History—20th century. | Collaborationists—
    Chile—History—20th century. | Collective memory—Chile.
Classification: LCC F3100 .L394 2018 | DDC 983.06/5—dc23
LC record available at https://lccn.loc.gov/2017046340

ISBN 9780299317249 (pbk.: alk. paper)

For **Julia**, **Ana**, and **James**—
los amores de mi vida

I think everyone involved, knows. . . . [And] because ordinary people know that [killing is] wrong, the human capacity for evil depends on our ability to lie to ourselves. Self-deception and cognitive dissonance [help to explain] how people are able to do things that are wrong.

Joshua Oppenheimer

Our willingness to become undone in relation to others constitutes our chance of becoming human.

Judith Butler

Contents

Illustrations

Acknowledgments

Throughout this book, words like *complicity* and *collaboration* carry a negative valence. Yet these words can also connote the professional and affective ties that bind us to one another and to collective projects whose impact, we hope, will ultimately be positive. Playfully, then, I wish to thank the many "accomplices" who inspired, supported, and accompanied me as this project developed.

Over the past twenty-plus years, Chile has become like a second home to me. I am deeply indebted to many colleagues and friends there who continually nourish my thinking and deepen my understanding. I will name a handful of them, knowing that I have left out many others: Luis Alegría, Jorge Arrate, Claudio Barrientos, Mónica Barrientos, Wolfgang Bongers, Eugenia Brito, David Bustos, Juan Camilo, Rubí Carreño, Ximena Carrera, Cristián Castro, Jeffrey Cedeño, Claudia Darrigrandi, Poli Délano, Jean de Certeau, Darcie Doll, Diamela Eltit, Rosana Espino, Nona Fernández, Carlos Flores, Ricardo Fuentealba Fabio, Inti Gallardo, Federico Galende, Milena Grass, Manuel Guerrero, Erika Hennings, Andrea Jeftanovic, Laura Lattanzi, Pedro Alejandro Matta, Pablo Morris, Patricio Navia, Cristián Opazo, Carlos Ossa, Tiziana Panizza, Leith Passmore, Carla Peñaloza, Iván Pinto, Isabel Piper, Eugenia Prado, Javier Rebolledo, Nelly Richard, Marcela Said, Alicia Salomone, Magda Sepúlveda, Macarena Urzúa, Marisol Vera, Gabriela Zúñiga, and the Gómez-Ortiz family.

In addition to colleagues and friends in Chile, others deserve special mention: Hassan Akram, Leonor Arfuch, Rebecca Atencio, Idelber Avelar, Manuela Badilla, Vikki Bell, Adriana Bergero, Fernando Blanco, Marta Cabrera, Pilar Calveiro, Alicia del Campo, Héctor Hoyos, Luis Cárcamo-Huechante, Ryan Carlin, Katia Chornik, Cath Collins, Verónica Cortínez, Juan Pablo Dabove, Greg Dawes, María de Vecchi Gerli, Lisa DiGiovanni,

Valeria Durán, Carl Fischer, Jean Franco, Antonio Gómez, Macarena Gómez-Barris, Katie Hite, Elizabeth Jelin, Gwen Kirkpatrick, Peter Kornbluh, Francesca Lessa, Cara Levey, Elizabeth Lira, Bernardita Llanos, Francine Masiello, Mabel Moraña, Paola Ovalle, Yansi Pérez, Jonathan Ritter, Ileana Rodríguez, Jorge Ruffinelli, Héctor Salgado, Valentina Salvi, Mónica Szurmuk, Diana Taylor, Heidi Tinsman, Vicki Unruh, Margarita Vannini, Erika Verba, Angela Vergara, Mariana Wikinski, and Peter Winn.

I am also grateful to many UC Davis colleagues who support my work and share the everyday conversations that make it better, especially those in the Department of Spanish and Portuguese (past and present), in particular Francisco X. Alarcón, Marta Altisent, Sam Amistead, Emilio Bejel, Leo Bernucci, Bob Blake, Cecilia Colombi, Linda Egan, Robert Irwin, Adrienne Martín, Cristina Martínez-Carazo, Rob Newcomb, Ana Peluffo, and John Slater. Additionally, I wish to thank colleagues in the Program in Human Rights Studies whose work dialogues deeply with mine: Marian Schlotterbeck, Chuck Walker, Heghnar Watenpaugh, Keith Watenpaugh, and Diane Wolf. I am inspired, too, by the insights and research of many students with whom I have had the pleasure to work in recent years: Renzo Aroni, Theresa Bachmann, Maureen Burdock, María Fernanda Díaz-Basteris, Emily Davidson, Emily Frankel, Manuel Gómez-Navarro, Erik Larson, Tania Lizarazo, Diana Pardo-Pedraza, Moisés Park, Sara Phelps, Arelis Rivero-Cabrera, Alejandro Rossi, Nicholas Sánchez, and Gustavo Segura Chávez.

Two New Yorkers had an enormous impact on this book and deserve special thanks. I am indebted to John Dinges for sharing his vast wisdom, sage advice, and invaluable archival materials. John provided me Mariana Callejas's personal, handwritten correspondence with Michael Townley, a series of documents that became the "smoking gun" for my argument in chapter 1. Michael Peppard, my great friend and fellow academic, came up with the title *Civil Obedience*. Everyone who has since heard Mike's/my title has loved it.

Thank you as well to Gwen Walker, editor extraordinaire; to the anonymous peer reviewers; and to Sarah Kapp, Sheila McMahon, Jeri Famighetti, and the whole team at the University of Wisconsin Press. Their professionalism, experience, and care for the books they publish shine through in the end result. Likewise, I am grateful to Steve J. Stern and Scott Straus, coeditors of the Critical Human Rights series, which I have admired for years and always knew would make the perfect home for this book. Steve's scholarship on Chile's fraught memory struggles has long been an inspiration to me, as it has for so many others. I cannot adequately express my gratitude to him for the careful, detailed, and learned feedback he gave me on my rough draft of this book.

This project has been a labor of love and a process of years. Without the support and encouragement of close friends, mentors, and family, I could never have done it. Mari Spira and Lupe Arenillas have been my *compañeras de ruta*. María Rosa Olivera-Williams has been one of my most important teachers and professional interlocutors, someone to whom I can always turn at any time and with any question. *Civil Obedience* also bears the traces of formative conversations enjoyed with my Princeton mentors, even years after graduate school, especially Arcadio Díaz Quiñones and Ricardo Piglia (whom we all dearly miss). Seth and Kelley. Uncle Jimmy and Aunt Sue, Kathie and Chris, and many others always told me I could do it. Aunt Pat, way back when my Spanish was rudimentary, gave me a lesson in her kitchen about the subjunctive mood. My parents, James and Virginia Lazzara, are there for me every step of the way, encouraging me to pursue my dreams and make a positive impact in the world through my work. And, of course, without the unconditional love of Julia, Ana, and James—who lifted me up every day when writing turned onerous— this book would simply not exist.

Shorter versions of chapters 2, 3, 4, and 5 appeared in the following publications: *Revista de Historia* 32 (2014): 17–26; *Radical History Review* 124 (Duke University Press, January 2016): 141–52; Francesca Lessa and Vincent Druliolle, eds., *The Memory of State Terrorism in the Southern Cone: Argentina, Chile, and Uruguay* (New York: Palgrave Macmillan, 2011), 87–106; *Rúbrica Contemporánea* 5, no. 9 (2016): 59–76; *A Contracorriente: Una Revista de Historia Social y Literatura de América Latina* 12, no. 1 (Fall 2014): 89–106; *Cuadernos de Literatura* 37, no. 18 (July–December 2014): 166–83; and *Bereginya. 777. Sova* 3, no. 18 (2013): 112–20. All the material upon which I have expanded appears with their permission.

My thinking benefited immensely from generous invitations to present earlier versions of chapters in places around the globe. Special thanks go to colleagues at the University of Manchester (England), Carleton College, Instituto Gino Germani (University of Buenos Aires, Argentina), Pontificia Universidad Javeriana (Bogotá, Colombia), Pontificia Universidad Católica de Chile, Universidad de Chile, Universidad Diego Portlaes, Universidad de Santiago de Chile, UCLA, Tulane University, and the University of Notre Dame. I learned much from conversations in all of these places.

All translations are my own unless otherwise indicated. For the most part, quotations appear in English only. However, in a few cases in which my arguments hinge on wordplay, I have provided the original Spanish as a point of reference.

Prologue

The Pending Debate on Civilian Complicity

My inspiration for this book was a gift that my friend Julio Oliva, a journalist, human rights activist, and leader of the popular justice movement known as FUNA-Chile, gave to me almost a decade ago.[1] Julio's father, a communist militant, was killed in a confrontation with General Augusto Pinochet's secret police in 1984. Since that devastating day, Julio, like so many other family members of Pinochet's victims, has spent years seeking redress for the irreparable suffering that the perpetrators of state terror inflicted on him and his loved ones.

While we chatted in 2008, Julio reached into his backpack and nonchalantly handed me a book he had written that bore the title *Informe Gitter: Los criminales tienen nombre* (The Gitter Report: Criminals Have Names, 2003), an artisanal publication meant to circulate hand to hand among human rights activists and concerned citizens.[2] His impressive investigation flew in the face of the government-sponsored Rettig Report (Gitter spelled in reverse), the official report of the Chilean National Commission on Truth and Reconciliation that in 1991 detailed the nature of, extent of, and historical context for the human rights violations that Pinochet and his collaborators inflicted during their seventeen-year reign of terror (1973–90). Incensed by what he believed to be the transition governments' insufficient efforts toward securing truth, justice, and livable reparations for victims and their families, as well as by the Rettig Commission's often-noted shortcomings—it refused to name the perpetrators directly or to address adequately the stark reality of torture as official state practice under Pinochet—Julio told me that he had written his book to *name names*, to "out" the protagonists of state terror, most of whom at the time remained shielded from judicial reprisal by the 1978 Amnesty Law and continued to live peaceful lives in impunity.

As I paged through Julio's investigation, impressed by blocks of photographs, long lists of names, and even state identification card numbers that seemed to signal to Chileans that perpetrators of egregious human rights violations might very well be living in the house next door to them, a section toward the end of the book especially caught my eye. It cited countless ministers, economists, judges, and other powerful figures who helped Pinochet both to consolidate his lengthy rule and to impose neoliberalism on the country by force. That barrage of names and faces, which included notorious figures close to the regime such as Sergio Onofre Jarpa, Hernán Büchi, Mónica Madariaga, Sergio de Castro, Jaime Guzmán Errázuriz, José Piñera, and a host of others, made me appreciate that for so long Chilean state memory had either understated or at times even outright ignored the crucial role that civilians played in aiding and abetting the dictatorship as well as in securing the long-term survival of its economic project. I imagined that this had been the case not only because defining complicity and condemning it (either morally or judicially) were exceedingly delicate matters for a nation whose transition to democracy had played out as a negotiated pact between the military and civilian authorities but also because Pinochet and his heirs continued to occupy positions of political and economic power for many years after the General ceded his rule to the center-left governments that later consolidated the transition, the Concertación de Partidos por la Democracia (Coalition of Parties for Democracy, subsequently called Nueva Mayoría, or New Majority).[3]

Seeing Julio's book prompted me to look back at the Rettig Report, official state memory's founding document, to see what it had to say about civilian complicity. My investigation uncovered a brief section in part 2, "Civilians as Political Actors under Military Rule," that calls attention to two "waves" of civilian supporters: a first wave composed of Catholic nationalists whose political ideas were inspired by prior authoritarian figures from Chile and Spain, in particular Diego Portales (1793–1837) and General Francisco Franco (1892–1975)[4]—a figure like Jaime Guzmán Errázuriz, Pinochet's most important civilian advisor might fit into this first wave—and a second wave of younger supporters, most of whom were under forty in the 1970s and all of whom were upper- or upper-middle-class professionals trained by Milton Friedman in neoliberal economics at the University of Chicago.

The infamous "Chicago Boys," many of whom emerged out of the conservative *gremialista* (guild-based) movement that Guzmán founded at the Catholic University (Pontificia Universidad Católica de Chile) in 1967, began supporting the idea of imposing neoliberalism via authoritarian means even before the September 11, 1973, coup. After the coup took place, they became well known for crafting a set of economic tenets, embodied in a document famously called *El ladrillo* (The Brick), that would then come to guide the regime's policy actions, most notably its surgical privatization of health care, education, labor, social security, and media communications, among other social goods.[5] Embraced by Pinochet, who saw in the young economists a vehicle for consolidating his power, the Chicago Boys, despite their differences, coalesced (according to the Rettig Report) around a set of "traditional liberal and democratic principles" cast with "an authoritarian slant" that would provide the basis for "rebuild[ing] Chile morally, institutionally, and materially, and [for changing] the attitude of Chileans."[6]

The Chicago Boys' ideas would later saturate the 1980 constitution — Pinochet and Guzmán's constitution—and would also come to undergird the country's social, political, and institutional order for decades thereafter. Throughout the transition and despite the Concertación governments' efforts to mitigate neoliberalism's blow to the poor by giving it a "human face," Pinochet's heirs would work stealthily to solidify the General's legacy by sacralizing hallmark principles such as "economic freedom, the primacy of private initiative, and the diminishing of the state's role" in the economy.[7] Even today the legacies of the gremialistas and the Chicago Boys remain firmly entrenched in the social fabric and have left indelible marks on the country's institutional infrastructure. This is why streets throughout Chile regularly teem with protestors fighting for greater degrees of equality and access to education, health care, a livable retirement, and other basic rights.

Situated, then, at a critical juncture, Chilean society currently finds itself embroiled in a bitter, ongoing struggle to break free of the dictatorship's imposed constitution while trying to determine a viable path forward. Still unclear, however, is whether that path will ultimately mean holding to the status quo, instituting reforms, or, as more radical voices espouse, convening a Constituent Assembly whose goal would be to pen an entirely new magna carta—a move that would place a vitally needed and perhaps definitive nail in the dictator's coffin.

The Rettig Report therefore acknowledges that civilians played a crucial supporting role during the dictatorship, but it does so in a manner that is on the whole innocuous and nonevaluative and that fails to hold civilians responsible for their knowledge of or contributions to human rights violations. This may come as no surprise given that the commission's restricted legal mandate limited its activities primarily to information gathering and suggesting concrete forms of reparation, while also making sure that the commission's work would not interfere with matters better handled by courts of law. Under no circumstances was the commission to take a position on specific individuals' responsibility for the human rights violations that occurred. Consequently, the report does not mention specific actors by name. Even more notably, it deploys overt language that downplays civilians' responsibility by blaming a generalized climate of deception and misinformation that, according to the commission's logic, made it extremely difficult for civilians—even those in Pinochet's innermost circle—to know the nature and extent of the human rights violations that were occurring. In its most accusatory move, the report credits civilians with promoting the country's neoliberal transformation, yet it avoids passing judgment on or even alluding to the many toxic effects that unbridled neoliberalism has had on society—the perpetuation of deep-seated socioeconomic inequality chief among them—or to question the role that civilians assuredly played in both passively and actively propagating state terror.

> It is not the Commission's role, let us repeat, to make value judgments on [all that we have stated to this point]. [We have provided this information] as a framework for understanding the role of the civilians who were connected to the military government vis-à-vis the issue of human rights and the DINA [Dirección de Inteligencia Nacional, National Intelligence Directorate] group. [Civilians] were no doubt somehow aware of the problem [of human rights violations] and of how harmful the group [DINA] was, but in general they did not have the means to deal effectively with the situation, and so they thought it would do more harm than good for them to [stop] supporting the military regime. Moreover, given the degree of [m]isinformation [that existed], it is possible that at some moments they may have sincerely (though incorrectly) believed that human rights violations had ended, or that they were declining to such an extent that they would soon no longer constitute any threat. Other civilians argued that their responsibilities were technical rather than political, and that concern for human rights was a matter for [which] those holding political responsibilities [should answer]. Some furthermore asserted that it was better and more productive to work silently through persuasion on a case-by-case basis rather than dra[w] attention publicly and [as a result damage] communication with the regime. Finally, some denied that any [human rights] violations [had occurred] at all and regarded them as propaganda, or contrariwise invoked the heated arguments of the pre–September 11 period . . . to "justify" any violation (*although to be sure they were often unaware of the true situation*).[8]

A careful consideration of these words quickly reveals that the Chilean transition's founding document promotes an official memory that largely exonerates civilians of responsibility for the regime's human rights violations. By placing the onus of responsibility upon DINA, Pinochet's first secret police organization, and by citing a climate of fear in which civilians were generally *unaware of* or *misinformed about* the extent of what was happening, the report is reluctant to attribute to civilians even an iota of moral or ethical responsibility for the support they gave to a criminal and murderous regime.[9] Perhaps the two notable exceptions to this rule are the judiciary and the media, though to differing effects and degrees of intensity.[10] If, on the one hand, the commission acerbically critiqued the judiciary, both military and civilian, for its failure to protect the rights of political prisoners and grant them due process, on the other hand, it pointed a subtle, though much less accusatory, finger at the media. References to the media focus mainly on the pre-1970–73 period—on how media sources of *both* the left and the right contributed to fomenting a climate of bitter political tension that eventually culminated in the coup. Regarding the postcoup period, the report mentions that the Pinochet regime frequently resorted to censorship to control the media's dissemination of information. On that point, responsibility remained squarely in the military's hands; never does the report allude to the *active* role that a civilian publication like *El Mercurio* newspaper, for example, played in supporting the government's ideology and repressive tactics.

It follows that for more than two decades after the Pinochet regime ended (the 1990s and 2000s), Chile lived a kind of uncomfortable tacit arrangement in which talking about civilian complicity was largely taboo. Unlike neighboring Argentina—and other postconflict societies in which the role of civilians has lately been a topic of open public debate and where civilians have sometimes even been convicted in court for their involvements with dictatorships, genocides, armed internal conflicts, and "dirty wars"—the particular negotiated conditions of Chile's transition made it such that civilian prosecutions were for a long time difficult, if not impossible, to achieve.[11] Only very recently— following the momentary memory boom that came with the fortieth anniversary of the coup (2013) and a series of noteworthy economic and political scandals (2014–present) that have implicated public figures linked to the dictatorship in financial crimes perpetrated during the transition—have we seen a growing interest in the topic: for example, the publication of a groundbreaking work of journalism, Javier Rebolledo's *A la sombra de los cuervos: Los cómplices civiles de la dictadura* (In the Ravens' Shadow: The Dictatorship's Civilian Accomplices, 2015), which has heightened awareness about the impunity of civilian accomplices.[12] Even more importantly, the Chilean Supreme Court in November 2017 at long last upheld the very first conviction of a civilian collaborator with dictatorship-era human rights violations. This watershed moment, with some luck and perseverance, may prove a harbinger of future convictions that could eventually signal a new chapter in the drawn-out saga of Chilean transitional justice.[13]

Books like Rebolledo's coupled with the first judicial conviction of a civilian accomplice are now beginning to *prove* something that we long suspected and perhaps even knew to be true: that civilians not only were *aware of* but also *did* much, in many cases, to contribute (by commission or omission) to Pinochet's reign of terror—much more, in fact, than the Rettig Report might lead us to believe.

A decade before Rebolledo's study, my friend Julio's *Informe Gitter* took a bold first step toward publicly vetting civilian complicity. Inspired by his lead, this book shares the conviction that *naming names* and deconstructing the contrived memories of countless civilians who stoked the regime and consolidated neoliberal hegemony remain pending challenges for Chile's protracted memory saga.

Civil Obedience

Introduction

Complicity, Complacency, and the Ethics of Saying "I"

Over the past thirty or so years, much of the work that "memory studies" scholars have produced has focused on the memories of *victims* and, to a lesser extent, *perpetrators* of egregious acts of political violence. Yet we know that the complexities of genocide, dictatorships, and armed civil conflicts defy facile binary constructions. While scholarship on victims' and perpetrators' memories continues to be of vital importance for Latin American societies grappling with the aftermaths of traumatic pasts, a new turn in memory studies—and an honest reckoning with history—requires that scholars now illuminate the many gray and morally ambiguous realms of experience that dictatorial regimes inevitably generate.

It is well known that the Pinochet regime (1973–90) radically transformed Chile and its citizens. To undo significant advances toward socialism that Salvador Allende's Popular Unity government (1970–73) effected, a military junta, supported by an apparatus of civilian, neoliberal ideologues and technocrats, as well as by the United States, turned Chile into a "test case" for neoliberal shock therapy. This shock therapy, as Naomi Klein convincingly argued, played out—quite literally—on the tortured bodies of revolutionaries and common citizens who dreamed of creating a more just and equitable society.[1] While tens of thousands of citizens were tortured, disappeared, murdered, or exiled, the stark and uncomfortable reality is that others benefited economically from their fellow countrymen's suffering.

Since the start of Chile's transition to democracy in 1990, the country has struggled to construct public memory and deal with the ugly dimensions of its recent history. Battles over memory, truth, and justice have been fierce—and the path long and rocky. Although scholars, activists, educators, human rights lawyers, and committed citizens have worked tirelessly to establish a culture of respect for human rights, it is also undeniable that silences, injustices, discrimination, and rampant socioeconomic inequality still exist. This is because Chile's transition governments, despite good intentions and tremendously noteworthy gains, have, in a broad sense, dedicated themselves to administering the neoliberal model that the Pinochet regime imposed and have not questioned it to its core.

It is no secret, of course, that civilians played a key role in upholding the Pinochet regime and advancing its neoliberal reforms. This role has been treated in the pages of books such as Rafael Otano's *Crónica de la transición* (Chronicle of the Transition, 1995), Víctor Osorio and Iván Cabezas's *Los hijos de Pinochet* (Pinochet's Sons, 1995) and Carlos Huneeus's *El régimen de Pinochet* (2000; English translation, *The Pinochet Regime*, 2007); satirized in the pages of the weekly newspaper *The Clinic*; and explored in recent films such as Carola Fuentes and Rafael Valdeavellano's *Chicago Boys* (2015), to cite just a few examples.[2] For a long time, however (and even now to some degree), Chilean society shied away from tackling the issue of civilian complicity analytically. Most books that touched on the topic were journalistic or informational in nature. Nor was the issue a matter of widespread public discussion in the country. Generally speaking, Chilean memory work did not concern itself with gray figures whose culpability or responsibility were not easy to define or whose connection to human rights abuses was often nebulous, indirect, or seemingly difficult to pinpoint. To a great extent mirroring Primo Levi's logic for the case of the Holocaust, the Chilean postdictatorship period tended to shun "half-tints and complexities," preferring instead a cleaner, Manichean rendering of history's "winners and losers."[3]

Consonant with such a binary approach to memory, struggles to achieve justice focused first and foremost on the military, the most obvious perpetrators whose symbolic condemnation was not only difficult to secure because of blockages by a still-powerful right but also a vital ingredient for a "successful" transition that might allow Chile's Concertación governments, haunted by the past, to "turn the page," "look to the future," and promote "national reconciliation." Moreover, throughout the early transition, to speak of civilian complicity was immensely difficult because many of the accomplices who upheld and promoted the General's neoliberal transformation of society remained all too present on the political scene. The media, as well, were (and are still) largely dominated by the political right, while many civilians who years ago supported the regime and promoted the dictatorship as the country's "salvation" from

Marxist degradation continue to hold noteworthy positions in politics, business, and other spheres. They vocally espouse their version of history at every available opportunity, even in the face of defiant opposition from large swaths of the population that are clearly disenchanted with and dismayed by things as they stand.

Given this state of affairs, this book proposes to explore in a focused way the nature, extent, and forms of complicity upon which today's Chile is built.[4] On its most fundamental level, it asks: Who are some of the accomplices, and what are some of the forms their complicity has taken? Yet the primary goal of this study is not to establish an exhaustive taxonomy of complicity. More than sketching a hierarchy of complicities and responsibilities, which would arguably always be incomplete and prone to refutation, my main goal is to attend to the narrative dynamics at play in the configuration of complicit subjects' memories. Doing this, of course, first requires naming certain complicit subject positions. But this, as I say, is only a starting point for asking the deeper questions that undergird this book: Given the myriad forms of complicity that dictatorships generate, what *fictions of mastery* shape complicit subjects' memories about Chile's "recent history"? Or put somewhat differently, what kinds of stories do complicit subjects tell to assuage the pangs of conscience or existential crises that their complicity inevitably generates? At the same time that I pose these questions, I also ask, in a secondary way, how other influencers of public opinion—for example, journalists, the media, and politicians—frame the accomplice figure, and to what ends. Pursuing this parallel line of inquiry opens space for me to offer some reflections on how Chilean society is dealing (or not dealing) more broadly with the reality of complicity.

At bottom, then, *Civil Obedience* sets out to decode certain complicit voices and signal the ethical complexities of their partial or self-serving acts of reckoning. Without ignoring that the theme of complicity has appeared at times in the work of fiction writers, particularly those of the postcoup generations, I keep my gaze decidedly fixed on reality-based genres (autobiography, testimony, documentary films, interviews) whose common denominator is the first-person utterance—the story of a life—that wants to be validated as "truth."[5]

Two Interwoven Arguments

A single book could never exhaustively treat the myriad complicit subject positions to which the Pinochet regime—or any dictatorial regime, for that matter—gave rise. For that reason, I plan to shed light on a limited, though heterogeneous, sampling of subjectivities that can speak in symbolic (and metonymic) terms to the *wide spectrum of positionalities* that constitute the gray zones of complicity with the dictatorship, on the one hand, and the neoliberal paradigm it espoused, on the other hand: specifically, complicit artists and intellectuals, the political right, economists, lobbyists, bystanders, marginal figures who were sucked into the dictatorial state's apparatus and became lackeys to the horror, and leftist revolutionaries who after the dictatorship underwent radical ideological shifts that plunged them into murky ethical waters.

All of these complicit civilians, in their own ways, have been "obedient" either to the dictatorship's violations of human rights or to the inequality-generating neoliberal model the Pinochet regime imposed, or both. In stark contrast to radicalized students, indigenous activists, families of the disappeared, members of human rights organizations, environmental and labor activists, advocates for sexual and gender rights, and others whose civil disobedience has long worked to attenuate neoliberalism's blow, the voices that concern me in this book have exercised instead a kind of *civil obedience* aimed at maintaining the status quo, while simultaneously striving to shield themselves, their privilege, and their self-image from harm. At every turn, they seek to render themselves invulnerable—an idea to which I return insistently. In so doing, they shy away from a fundamental concern for the "other" or the wider community. Owing to their lack of vulnerability, their narrative accounts, which are largely self-deceptive and self-aggrandizing, fail, in my opinion, to meet an ethical standard.

Two main argumentative threads run through the case studies I treat: the first historical and political in nature, the second literary and philosophical.

My first argument holds that Chile today, in a broad sense, is a product of *complicity* and *complacency*. On the one hand, we find the complicity of those who, via state terror, imposed (through the active or tacit approval of unspeakable violence) an economic system that has generated profound socioeconomic inequality—riches for some, poverty or extreme indebtedness for others. On the other hand, we find the complacency of those who endorsed and promoted that system both *during* and *after* the regime, either by inventing it or by administering it with implacable fervor. To study these two interrelated phenomena, I have chosen to focus on the present—Chile's present, "our" present—while always keeping a close eye on the historical forces that shape the here and now. My approach foregrounds how figures who acted complicitously years ago rationalize and communicate their experiences today. Because of this, I focus almost exclusively on texts published during the transition to democracy, that is, after 1990. But at the same time, I am also interested (particularly in chapter 5) in decoding the voices of a series of "complacent" figures: former revolutionaries who today are stalwart capitalists, who wield significant power, and who, since the 1990s, have played key roles in obediently managing and justifying the country's neoliberal turn.

I claim that while complicit subjects of the 1970s and 1980s created the conditions of possibility for today's Chile, complacent subjects in the 1990s and 2000s have contributed to propagating Pinochet's legacy by steadily nurturing the status quo and by espousing only incremental reforms. To be clear, complicity, as I conceive of it, implies *direct involvement* in wrongdoing (with varying degrees of agency and at either greater or lesser removes from actual crimes). Complacency, in contrast, means (through either action or inaction) upholding the status quo, resisting change, and acting in a self-interested manner, all the while attenuating or downplaying the foundational violence that led to the current state of affairs. Interestingly, if we return to the Latin root *com-placere*, we find the idea of "pleasure" bound up in the very idea of complacency. Those who are complacent are so because they benefited (economically or existentially) from the very system that the dictatorship created.

By juxtaposing these two separate, though related, concepts—complicity and complacency—I seek to fuel a bold reading of how Chile has become what it is at present: an embattled terrain in which the interests of students, indigenous peoples, women, sexual minorities, workers, and other groups advocating for equality and democratic change constantly collide with the interests of those who created the dictatorship, negotiated the transition, and feel most comfortable maintaining the neoliberal status quo. In so doing, I by no means wish to imply that complicity and complacency are equally egregious ethical conundrums or at all equivalent terms; in fact, they are markedly different and distant from each other on the overall continuum of complicities. Instead, as I explain more fully in chapter 5, I propose that the two phenomena, taken together, evoke *a broad spectrum of moral and ethical forms of responsibility* that beg consideration. The points along this spectrum may be clearly distinguishable from one another, especially when the distance separating them is great; yet it is vital to remember that they always exist *in relation to* one another, each never ceasing to occupy its place in the matrix.

Complicity and complacency thus feed each other like a two-headed hydra whose heads nourish a single organism—in this case, neoliberal rule. I believe that juxtaposing these concepts, without equating them, can prove critically fruitful because doing so allows the present to touch the past, and vice versa; it allows us to think about how certain attitudes and ideological positions that impede the abatement of today's socioeconomic inequality have their roots in the violent legacies of dictatorship.

My second argument, more literary and philosophical in nature, speaks to the ethics—or lack thereof—of complicit and complacent memory narratives. I hold that such narratives fail to meet an ethical standard because they bring us face to face with subjects whose autobiographical acts are generally self-protective and individualistic rather than selfless, vulnerable, and *for an-other*. Inspired by the theorizations of thinkers such as Emmanuel Levinas, Judith Butler, Shoshana Felman, and Michel Foucault, as well as by others who have thoughtfully considered the complexities of the first-person utterance, I advocate for a utopian conceptualization of first-person accounts as *acts of individual responsibility toward an-other* born out of a social responsibility to heed the other's "call" to speak truthfully and to assume any potential consequences that may stem from one's actions. Under optimal circumstances, to "account" for oneself, as Judith Butler asserts, means to heed a call to transparency and truthfulness in the interest of forming or strengthening community—that is, in the interest of a greater good that lies beyond the self.[6] It means rendering oneself vulnerable to another and a willingness to assume responsibility for who one is and what one has done (or has not done). In this sense, constructing truthful societies begins with truthful individuals being true to themselves.

But just as I advocate for a need for certain complicit and complacent actors to render themselves vulnerable through their speech acts—something they almost never do—I also want to suggest that complicit and complacent subjects' speech acts are perhaps best understood when we recognize that they are intertwined with the very structures of neoliberalism and its individualizing ethos. Contrary to the utopian conceptualization I espouse of what ethical self-narratives *might potentially be* (that is, self-reflexive, vulnerable, and for an-other), the complicit and complacent autobiographical acts I study in this book derive from and participate in the structures of neoliberalism in at least two ways.

First, narratives penned or spoken by accomplices can be understood as *products* attempting to compete in a varied landscape of cultural memory offerings, as accounts vying for acceptance on the societal battlefield of memory.[7] Reflective of this idea, it never ceases to amaze me that the shelves of Chilean bookstores, more than forty years after the coup, remain littered with narratives by complicit or complacent autobiographers who try to sell their versions of history and gain validation from their fellow countrymen. These voices dangerously sell partial histories, eager to connect with readers who will overlook accomplice figures' past "peccadilloes" and instead accept their normalized, present-bound versions of the self, however riddled those may be with half truths, excuses, and glaring silences.

Second, because neoliberalism—as a "normative order of reason"—commodifies *everything*, including forms of knowledge and self-knowledge, complicit and complacent autobiographers, interested primarily in bolstering their self-image, may very well be understood as instantiations of the neoliberal subject par excellence.[8] Products of the times in which they/we live and of what Leonor Arfuch has called the "biographical space"—that is, the "I"-obsessed culture that dominates Western, neoliberalized societies—complicit and complacent authors self-promote and, on some level, fail to heed a call to responsibility toward the greater community.[9] Instead, they are content to seek "buy-in" from readers via what Philippe Lejeune long ago referred to as the "autobiographical pact."[10] To push this neoliberal metaphor one step further, we might say that complicit and complacent autobiographers create self-appeasing fictions that they hope can "attract investors" and bolster their "figurative credit-rating,"[11] while at the same time doing whatever they can to fashion themselves in ways that skew their own attention away from certain anxiety-causing experiences and instead promote inner, subjective harmony.

What at first, then may seem like two discrete lines of argumentation—one historical and political, the other literary and philosophical—really have everything to do with one another. Ultimately, I want to show, using concrete cases, how social dynamics and narrative dynamics mirror each other: that is, how the neoliberal culture that the dictatorship originated and the transition endorsed has symptomatically precipitated a set of self-interested, eminently individualistic memory narratives whose "I"-centered nature forsakes autobiography's intersubjective dimension and instead reflects neoliberal rationality. In the end, what we find in the complicit and complacent memory narratives I study are first-person *marketers of the self*: writers selling a product they hope can compete with and speak louder than other products in the marketplace—products that, at the same time, attempt (probably futilely) to bring to these subjects a modicum of tranquility when confronted with the contradictions of their lives.

Having asserted this, I want to be careful not to push the marketing metaphor I am using too far so as to avoid its sounding trite or reductive. Indeed, the dynamics at play in all the texts I examine in this book are quite complex and driven by much more than a facile impetus to sell a version of the self. Complicit and complacent autobiographers, beyond their desire to self-sell, also seek to appease themselves, to mitigate angst in psychologically nuanced ways, to advocate for particular visions of history, and to offer versions of the truth that reduce potential cost (e.g., blame, suffering, shame, even possible judicial consequences) that might be imputed to the speaking subject.

In point of contrast to the instrumental versions of memory (and of history) that we find in texts by complicit and complacent narrators, I argue with Butler and others that what is really needed is candor and vulnerability: truth spoken in the name of responsibility toward an-other, in the interest of the collective, and with willingness to assume the consequences of one's actions (social, judicial, or otherwise). To be sure, those are the memories that will ultimately strengthen democracies.

A Vast Spectrum of Complicities

To speak of complicity carries an inherent risk: that of conflating all types of accomplices into a generalized, undifferentiated cast of characters whose acts of commission or omission are equivalently questionable. I wish to avoid such a risk and make clear from the outset that situations of dictatorship and extreme political violence generate a "messy moral landscape"[12] in which characters such as complicit intellectuals play their part alongside businessmen who funded the secret police, underlings who worked in detention centers, neighbors who knew of torture but said nothing, and common people who simply supported the dictator's mission in ways large or small.

Such diverse positionalities beg a series of difficult questions: How serious is the complicity of each actor? To what extent are individuals responsible for their actions during states of exception? When "systems" like authoritarian regimes or even neoliberal states exercise powerful holds on subjects, what spaces remain for resistance, moral action, and individual responsibility? If the lines separating victim, perpetrator, accomplice, bystander, and complacent subject can become easily blurred, at what point does complicity turn into culpability? And might there, in fact, exist a point at which complacency becomes complicity? Mindful of these questions' moral complexity, the case studies I examine seek to reflect on them in different ways without pretending to resolve them fully. This book, in that regard, is not meant to function in the manner of a court of law that adjudicates on every detail of each case, but rather it intends to stand as a signpost that can signal a set of complicitous political, social, and cultural dynamics that have contributed to the creation of today's Chile. I do this to decode how such dynamics manifest, are dealt with, or are silenced in complicit and complacent subjects' self-fictions.

New studies in moral philosophy have worked to advance a nuanced understanding of complicity and to avoid its inchoate deployment as a "catch-all term."[13] Chiara Lepora and Robert E. Goodin, for example, lay out a series of related terms—including conspiracy, cooperation, collusion, collaboration, connivance, condoning, consorting, and contiguity—all of which differ with regard to "the ways in which one is contributing, the extent to which one is contributing, the willingness with which one is contributing, and the extent of common planning among the agents involved" in the commission of a given act of wrongdoing.[14] As a result, all accomplices are not equally condemnable, responsible, or punishable. Some cases are clearer-cut than others.

Allow me to give two examples derived from this book that draw out this complexity. Sometimes, as I say, defining complicity can be a rather clear-cut exercise. The case of Mariana Callejas (chapter 1) confronts us with a woman who participated directly in the planning and execution of a notorious car bombing, that of General Carlos Prats (who opposed the coup and remained loyal to Allende) and his wife, Sofía Cuthbert.[15] Applying Lepora and Goodin's taxonomy, Callejas would likely be deemed a "conspirator" in the Prats assassination, and we would thus tend to view her complicity unambiguously, particularly because of its active nature: she was physically present at the moment the crime was committed and even played a role in the crime. We would consequently locate her somewhere toward the more overtly complicitous end of the broad spectrum to which I am referring.

In contrast, at the opposite end of the spectrum, we find other, more nebulous derivations of complicity—"conceptual cousins"[16] of it, in Lepora and Goodin's terminology—in which the subject's responsibility is far less clearcut. Consider the example of Hugo Zambelli (chapter 3), the gay lover of another direct accomplice to the Prats crime, Jorge Arancibia Clavel, an employee of DINA. Many years after the crime, when Arancibia's case finally went to trial, Zambelli brazenly lied on the witness stand to protect the man he once loved. Classified according to Lepora and Goodin's rubric, Hugo Zambelli might on first glance be labeled a "conniver": one who "overlook[ed] or ignor[ed]" an offense though without taking part in the plan directly.[17] Nevertheless, doubt remains regarding the real nature and extent of his involvement. We will never know for sure exactly how much Zambelli knew about the crime at the time it was committed. Moreover, his proximity to one of its material perpetrators necessarily raises concerning questions that, depending on the answers we uncover, might persuade us to construe his connivance as effectively complicit. In addition, Zambelli's repeated acts of lying (in life and in court) to protect his lover might also render him an accessory after the fact. The case of Zambelli is therefore instructive insofar as it proves that even when a causal link to a crime cannot be definitively established—and such a causal link is, at least according to Lepora and Goodin, a precondition for unambiguously defining complicity in the first place—other derivative forms of *contributory agency* linked to complicity may, to recall Anthony Appiah's term, cast a shadow of "moral taint" on a given actor or require that he answer for his actions in moral terms.[18] In Zambelli's case, staying silent or doing nothing in the moment, coupled with lying after the fact, might suggest that a simple conniver could under the right circumstances be deemed a contributory actor.

From a legal perspective, cases like Zambelli's (if we momentarily bracket his perjury) tend to escape prosecution because the law generally does not account for passive subject positions. If one cannot point to some concrete act that a given person has committed, then the definition of that person's complicity becomes less precise, less legally condemnable. The accomplice, as Gregory Mellema notes, is usually thought of in *active* terms, as one who "knowingly, voluntarily, and with common intent unites with another to commit a crime, or in some way advocates for the commission of a crime."[19]

Moreover, when it comes to civilian complicity (specifically), scenarios such as the "failure to prevent wrongdoing" or the silencing of that wrongdoing typically do not carry a legal burden of responsibility.[20] One noteworthy exception concerns chain-of-command situations: Article 28 of the 1998 Rome Statute of the International Criminal Court states that military and other types of commanders who knew about and failed to prevent wrongful acts can be held criminally responsibility for their failure to intervene.[21] Yet, from a practical standpoint, the sheer load that legally prosecuting "lateral" forms of complicity such as civilian complicity might place on courts would make the meting out of transitional justice a near impossibility. It thus becomes clear why transitional justice, and the law more generally, tends to be selective in pursuing complicit defendants, careful not to stray too far afield from the "most responsible" actors.

Recognizing the limitations and boundaries that the legal sphere imposes on defining and prosecuting complicity, Mellema adds that moral philosophers tend to favor a more capacious definition of the notion. For the moral philosopher, not only one who actively contributes but also "one who covers for a principal actor is commonly referred to as an accomplice."[22] Harking back to early, medieval reflections on complicity, Mellema observes that the conception of *what counts* as complicity has always been much more broadly defined by moral philosophers than by practitioners of the law and, in fact, even comes to include certain passive subject positions (or positions of omission) that usually fall outside the law's purview. He gives the example of Thomas Aquinas, who identifies nine ways in which a person can be complicit in another's wrongdoing: "by command, by counsel, by consent, by flattery, by receiving, by participation, by silence, by *not* preventing, and by *not* denouncing."[23] All these positions—even when not legally prosecutable—imply at least some degree of moral responsibility on the subject's part.

If we extrapolate all this to the realm of transitional justice, we find that the idea of moral responsibility has played an important role in certain contexts. The South African truth commission's final report, for example, ultimately acknowledged that moral responsibility runs even "deeper than legal and political responsibility."[24] In making such a claim, the commission in no way denied the necessity of political and legal responsibility. Nevertheless, it concurrently advanced the bold idea that a moral reckoning with certain aspects of the past (and present) is a fraught, though essential, task for societies struggling to come to terms with difficult and violent pasts.

While I admit, then, that the legal prosecution of certain types of accomplices may go a long way toward contributing to the health of postdictatorial societies transitioning from overt, state-sponsored violence—and should, for that reason, be enthusiastically pursued—I am more interested in this book in thinking about complicities (and specifically complicit narratives) from the standpoint of morality and ethics. Examined through this lens, I propose that complicities—no matter what form they take or degree of gravity they evidence (complicity, complacency, or any other number of possibilities)—always imply, or should imply, a responsibility to reckon and account for one's actions. When one's comportment has been ethically questionable in any way, a need to *answer for oneself* arises. How one chooses to do that, to heed the call to accountability *for himself* and *to another*, therefore becomes determinant of the ethics of his speech act.

Having said this, my conceptualization of complicity now demands that a further complication be addressed: that of *defining the wrong* with respect to which a given subject is complicit—a particularly difficult question for the Chilean case. As I mentioned earlier, moral theorists, including Lepora and Goodin or Mellema, seem to agree that for someone to be complicit with a wrong, it is first necessary to name that wrong prior to placing blame or assigning responsibility. Thinking in a similar vein, the philosopher Christopher Kutz usefully reminds us that complicity is, at bottom, a collective notion insofar as it "results when individuals [working together] orient themselves around a *joint project*."[25] To be deemed complicit, people acting in concert with a given project must meet certain minimal criteria that include a willingness to participate in that project and an acceptance (either tacit or active) of the project's mission. To speak of complicity with the Pinochet regime's "joint project" therefore begs asking what, specifically, the joint project was that the military and the regime's civilian collaborators were carrying out.

On a surface level, the answer seems clear. Viewed in its Cold War context, the Pinochet regime's primary, stated goal was to eliminate a perceived Marxist threat—often referred to by the regime as a "Marxist cancer"—from the body politic. To achieve the elimination of a perceived internal enemy, the regime resorted to torture, forced disappearances, murder, and exile; it governed with fear, stifled democracy, and severely curtailed freedom of expression. All these elements, to be sure, constitute major aspects of the dictatorship's project. But this project, as I have already remarked, also included the installation of unbridled neoliberalism and the creation of a constitution that would turn the country, upon return to civilian rule, into a "protected democracy" governed by an economic and institutional arrangement that would skew wealth to the top. If one accepts this second aspect—which, as I maintain at every moment in this book, is always already inseparable from the first—then the definition of the regime's end game and who was complicit in it becomes much more nuanced and open to interpretation.

An expanded definition of the Pinochet regime's "joint project" thus causes the spectrum of complicity to grow. That spectrum now ceases to include only those who bore some direct or active relationship to the machinery of state terror and comes to include all those who tacitly supported the regime and its violent uprooting of Allende's socialist project—perhaps by turning a "knowing" blind eye to the violence either out of fear or because of the benefits to be gained from doing so, or both.

In his famous essay "The Question of German Guilt," the philosopher Karl Jaspers grappled with the breadth of this spectrum by seeking to define *who* was morally guilty of complicity with the Nazis' project of National Socialism. Among the many specific cases he cites, Jaspers calls attention to that of Germans who thought certain aspects of Hitler's project deplorable but still managed to adjust their worldview to claim publicly that, despite the horror, "there was some good to it."[26] Jaspers's evocation of those who managed to rationalize certain aspects of the Nazi project so as to accept its overall "good" runs remarkably parallel to those in Chile who have repeatedly tried to separate the dictatorship's violence from its neoliberal "miracle" (see chapter 2). It reminds us of certain actors, such as those of the political right, who have repeatedly misappropriated or diluted human rights discourse to downplay the Pinochet regime's crimes. In the face of such contradictory logic, however, Jaspers correctly observes that one cannot accept the outcome of a violent regime without also accepting the violence that gave birth to that outcome: "The truth," Jaspers wrote, "could be only a radical 'either-or': if I recognize the principle [that is, the regime] as evil, [then] everything is evil and any seemingly good consequences are not what they seem to be."[27]

Consequently, we must acknowledge that even though complicity may stem from impossible choices (or perhaps from a lack of real choices at all), this impossibility does not relieve complicit actors of a moral obligation to answer for themselves after the fact—in the interest of society's greater good. My thinking on this matter ultimately sides with Jaspers, Hannah Arendt, and others who argue that *individuals* are indeed the ones who must be taken to task and compelled to answer for their various commitments. While it is possible to say—in a rhetorical turn of phrase—that, on some level, an entire country is collectively responsible for certain decisions made by the state, individuals are ultimately the ones who must respond for their own actions or inactions in any given situation or set of circumstances. "It is nonsensical," Jaspers observes, "to charge a whole people with a crime. The criminal [or the accomplice, we might say] is always only an individual."[28] And so, the individual must account.

Memories of Complicity

The act of saying "I" is shot through with complexity. Literary critics have dedicated reams of theoretical writing to the subject.[29] Given the vastness of the critical literature, I will limit myself to highlighting three operative ideas that have shaped my thinking on the matter and that are relevant to the readings I develop throughout this book.

First, the "I" who speaks in autobiographies, interviews, documentaries, or other similar genres is by nature a dynamic entity. The "I" performs a version of the self at a given moment in time, guided by particular motivations and with a specific, perceived audience in mind. The version of the self that appears on the written page or on screen tends to be less reflective of the speaking subject's private, intimate life (although elements of that intimate life inevitably seep into the narrative, either wittingly or unwittingly) and instead generally projects an "exemplary" self-image that the subject wishes others to validate.[30] We find that this tendency toward exemplarity manifests in much self-referential discourse despite the fact that, as Sidonie Smith and Julia Watson observe, the "unified" subject is, at bottom, a myth: "Readers often conceive of autobiographical narrators as telling unified stories of their lives, as creating or discovering coherent selves. . . . [But] there is no coherent 'self' that predates stories about identity and about 'who' one is. Nor is there a unified, stable, immutable self that can remember everything that has happened in the past. We are always fragmented in time, taking a particular or provisional perspective on the moving target of our pasts, addressing multiple and disparate audiences."[31] When one says "I," one therefore does so bearing witness to a set of tensions among who one was, who one is, and who one ideally would like to be. One also does so in an attempt to "figure" or inscribe a new iteration of the self in a particular context—always inevitably subject to the vicissitudes of memory and influenced by a series of mediating factors (historical, political, moral, institutional) that compel or allow one to speak in certain ways.[32]

In the specific case of the complicit and complacent narrators I study, all of them say "I" from the present of Chile's transition to democracy, temporally removed from morally fraught experiences or choices (of varying kinds) that left indelible marks on their subjectivities. Their present-day speech acts channel a desire to make sense of their lives, to bring coherence to incoherent experiences, and to alleviate difficult tensions between past and present. In doing this, they create "diversionary schemas"—whether they are aware of it or not—that shift their attention away from anxiety-producing realities.[33] Such schemas manifest textually as silencing, masking, forgetting, spinning, or justifying, among other narrative mechanisms, that aim to relieve dissonance within their psychic worlds. Despite all efforts at evasion or deflection, however, the "I" remains indissociable from a past that haunts it.

A second complexity that plagues self-referential discourse concerns the relationship between the speaking subject and "truth." Theorists from Michel Foucault and Paul de Man to Stanley Fish and Judith Butler, among countless others, have opined on this question, leaving us to ponder, as Ángel Loureiro once put it, that the "only truth we can expect from autobiography [is] the writer's belief in his or her [own] truth, but not truth as adequation to past experience."[34] If we accept that the autobiographer's truth is a personally motivated truth full of potential blind spots, then examining self-referential discourse necessitates that we work to understand, deconstruct, contextualize, and perhaps even counter the logics to which the autobiographical subject adheres. Smith and Watson astutely observe that "any utterance in an autobiographical text, even if inaccurate or distorted, is a characterization of its writer."[35] What should therefore concern us when examining self-referential works is to determine precisely *why* the subject of reference characterizes herself as she does and to think about that individual's truth vis-à-vis a wider universe of truth claims. Put another way, we might say (with Foucault) that one of the main tasks that the critic of self-referential genres faces is to understand the *technologies of the self* that shape speaking subjects and give rise to their historically situated acts of truth-telling.

If we accept these basic observations, it then seems necessary to signal a risk: that of accepting an autobiographical utterance as irrefutable simply because it "belongs" to the speaking subject and represents a set of experiences that are the subject's alone. If indeed the self-referential "I" speaks a truth that is his alone, then how can the subject of autobiography be held to any truth standard at all? In other words, if all one can expect from one who says "I" is a self-interested, personally motivated narrative, then is it even possible to speak of *ethics* when it comes to self-referential discourse?

This question leads to a third and final complexity, perhaps the most important one to consider when thinking about complicit and complacent narrators: the *intersubjective nature* of self-referential discourse. Judith Butler's thought-provoking book *Giving an Account of Oneself* (2005) has proved deeply influential for my thinking on this matter. Butler theorizes the autobiographical "I" as fundamentally relational, as a textual manifestation of a social being whose speech act arises, following Levinas's reflections, in response to a "call" from the other. She wrote: "When the 'I' seeks to give an account of itself, it can start with itself, but it will find that this self is already implicated in a social temporality that exceeds its own capacities for narration; indeed, when the 'I' seeks to give an account of itself, an account that must include the conditions of its own emergence, it must, as a matter of necessity, become a social theorist."[36]

Most of the time, as we know, the "I" speaks self-interestedly and thus does a poor job of fulfilling its role as a "social theorist" capable of discerning how its own subjectivity is both implicated in and responsible to the broader collective. Normally, as Nietzsche and Freud would have suggested, the one who is *called to account* for some morally ambiguous behavior tends to speak self-defensively, primarily motivated by a desire to avoid punishment rather than by altruism or a wish to contribute to the greater social good.[37] Butler, to the contrary, holds the autobiographical subject to a much higher standard. She argues that anyone who says "I" should approach the act of self-telling as an invitation to write or speak responsibly, in the interest of others more than in the interest of the self. Even though, as she admits, the speaking subject can never be expected to know itself fully—that certain aspects of the "I" will always inevitably remain opaque to it—this by no means absolves the subject of its responsibility to probe that opacity and consider the contradictions inherent in its own *coming into being* as a subject. "From the outset," Butler states, "what relation the self will take to itself, how it will craft itself in response to an injunction [the other's call], how it will form itself, and what labor it will perform upon itself is a challenge if not an open question."[38] How the "I" heeds that challenge therefore ultimately serves as the litmus test against which we must measure its act of truth-telling.

Consequently, the "I," who speaks ethically, for Butler, is not the "I" who pretends to communicate his or her life in a finished or polished form but rather one who acknowledges that one can never fully know or understand oneself. Nevertheless, the "I" does everything it can—out of responsibility to another—to narrate the conditions of its own life critically, vulnerably, reflexively, and in a manner that others might deem something other than self-interested. To make oneself vulnerable, that is, to be willing to probe one's contradictions as a subject, is thus key to understanding the ethics of saying "I."

A concept of self-referential discourse steeped in the notion of *vulnerability* can serve as an invitation to combat certain kinds of "individualistic doctrines" (such as neoliberalism in this case) that are more preoccupied with "praising the rights of the 'I'" than with thinking about the ways in which human beings are and must remain responsible to/for one another. Rendering ourselves vulnerable makes us feel uncomfortable. It is certainly easier to recoil into invulnerability and protect oneself at all costs. But this book claims, in concert with the ideas of Butler and other thinkers, that to account for oneself must imply a willingness to pay a price—to break out of "excessive individualism"[39] (a patently liberal ideal)—and instead seize upon the autobiographical impetus as an invitation to ask how the "I," when it speaks, can and should fulfill its responsibility to the other and to greater society.

In the case of complicit subjects who played particularly noteworthy roles in stoking or perpetuating state-sponsored forms of violence, to do anything other than render themselves vulnerable is, in a sense, to subject the social body to a further act of violence by deepening a wound in its historical memory.

Chapter Overview

Throughout Chile's transition to democracy, a number of prominent figures—either direct accomplices or ideologically metamorphosed, complacent subjects—have produced life narratives that seek to justify their actions vis-à-vis the neoliberal present. The five chapters that comprise this book work with a carefully selected corpus of such self-referential texts with the goal of unpacking the instability of first-person narrators who bear witness to their lives partially, interestedly, or in a contrived manner. An epilogue then reads this phenomenon *outward* to think about complicity in a more global key.

The life narratives I study, uttered by subjects hailing from different spheres of society, bring into relief—like a societal X-ray—aspects of the broad spectrum of complicities that I described earlier. With an eye toward the variegated nature of that spectrum, each discrete analysis seeks to highlight the complex, selective processes of self-articulation and negotiation that complicit or complacent memory-texts evince: denial, silence, self-aggrandizement, mitigation of shame, self-justification, manipulations of all kinds, pseudo-confessions, cover-ups, and so on. In every case, I think about these subjects' acts of truth-telling with an eye toward ethics, considering how they might be read in relation to concepts such as avowal or disavowal, vulnerability or invulnerability, and responsibility.

Chapter 1, "Fictions of Mastery (Mariana Callejas)," encapsulates and theorizes one of the book's main arguments: that complicit subjects proffer fictions of mastery in an attempt to "normalize" themselves and their actions and that, when they do so, their self-defensive narratives fail to meet an ethical standard. To draw out the subtleties of this argument, I focus on an intriguing figure taken from the intellectual-cultural realm: Mariana Callejas, a literary writer who married the American-born DINA henchman Michael Townley, infamous for his complicity in the deaths of Eduardo Frei Montalva (a former president), Orlando Letelier (a government minister during the Popular Unity years), and General Carlos Prats (a general loyal to Allende). Callejas played direct roles in the Prats and Letelier crimes and even served a brief jail sentence for her complicity in the Prats assassination.

My analysis paints a portrait of Callejas as an ideological chameleon—she claims to have been a leftist in the 1960s, a rightist in the 1970s and 1980s, and a moderate in the 1990s and 2000s—and reads her autobiographical account *Siembra vientos* (You Reap What You Sow, 1995) in counterpoint to the fiction she wrote in the 1980s, in particular an intriguing short story collection titled *La larga noche* (The Long Night, 1981). I claim that Callejas's secret shame can be found buried within the structure of her fiction and that this masked shame offers a window onto subconscious anxieties that her autobiographical account, written ten years later, blocks out. Any acknowledgment of responsibility on Callejas's part—which might serve as the key to a genuine, transparent, honorable accounting in the interest of the collective—is entirely absent from her autobiographical act.

If Callejas serves as a rare example of a complicit subject who appears to feel some degree of shame, others appear shameless or even boastful about their participation in Pinochet's "salvation" of Chile from Marxist tyranny. Chapter 2, "Specters of Jaime Guzmán (Pablo Longueira Montes, Sergio de Castro, Ignacio Santa Cruz)," explores how several figures who have political or familial links to the founder of the Unión Democrática Independiente (Independent Democratic Union, UDI), Jaime Guzmán Errázuriz, have grappled with his ghost and with the vexing tension between the dictatorship's human rights violations and its neoliberal "counterrevolution."

The chapter juxtaposes three cultural objects. The first, Pablo Longueira's *Mi testimonio de fe* (My Profession of Faith, 2003), is, at its core, a dialogue with Guzmán's specter in which that ghost is actualized and instrumentalized to confront a profound crisis of legitimacy that the ultra-right UDI party, of which Longueira was a founding member, was starting to face in the early

2000s. To divert public attention from political scandal, Longueira's book, autobiographical at its core, deifies Jaime Guzmán while also manipulating Guzmán's figure to justify UDI's (curious) initiation of a dialogue on economic reparations with the families of the disappeared. My reading emphasizes the evasiveness undergirding Longueira's autobiographical act.

To follow up on and add new layers to Longueira's "salvific" reading of Guzmán, I then turn to Carola Fuentes and Rafael Valdeavellano's film *Chicago Boys* (2015), in which five prominent Chicago-trained economists, most prominently Sergio de Castro (who became a key ally to Guzmán), talk about their lives and defend their participation in the dictatorship's neoliberalizing mission. I argue that the economists' memories dramatically channel what the sociologists Kathya Araujo and Danilo Martucelli call *homo neoliberal*: the "new" Chilean citizen who stakes his identity primarily on individualism, competition, and the capacity to acquire material goods and less on an awareness of his role in or responsibility toward the collective. To become *homo neoliberal*, for the protagonists of *Chicago Boys*, serves as another kind of self-defensive mask that conveniently allows them to skirt the core violence, the "state of exception," that made their lives "exceptional" in the first place. Put differently, they are the exceptional beings whose imposed state of exception ultimately made Chile exceptional—or so their story goes. As in the cases of other complicit or complacent subjects whom I study in this book, a key to understanding de Castro's and the other Chicago Boys' memories hinges on the *depoliticizing* of their subjectivities. Their fiction of mastery is to portray themselves as altruistic neoliberals and *not* as ideologues or participants in a vast machinery of state terror.

The chapter's final section analyzes the film *El tío* (My Uncle, 2013), directed by Mateo Iribarren and produced by Guzmán's own nephew, Ignacio Santa Cruz. The movie, which casts Santa Cruz in the role of his controversial uncle, stages a fascinating metacinematic process in which a member of Guzmán's own family, who was only eleven years old when Guzmán was assassinated by a leftist insurgency group, tries to come to terms with who his uncle was and with the ways in which his uncle's ideas transformed Chile. If indeed *El tío* offers a fascinating intergenerational counterpoint to Longueira's narrative and goes much further toward a true "accounting" (Butler), in the end it (perhaps somewhat predictably) proves unwilling to betray Guzmán's ghost.

In sum, three "dialogues" (implicit or explicit) with Jaime Guzmán's specter by three figures from different generations—two *of* the pinochetista right, the other a familial descendant of it who is trying to break free of its legacy—yield instrumental (though *differently* instrumental) uses of that ghost, of the self, and of the very notion of human rights.

Having looked in the first two chapters at the complicities of culture workers, economists, and the right-wing political class and its heirs—all of them identifiable public figures—chapter 3, "Boundedness and Vulnerability (Hugo Zambelli)," turns attention to a minor figure, a passive accomplice and "bystander" (actually Argentine by nationality) whose relationship to the Pinochet regime's violence is "by association." Of course, there are almost no written accounts in Chile that deal with the complicity of average people: the bystanders who erred by omission, either through silence or by overtly covering up the crimes of others. This chapter attempts to touch on the topic via a reading of the Chilean writer Diamela Eltit's nonfiction book *Puño y letra: Juicio oral* (In My Own Handwriting: An Oral Trial, 2005), an investigative project dealing with the 1974 assassination in Buenos Aires of Chilean general Carlos Prats and his wife, Sofía Cuthbert.

The book's centerpiece is an elliptical and falsified legal deposition given by Hugo Zambelli, the Argentine gay lover of Enrique Arancibia Clavel, a Chilean man who was tried in Buenos Aires in 2000 as a co-conspirator in the Prats assassination plot. My reading of Eltit's book focuses on her selection of a marginal character (Zambelli) as a representative voice through which to interrogate the theatricality of the juridical "scene," in the style of Hannah Arendt's *Eichmann in Jerusalem* (1963). Eltit spent months observing Arancibia's trial in Buenos Aires, much as Arendt witnessed Eichmann's trial. Throughout my analysis, I focus on what I call the "boundedness" of Zambelli's discourse: he was a fearful subject who tried to protect himself and his partner from judicial reprisal at all costs. In contrast to the boundedness of Zambelli's deposition, I explore various strategies through which Eltit signals a need for the complicit subject to render himself vulnerable. Doing this allows me to explain more fully how I understand vulnerability in relation to this book's central arguments.

Following up on my analysis of the bystander figure, chapter 4, "Framing the Accomplice (Jorgelino Vergara)," looks at the complicity of a poor Chilean man whose life circumstances and desire to earn a living led him to work within the apparatus of state terror. Jorgelino Vergara, known in Chile as "El Mocito" (The Little Butler), served coffee as an adolescent to the former head of Pinochet's secret police, General Manuel Contreras, and later carried out horrifying tasks in the notorious torture center located at 8800 Simón Bolívar Street, in Santiago. Falsely accused in 2007 of killing the well-known Communist leader Víctor Díaz, Vergara emerged from a clandestine life and testified in court to clear his name. How did Vergara construct his truth? How did Chilean society, forty years after the coup, frame and understand this truth? My analysis seeks to answer these questions by comparing several representations of "El Mocito" in film (Marcela Said and Jean de Certeau's *El Mocito*,

2010); in print journalism (Javier Rebolledo's *La danza de los cuervos* [The Dance of the Ravens], 2012); and on television (Tomás Mosciatti's interview with Vergara on CNN Chile, 2012; Jean-Philippe Cretton's interview with him on *Mentiras verdaderas* [True Lies], 2013; and the Australian journalist Sally Sara's interview with him on ABC News Australia, 2013). Multiple framings of Vergara in different genres yield radically different uses and abuses of the accomplice figure ranging from balanced representation to reconciliatory framings to outright exploitation of a "popular" subject who was seduced by fascist ideology.

To close out the book, chapter 5, "Complacent Subjects (Max Marambio, Eugenio Tironi, Marco Enríquez-Ominami)," focuses on specific actors whose morally ambiguous character is bound up in the subjective metamorphoses they have undergone. I start by examining self-representations by two "complacent" autobiographers, Max Marambio (a former militant of MIR [Movimiento de Izquierda Revolucionaria], Leftist Revolutionary Movement) and Eugenio Tironi (a former militant of MAPU [Movimiento de Acción Popular Unitaria], Popular Unitary Action Movement), both of whom advocated for armed struggle in the 1970s but who have since abandoned their former radicalized positions and become what in Chile today are known as "renovated leftists," that is, leftists who embrace the neoliberal free market. Marambio, for example, is now a financier and one of the richest men in Chile; Tironi is a sociologist and a lobbyist who owns his own public relations firm. Through readings of Marambio's *Las armas de ayer* (The Arms of Yesterday, 2008) and Tironi's *Crónica de viaje: Chile y la ruta a la felicidad* (Chronicle of a Journey: Chile and the Road to Happiness, 2006), I explore how these complacent subjects narrate and justify their ideological shift. I read both of these books as attempts by former advocates of armed struggle to normalize (and contextualize) their revolutionary "I" so that it can thrive in the present as a neoliberal subject.

The last chapter concludes by once again introducing an intergenerational perspective, as I do in chapters 2 and 4. Concretely, it speaks to the clash between two epochs—the revolutionary and the neoliberal—by focusing on the figure of Marco Enríquez-Ominami (ME-O), the son of the legendary MIR leader Miguel Enríquez and three times a candidate for the presidency (in 2009, 2013, and 2017). ME-O's biography calls up a tension between armed struggle and radical change, between the father's 1970s beliefs and the son's "reformed" (neoliberalized) leftist politics in the twenty-first century. My analysis draws this tension out of two cultural products: ME-O's film *Chile, los héroes están fatigados* (Chile, the Heroes Are Worn Out, 2002), in which he shockingly questions and rejects his father's political strategies, and a book called *Animales políticos: Diálogos filiales* (Political Animals: Conversations between a Father and a Son, 2004), coauthored with his stepfather, the Socialist senator Carlos Ominami. My interpretation of these materials reveals that ME-O perhaps struggled just as much to reconcile with the ghost of his iconic, revolutionary father as Ignacio Santa Cruz (Jaime Guzmán's nephew) or younger politicians in UDI struggled, each in his own way, with a figure like Jaime Guzmán (chapter 2). In all these cases, we observe a tendency toward a normalization of subjectivity that adapts to the neoliberal present and shies away from radicalized positions of both the right and the left.

Taken together, all the "characters" I treat in this book by no means exhaust the spectrum of complicities. Certainly many other kinds of complicities demand to be investigated in essays or books still to be written: for example, the complicity of a large swath of the Christian Democratic party with the September 11, 1973, coup; the complicity of the press, in particular *El Mercurio* newspaper, with the cover-up of human rights violations; the complicity of big-business interests with the machinery of human rights violations; the complicity of neighbors who lived beside torture centers; and many other variations on the theme.[40] If I have chosen certain characters and not others, it is for a simple reason: because they are among the few accomplices who have written or spoken publicly and, in so doing, they have implicitly invited a debate regarding how they configure their memories.[41]

Given the force of current popular discontent with the political and economic classes (on the right and the left) that for years have protected Pinochet's legacy, the "pending" debate about complicity in Chile is now beginning to take place in a more complete and nuanced way than ever before. I will be content if my analyses of certain complicit and complacent voices can help to push that debate forward by sparking deeper conversations about the historical, societal, and psychological forces that shape complicit and complacent memories and if they can also get us thinking about how the dynamics we observe in Chile transcend its borders and inspire questions about how forms of complicity and complacency with neoliberalism pervade all of our lives in ways that we are often reluctant to admit. I hope that by revealing the neoliberalized impulse, normalized nature, and lack of vulnerability that underlie the telling of certain life narratives, I can shed some light on why it has been so exceedingly difficult for Chilean society to reconstitute community in the postdictatorship.

To "out" complicit and complacent memories should, in the final assessment, be understood as a calling to account, a strategy for shaking us all out of complacency—an invitation to decode the "I" so as to see beyond it, in the interest of "us."

1

Fictions of Mastery

(Mariana Callejas)

want to begin with the stories—both public and private—
that complicit subjects tell to appease their consciences:
the rationalizations, half truths, and vital lies they rehearse in private to construct inviolate visions (or versions) of the self, the performative narratives
they tell publicly to bolster their credibility in the eyes of others.

When an accomplice has "lost face," because of either action or failure
to act, he often feels compelled to construct *another face*, one that can mask
shame or alleviate pangs of conscience—if and when pangs of conscience exist
at all (this, of course, is not always the case).[1] Constructing such an alternate
face becomes easier than or preferable to telling the truth or taking responsibility for what one has done. (From the outset, then, it is worth pausing to note
that, interestingly, the Spanish language equates the very concept of "taking
responsibility" with the gesture of "showing one's face"—*dar la cara*).[2] Mired
in a crisis of face, complicit subjects therefore attempt—whether consciously
or unconsciously—to assuage the nagging cognitive dissonance that arises when
the reality of who they are (or were) conflicts with who they ideally would like
to be or with how they hope to be perceived by others. I refer to the complex
psychic and narrative operations through which complicit subjects try, in the
present, to "save face" as *fictions of mastery*. Such fictions, I maintain, are crucial
for preserving the ashamed accomplice's mental equilibrium and for constructing future-oriented self-narratives that allow the accomplice to navigate and
take control of his life. These fictions, however, do not necessarily equate to
falsehoods. More correctly, they are versions of the truth: self-satisfying memory
scripts that may indeed contain some factual accuracies but that are also riddled
with glaring blind spots and self-deceiving conceits.

Fictions of mastery stem from inner psychic processes—sometimes but not always consciously initiated by the subject—that compartmentalize experience or generate diversionary schemas that can mitigate the impact of anxiety-producing realities.[3] Much like the perpetrator narratives that Leigh Payne discusses in her compelling book *Unsettling Accounts: Neither Truth nor Reconciliation in Confessions of State Violence* (2008), the outward, performative manifestations of accomplices' self-fictions, like those of perpetrators, assume a range of forms that include but are not limited to "denial, justification, excuses, and euphemisms that hide their acts from themselves or others."[4] Occasionally, though very rarely, complicit subjects experience remorse. However, as all the case studies in this book show, almost never do they apologize for the harm they caused, and almost never do they deeply and meaningfully acknowledge the ramifications that their actions had—or continue to have—on others or on society at large. Because of accomplices' frequent lack of remorse, expiation, or willingness to pay a price for their actions (judicial or otherwise), it would be inaccurate to classify their narratives as confessions. To confess, in my understanding, implies a willingness to take responsibility and assume the consequences for what one has done.[5] For this reason, I prefer to call accomplices' public accounts fictions of mastery so as to avoid the saturated, Christian language of confession.

Of course, not all complicit subjects experience shame. In fact, many are convinced that their actions or omissions under dictatorship ultimately served to further the common good. In the specific case of those who supported Pinochet, we are by now quite familiar with the well-worn "salvationist" memory framework that holds that on September 11, 1973, the military saved Chile from the throes of Marxist tyranny and liberated the country from impending civil war.[6] Within a conflicted field of "competing selective remembrances"—which is very much what the transition to democracy has been—such rationalizations have allowed complicit subjects to orient their memories in ways that resonate with those of like-minded individuals.[7] By framing personal life experiences within a collective "salvationist" framework, for example, complicit subjects who supported the Pinochet regime find communities or networks of social legitimacy that help them ward off potential feelings of shame. They surround themselves with others who see eye to eye with them morally or ideologically, and in such circumstances their ability to be self-reflective diminishes. Protected by their cohort, they also become less receptive to the victims' pain, even when that pain, whether they like it or not, interrogates them insistently *from the outside* and in myriad ways (e.g., through the media, art, or even legal verdicts that punish others in their peer set).

An awareness of accomplices' self-induced protectionism leads from there to a critical insight: if the accomplice is unwilling to become exposed, vulnerable, naked, so to speak, before her fellow human being, if she adorns herself in external (rhetorical) trappings that shield her from potentially shameful acts and thoughts, then the subject is indeed *shameless*—that is, without shame. And a subject without shame becomes stuck, recoils into herself, fearful and brazen at the same time, thoroughly unable to experience any kind of transformation in the eyes of the self or of another.

In contrast to such brazenly shameless subjects (who do, indeed, exist and perhaps constitute the majority of accomplices), I restrict my focus in this chapter to an accomplice who *does*, in fact, seem to blush when she thinks about her past actions and, as a result, weaves intricate textual edifices or elaborate self-fictions whose goal is to make that blush fade away.

I have chosen to concentrate on one shady and intriguing character whose cultural symbolism has been explored diversely in fictional texts by Roberto Bolaño, Pedro Lemebel, and Roberto Brodsky; more recently in the hit television series *Los archivos del cardenal* (The Archives of the Cardinal, 2011, 2014); and also in Nona Fernández's 2012 play *El taller* (The Workshop).[8] I am referring, of course, to Mariana Callejas (1932–2016), the former wife of a US-born DINA functionary, Michael Townley (b. 1942), infamous for her complicity (with Townley) in the 1976 assassination of General Carlos Prats and his wife, Sofía Cuthbert, in Buenos Aires, among other egregious crimes.[9]

The persona adopted by Callejas, a literary author whose talent for short-story writing had put her on the map by the mid-1970s, in symbolic terms points toward the complicities that linked certain members of the artistic and intellectual community to the dictatorial state. In one sense, she was clearly a figure of cultural or intellectual complicity; in another sense, her connection to Townley metonymically evokes the insidious marriage between General Pinochet's dictatorship and the United States—one of the great complicities of the Cold War era in Latin America.[10] (We should recall that not only did the United States support the coup in 1973; it also tried to foil Allende's rise to power from the time of his first presidential bid, in 1952.) Callejas's figure is therefore particularly striking because it metaphorically embodies the ties that existed between certain right-wing cultural figures and the Pinochet regime as well as those between the United States and Chile during the Nixon–Kissinger years.

Callejas's story, tied to Townley's, is fairly well known, though many of her actions still remain shrouded in secrecy.[11] As a young girl, she fervently embraced leftist causes, marching against the US war in Vietnam and even joining the Chilean Communist Youth at age fifteen. In 1960 she separated from her second husband, a New Yorker named Allen Ernest who turned her on to the Zionist cause and with whom she went to live on a kibbutz in the Negev Desert, in Israel, when she was twenty-eight years old. Shortly thereafter, in 1961, she married Michael Vernon Townley, the son of a Ford Motor Company employee. Townley's father worked as part of the American business community in several Latin American countries, had connections to the Central Intelligence Agency (CIA), and weened his son on his own deep-seated, anticommunist views. Never able to live up to his father's example, Townley grew up to become a wannabee Cold Warrior who at several points in his young life flirted with the CIA but was never able to become a full-fledged operative. His visceral anticommunism and desire to participate in the anti-Allende fight eventually led him and Callejas to join Patria y Libertad (Fatherland and Liberty), an ultra-right-wing paramilitary organization. Both of them, in early 1974, would then become civilian contract employees for DINA at the request of Lieutenant Colonel Pedro Espinoza Bravo.[12] Not only did DINA find attractive the passionate anticommunism that Townley and Callejas exhibited as members of Patria y Libertad; it also considered the American's ability to move in and out of the United States freely and his finely honed skills working with electronics and explosives to be important strategic assets. According to Dinges and Landau, "Espinoza hired both Townley and [Mariana] Callejas for a combined salary of about $600 a month."[13] As part of their compensation package, Espinoza also provided the couple with a house in Santiago's upscale Lo Curro neighborhood, a house that they never owned but in which Callejas lived until the mid-1990s.[14]

From that infamous Lo Curro mansion—which DINA referred to as Cuartel Quetropillán and in which DINA is known to have tortured prisoners and produced lethal gases and false documentation—Callejas led a deplorable double life: that of a literary author directing workshops for aspiring writers and that of an international spy deeply complicit with some of the worst crimes that the dictatorship committed abroad: the assassinations of Carlos Prats and his wife, Sofía Cuthbert (Buenos Aires, 1974); the assassination attempts on Bernardo Leighton, an opponent of the Christian Democratic regime, and his wife, Anita Fresno (Rome, 1975); and the assassinations of Orlando Letelier, a socialist who held several key cabinet posts under Allende, and his coworker Ronni Karpen Moffitt (Washington, DC, 1976).

It was Callejas who sat next to Townley when he pushed the detonator that exploded Prats's car (she fumbled the button and lost the courage to press it before handing it off to Townley); Callejas who fraternized with and played host to the Italian terrorist and neofascist sympathizer Stefano Delle Chiaie and his anti-Castro Cuban cronies both before and after the Leighton crime; and Callejas who received the phone call that relayed to DINA that Letelier

Mariana Callejas, Michael Townley, and their children. Photograph courtesy of the *La Nación* newspaper archive, Universidad Diego Portales, Chile.

was dead in Washington, DC. Masquerading under false names such as María Luisa Pizarro, she also participated in two failed operations, both of which took place in 1975 (in Mexico City and in Europe), whose goal was to kill iconic figures of the center and the left such as Hortensia Bussi (Allende's wife), Carlos Altamirano (General Secretary of the Socialist Party), Volodia Teitelboim (a writer and Communist senator), and Patricio Aylwin (president of the Christian Democratic Party during the Allende years).

As a writer, Callejas had crafted fiction since the 1960s, but her "breakout" moment onto Santiago's literary scene came in 1975 with the publication of her short story "¿Conoció usted a Bobby Ackerman?" (Did You Know Bobby Ackerman?), which won a literary prize from *El Mercurio* newspaper.[15] In those years, the prominent right-wing writer Enrique Lafourcade, in whose literary workshops Callejas participated, touted her as one of the most promising young writers of her generation. She would soon begin to run her own literary workshops using the Lo Curro mansion as her home base and would mentor other aspiring writers such as Carlos Franz, Gonzalo Contreras, and Carlos Iturra, whom she affectionately called "mis chiquillos" (my little ones). Other well-known writers, including Pía Barros, Pedro Lemebel, and even the legendary Nicanor Parra, found themselves at the mansion at certain points but abandoned and rejected Callejas once they became aware of her sordid double life as a political terrorist. In Callejas's twilight years, Iturra was perhaps the only writer from her younger days who maintained regular contact or something of a friendship with her.

While Callejas wrote, drank, and smoked marijuana with her friends, right under her nose—and likely with her full knowledge—DINA tortured and killed the Spanish diplomat Carmelo Soria with sarin gas and made 119 false passports to cover up the murders that would be carried out in 1975 under the code name "Operation Colombo."[16] Thirty-four years after the Prats killings, in 2009, she would be convicted and sentenced in Chile to twenty years as an accessory to murder. Eight months later, in 2010, Chile's Supreme Court would reduce that sentence to five years without jail time. After that, until her death in 2016, she was free.

To think about the ways in which the accomplice's self-narrative maneuvers around shame and, in the final assessment, fails to achieve an ethical standard, I assess two works that Callejas wrote in different moments: *Siembra vientos* (You Reap What You Sow, 1995), a nonfictional memoir in which she strives to account for her past actions yet consistently engages in self-deception and cover-up; and a collection of fictional short stories titled *La larga noche* (The Long Night, 1981), which I read, strategically, as a window onto the secret shame and psychological torment that *Siembra vientos* tries to smooth over at a fourteen-year temporal remove. With this unusual pairing of texts, I hope to highlight that while the autobiographical work (written in the mid-1990s at a moment when Callejas had not yet been prosecuted for her role in the Prats assassination) masks the truth and engages in contrived testimony in an attempt to "save face" publicly, the fictional text, written nearly a decade and a half earlier (and which took her two years to complete), curiously approximates something more akin to (partial) avowal—though certainly not at all a fully realized act of avowal owing to its lack of expiation, lack of willingness to assume responsibility, and lack of willingness to pay a price. Interestingly, in Callejas's case, fiction—not the memoir—reveals deeper truths about the complicit subject's inner psychic life and brings into sharp relief the contrived nature of her autobiographical act.

This juxtaposition of texts—one fictional, one nonfictional—also reminds us that *genre* as well as *perceived audience* matter when it comes to confronting shame through narrative. Callejas's memoir, like virtually all memoirs, was written for public consumption and thus seeks to bolster her figurative credit rating in the eyes of the reader-consumer.[17] That *Siembra vientos*, the memoir, would read as a skewed and contrived discursive act is therefore probably not all that surprising.[18] Like her memoir, Callejas's short stories of the 1980s were meant for public consumption; nevertheless, their publication occurred on a much smaller scale and was likely geared toward a more narrowly defined audience, perhaps only fellow writers and close friends. The self-published nature of *La larga noche*, which bore the imprint "Editorial Lo Curro" (Lo Curro Publishing House) and was written during years in which censorship reigned and literature could be published only with considerable difficulty, attests to the more limited scope of its audience. *La larga noche* therefore emerges from an intimate place and is much less oriented toward the reader-consumer. Indeed, Callejas always fancied the space of fiction her true home. For that reason, fiction provided the accomplice a place of relative comfort in which to bare her most intimate thoughts; it also facilitated, as I will show, an array of distancing mechanisms that permitted her to treat her experience elliptically but also—in a somewhat paradoxical sense—more directly than in the memoir genre, which is a priori a genre grounded in a perceived expectation of factual exposition.

Methodologically, I want to track a reverse movement from the present-bound, guarded discourse of Callejas's memoir toward the intimate fictional world of an ashamed mind still caught in the eye of the storm, still reeling from her participation in the crimes. This move, I think, can prove instructive for understanding how shame persists in different moments and how it generates diverse narrative reactions that are at once contingent on perceived audience and responsive to shifting social, political, and historical circumstances. I suggest that the fictional mode, less regulated by strictures and narrative control than the memoir genre—which also, admittedly, has decidedly fictional qualities—became the space in which Callejas's secret shame is most visible and palpable to readers.

Before analyzing these two texts, however, a brief detour into the landscape of shame will allow me first to define it for purposes of my analysis and then to propose some possible ways of reacting to it that can help us arrive at some eventual conclusions regarding the textual universe Callejas creates vis-à-vis her complicity.

Shame

In an essay titled "On Escape," Emmanuel Levinas suggests a simple definition of shame that can provide a useful starting point: "Shame arises each time we are unable to make others forget [*faire oublier*] our basic nudity. It is related to everything we would like to hide and that we cannot bury or cover up. . . . What appears in shame is thus precisely the fact of being riveted to oneself, the radical impossibility of fleeing to hide from oneself, the unalterably binding presence of the I to itself [*du moi à soi-même*]."[19]

Shame is an emotion, a blush that washes over a person when her concept or ideal vision of herself is out of sync with the person she knows herself to be.[20] Unlike guilt, which often carries legal connotations and primarily concerns the deeds or acts that one has committed (e.g., "I am guilty of having done such and such an act"), shame concerns the whole person and has to do with the subject's overarching sense of identity, morals, or ethics (e.g., "I am ashamed of my*self*").[21] Both shame and guilt are linked to conscience and to the feeling that some external authority's eyes are upon us; often that judging eye becomes internalized, and it is from that scrutinizing eye that the subject wants desperately to flee, often to no avail.

To separate shame from guilt, however, does not mean that both feelings do not frequently coexist within one subject. This can indeed be the case. The language people use to refer to shame and guilt often seems ambiguous: the word *culpa* in Spanish, for example, can simultaneously connote blameworthiness, shame, or guiltiness that is punishable in some way. But for the purpose of my discussion here, I think it useful to distinguish conceptually between the two terms specifically because Callejas admits only to shame, not guilt (even though she does, in fact, use the word *culpa* on occasion as a stand-in for shame): in that regard, until the moment of her death (in 2016) she never felt that she should be held legally responsible or beholden to an external authority for her complicity in the crimes of DINA. She was wholly unwilling to assume the consequences of her actions in any way other than subjecting herself to the moral torment of shame. Given, then, that Callejas evades guilt, her protracted psychological torment, which I define as shame, corresponds to an internalization of the feeling that she has transgressed her own (and perhaps society's) code of ethics and that she has consequently become dishonored.[22] In a word, she experiences her past in the present as a *crisis of face*.

Agnes Heller, in *The Power of Shame: A Rational Perspective* (1985), writes that "losing honour means losing *face*. The expression 'losing face' aptly describes the visual character of shame."[23] The philosopher Claudia Welz also picks up on this visual element: "One feels eyes upon oneself and ends up observing oneself as if one could see oneself from outside, shifting viewpoints and comparing oneself with others."[24] Naked before the self, the ashamed subject's basic instinct is "to hide from others, but also from [the] self."[25] In Callejas's case, she goes to great lengths to flee from her intimacy, to robe herself in metaphorical clothing that might cover up what she does not wish to see. Her situation overtly concretizes Levinas's insight that "shame is, in the last analysis, an existence that seeks excuses. What shame discovers [*découvre*] is the being who *uncovers* himself [*se* découvre]."[26]

From the autobiographer's or memoir writer's perspective, to hide shame is to construct a new (public) face, a textual face that can mask nakedness before oneself and the other and that can ideally bring a modicum of peace — though certainly an equilibrium that is always incomplete and on some level unsatisfactory. Complicit writing therefore engages in selectivity and self-deception, in putting up walls or boundaries that can protect the subject from harm. And to do this, as many psychologists, including Freud, have noted, is perhaps unsurprisingly attributable to human instinct: "the self-system protects us against anxiety by skewing attention."[27] In fact, people often do such a good job at repressing what is painful or shameful in their lives that they forget exactly when the operation of repression first occurred; in some cases, they are not even aware that it occurred at all.[28] Later, when one who experiences shame faces the task of avowal or of self-analysis, she is unable to verbalize the nature of the self-defense she is carrying out. She turns inward and narcissistically bolsters her self-image. In the process, certain defense mechanisms — including denial, rationalization, sublimation, and repression — become naturalized, part and parcel with her being, and are therefore not something that can easily be tamed or explained away through abstract reasoning.

It is also worth noting that the need an accomplice feels to assuage shame at certain junctures in her life — in Callejas's case, in the *present* of her 1995 memoir—may, in fact, have been much less necessary in previous moments. Social norms and definitions regarding what constitutes "acceptable" behavior shift from one historical epoch to another. Under dictatorship, terrorist states find ways of rationalizing that it is acceptable to kill the "other" for political reasons. In this sense, actions that may have seemed reasonable or even honorable to a subject such as Callejas in the early to mid-1970s probably ceased to be so after the state of exception was lifted, that is, after actions that the regime at one point considered noble became widely understood by mainstream society as crimes.

To attribute shame to Callejas, however, is not merely a matter of critical speculation. Tellingly, she used the term to describe her own state of being in a series of intimate, personal diaries—never meant for public consumption—that she wrote in mid-1978 while visiting Michael Townley as he awaited trial in the United States.[29] These diaries allude to an already shifting conception of the self and reveal that Callejas had by then started to engage in a process of recalibrating her ethical compass.

> I feel that life is lived in stages At least mine has consisted in many stages, and today, after a long conversation with Michael and his lawyers inside the prison walls, I understand that when I leave for Chile I will be finishing one stage and beginning another—one of great loneliness and anguish, because even though I know I have many friends who will support me no matter what happens, the *shame that floats in the air will affect me more than anyone*. I know, nevertheless, that no one will remember me as a DINA "agent" *because I never participated in any mission in Chile*, and my Marxist friends or acquaintances know that I didn't give them up or try to get information from them. To do that, simply put, would be *out of sync with my character*.[30]

Notice that in the same breath in which Callejas admits to feeling shame, her pen displaces the origin of that shame onto an undefined *outside*: the "shame that floats in the air." Indeed, she feels shame but does not fully claim its origin as existing within her. She therefore begins to proffer excuses and justifications that silence or downplay the gravity of her ideological affiliations: for example, she claims to have done the least possible harm because she was never responsible for the capture or torture of any of her "Marxist friends." It also becomes clear in this passage that the ashamed accomplice bears within her an undefined though benchmarked idea of *character* against which she measures all her actions. Curiously, she does not deny that she worked as an agent for DINA. She merely downplays her role in DINA, stating that no one in Chile will remember her as an "agent" because she never participated in any mission *in*

Chile. And this is indeed correct: all the crimes she helped facilitate took place abroad—Prats, Letelier, Leighton.

In every moment, then, no matter how dire the circumstances, the self seeks integrity, a rational life plan.[31] But articulating such a life plan requires that the "I" accept certain unresolvable contradictions, that it create a coherent (or better put, semicoherent) vision of the self while acknowledging that certain zones of the self will always remain opaque to it or hidden from it. At best, a rational life plan can only ever be partial, a kind of evolution in self-knowledge that stems from the possibilities and limitations that the present moment of enunciation inflicts.

In all of this, the question of accounting for oneself and one's actions, of assuming responsibility for past wrongs and commitments, is crucial. In Chile, a series of mea culpas has emerged over the years, primarily from the different branches of the military and from some politicians for whom taking responsibility has seemed more an instrumental maneuver than a heartfelt action. Discourses that deeply reflect or repent have been virtually nonexistent. In contrast to this scenario, I want to consider the (perhaps utopian) possibility that one might manage to make amends for past wrongs by telling the truth, revealing one's nakedness—one's true face—and making oneself vulnerable before another. Agnes Heller opened a door to this scenario in her study of shame by linking atonement for shame to the idea of social justice: "Normally a violation of external authority can be requited with atonement, that is to say, by inflicting some suffering on ourselves (or by accepting suffering inflicted on us by others) which restores *social justice*."[32] One must therefore pay a price. She must assume the full consequences of her actions to make things right.

If we follow Judith Butler's insights on the ways in which subjects *account* for themselves, we find that to construct an account of one's life does not just mean telling a story. Accounting implies *accountability* to another: an ethical responsibility to tell the truth and assume the consequences of one's actions, whatever those may be.[33] To account for oneself implies an a priori ethical relation to the other, a willingness to heed the call that comes to us from outside, from the Levinasian "face."[34] Although textual control may be a natural tendency for autobiographers who are trying to find ways to live with themselves, Butler suggests that, on the contrary, "our willingness to become *undone* in relation to others constitutes our chance of becoming human."[35] She continues: "The account is an act—situated within a larger practice of acts—that one performs for, to, even *on* another. . . . This account does not have as its goal the establishment of a definitive narrative but constitutes a linguistic and social occasion for self-transformation" and, I would add, for societal transformation.[36] If a self-referential text is not open to this transformative dimension, if the subject is not willing to become vulnerable or undone through a truly honest reckoning, then the narrative fails to meet a standard of ethics.

Revelations of intimacy are not enough. To "confess" one's shame—to reveal the private, the sentimental, or the emotional—does not automatically make the subject ethical. Rather, there is a need for utter candor, spoken in the name of responsibility toward another, in the interest of community, and with the important ingredient of being willing to assume responsibility for one's action's (judicial social, or otherwise).

Let us now take these ideas about shame—a shame to which, as I have shown, Callejas admits overtly—and use them as a basis for analyzing how she responds to shame differently in her 1995 memoir and in her 1981 short-story collection.

Siembra vientos: De-ideologizing the "I"

The fragmented, episodic narrative that is *Siembra vientos* begins in medias res, in 1978. Salvador Allende's former minister, Orlando Letelier, is already dead, and Townley is awaiting extradition to the United States for his involvement in the killing, hoping that General Contreras, the now-deposed head of DINA, will save him. During this same period, fearing that detractors might kill Townley *and* her, Callejas follows her lawyer's advice to maintain high public visibility and appear often in the media: "I took it upon myself to lie, to make things up, to make stupid statements that brought me shame," all in the interest of protecting Townley and maintaining loyalty to Pinochet and Contreras.[37] (Although she was upset with Pinochet for having let Townley take the fall for the killing, her loyalty to the regime and to the General, in macro terms, remained unflagging.) She later notes that she lied so often in public that, eventually, no matter what she said, no one would believe her. All but a few close friends abandoned her, and she became an outcast in her own country. By 1995, the present time of textual enunciation, we see her as an aged, paranoid, pathetic subject rotting away in the Lo Curro mansion: "I grow old, alone in my personal, ruinous mausoleum."[38]

Siembra vientos thus begins with a discredited witness who, roughly a decade and a half after the original crimes, purports to want to tell the truth. She is doubly ashamed: ashamed for having participated in the crimes and ashamed for having lied incessantly in the media to cover them up. As in almost all narratives of its kind, we find an expression of desire in Callejas's memoir to set the public record straight: "I have not written this narrative to defend myself or express opinions. I have written it to tell the truth, my truth, to those who wish to hear it."[39] However, despite this disclaimer, the book is obviously an exercise in self-defense and a wish for historical absolution. Its truths are partial.

Inevitably, as Shoshana Felman observed regarding the 1987 discovery of Paul de Man's wartime writings for a Belgian collaborationist newspaper, there is "a demand for absolution that every confession necessarily implies."[40] Yet in Callejas's case, this demand for historical absolution comes without apology. She claims to assume "responsibility" for her actions but never spells out precisely what those actions were or why she feels it necessary to take responsibility in the present; instead, she concentrates on disavowing actions that she feels others have attributed to her unfairly.[41] For Callejas, then, evoking "responsibility"—on the few occasions on which she does, in fact, evoke it in the book—amounts to little more than vacuous rhetoric. Unlike an honest reckoning with the self that is oriented toward an-other to make amends (Butler), the book bears witness to the *internal psychic disorder of an ashamed subject trying to put order to her life.*

Because Callejas's past self is on some level intolerable to her present self, she engages in rationalizations that allow her to "integrate" her fissured subjectivity. Significantly, Salvador Dalí's painting *The Hour of the Crackled Visage* (1934) adorns the book's cover: it depicts a faceless, fissured, female form, reflective of the psychic mayhem and desire for order that plague Callejas and that the reader acutely senses in the pages of her text. To rationalize the ideological inconsistencies that characterize her story, the autobiographer constructs her narrative by overtly *de-ideologizing* her own subjectivity. Her fiction of mastery hinges on the exceedingly implausible argument that at no point in time did she ever adopt an ideology or act in accordance with it. If we are to believe her, we must also accept that in all cases she simply reacted to "facts" (the term is hers), that is, to "circumstances." Her supposed lack of ideology or any solid political grounding thus becomes the narrative logic and mask that she wears to hide from her naked self. She wants readers to take pity on her—to see her as a normal person who, by mere chance, became involved with the wrong man and was sucked into the vortex of history.

And how did we, common people with everyday concerns and modest ambitions, get ourselves into such an absurd situation? I tend to blame myself for my obsession with Causes, the big Causes, which began when I was a very young girl, or perhaps it is a congenital defect—Causes that at times have seemed crazy and that have not taken a consistent political path because I have changed according to circumstances, not ideological concepts. My participation in anti–Vietnam War protests made me appear [*me hacía aparecer*] to be on the left; fighting against the Marxist government would make me a right-winger. But the truth is that my actions were directed either in favor of or against facts and never had to do with ideology.[42]

We know relatively little of Callejas's life before she met Townley, but what we do know of her origins paints a picture of an ideological adventurer whose loyalties at different points in her life, though radically at odds with one another, were never in question. Contrary to what she says, ideology seems to have driven her behavior at every turn. In a short section toward the end of the book, she reveals that her father was a "radical, a declared enemy of the Church, anticommunist, and anti-Nazi," yet "tremendously authoritarian."[43] These details would seem to "explain" the more liberal political leanings of her youth. From her father, through socialization, Callejas became grounded in certain "values" (her word choice) that remain entirely nebulous and undefined in the text, such that the word *values*—like the word *responsibility*—functions as another empty signifier.[44]

What we do know is that, having joined the Communist Youth at age fifteen, Callejas was expelled from school at age sixteen for possessing communist literature. Later, she abandoned her native Chile and went to live on a kibbutz in Israel. From the present of enunciation in 1995, she strangely expresses regret over having abandoned the collective, "socialist" life: "I think I still lament not having stayed on the kibbutz. But idealistic youth demands perfection, and after two years I left, disillusioned with socialism for totally infantile reasons."[45] This is a curious way of channeling her shame for having become a stalwart Pinochet supporter and a criminal, particularly because after living on the kibbutz, as John Dinges and Saul Landau point out, "her anticommunism was to have that special cast of hatred and fanaticism characteristic of former devotees."[46]

Callejas's personal diaries, written in mid-1978 while Townley was detained in the United States, reveal the solidity and depth of this fanaticism, which continued unwavering even after Townley took the fall for the Letelier assassination.

[I] insist that Michael was not a common delinquent, an adventurer or a stakeholder [in DINA]. Instead he was a naïve idealist who was extremely loyal to his superiors. I know there are people who reproach us for lying. I recognize that I have lied. But aren't the reasons why we lied clear? Not only were we trying to protect ourselves but also the [Intelligence] Service for which Michael worked, a Service that was loyal to Pinochet's government, a government that despite all that people say against it maintained the peace that so many of us Chileans desired. I don't know if this was good or bad; all I know is that it was effective, and I deeply fear that we will return to the times of graffitied walls, disorder in the streets, pamphlets, and posters.[47]

In the cited passage, we sense Callejas's fear of a return to the "chaotic" time of Popular Unity and a gratitude for the "order" that the Pinochet regime brought to Chilean society. Her perspective, quite typical of the pinochetista salvationist memory script, speaks to ideological allegiances that have shifted 180 degrees from those of her youth. This shift is rooted in self-serving pragmatism, fear, and, if we read between the lines, gratitude toward Pinochet for having "maintained the peace" in Chile. In short, Callejas's textual "I" over time is unstable, ungrounded, chameleonic, that of an ideological adventurer—though she denies it—although still in 1995 (as in 1978) unabashedly pinochetista.

At the beginning of chapter 6, likely alluding to herself, Callejas relays a revealing anecdote about a family she once knew whose members were Christian Democrats in the late 1990s and fervent Allende supporters in the early 1970s and who, after the coup, became rich and even erected a flag in front of their house to honor the coup plotters. Assuredly seeking absolution from the reader for her own chameleonic behavior, she notes, ironically: "I cannot reproach anyone for changing his or her mind; I have changed mine more than once."[48]

The cultural critic Nelly Richard attunes us to the rhetorical strategies that female confessional subjects—or, in Callejas's case, we might more correctly say *pseudo*-confessional subjects—sometimes use to portray themselves in a positive light. Richard claims that women who supported the Pinochet regime frequently write in a stereotypically feminine key ("en clave femenina"), meaning that they hide the true essence of their "selves" and take refuge instead behind masks of irrationality and emotion.[49] Rather than avow conviction or political commitment—understood, by contrast, as stereotypically masculine qualities—Callejas takes sanctuary in her loyalty to her man, her duties as a wife, and the self-proclaimed inchoate nature of her political leanings. Her autobiographical act, in this sense, becomes distracting to readers whose tendency is to view a figure like Callejas, who admittedly has a lot of hyperbolic and unbelievable qualities, as a pathetic anomaly. We gaze at her somewhat voyeuristically as an "isolated" case, when it would really be more useful to understand her as a dramatization of larger secrets of the state and of the schizophrenia undergirding pinochetista rhetoric, that is, as a symbol of the lack of candor and accountability that has characterized a certain sector of Chilean society.

Michael Townley and Mariana Callejas. Photograph courtesy of the *La Nación* newspaper archive, Universidad Diego Portales, Chile.

In that sense, Callejas provides a window into the postdictatorship period as a time in which complicit subjects can claim to support human rights, while at the same time they have been assassins, either actively or tacitly. In Callejas's case, a compartmentalization of subjectivity occurs. On the one hand, she sat in the car and held the detonator, intending to kill Prats; on the other hand, she claims in her book to have supported the anti-Pinochet "No" vote in the October 1988 plebiscite and to have stood side by side in solidarity with the shantytown dwellers of La Pintana throughout the transition to democracy.[50] Without sacrificing her pinochetista subjectivity, then, she tries to attenuate it by advancing an amorphous relationship with something called "human rights." It is by this same logic that former right-wing president Sebastián Piñera (2010–14), a direct descendant of Pinochet's Chicago Boys, could visit and applaud Santiago's Museum of Memory and Human Rights; it is by this same logic that various former Pinochet supporters rationalize their past complicities or publicly perform apologies for politically instrumental reasons.[51] It is only by bracketing human rights—by disconnecting them from the larger project of imposing neoliberalism—that such incongruous narratives can emerge.[52]

Literary critics have shown that autobiographical writing contains a number of prominent elements. Philippe Lejeune's paradigmatic idea of the "autobiographical pact" long ago established that the autobiographer writes because she wants to be believed by the reader.[53] Leonor Arfuch added that autobiographers seek complicity of understanding and acceptance from readers:

autobiographers expect readers to "buy" the "exemplary life" they sell on paper, which may or may not coincide with or reveal anything about their intimate, "private life."[54] Complicit autobiography is therefore a performance of the self through writing in which the complicit autobiographer who has done some wrong tries to "conceal from [her] audience all evidence of 'dirty work'"; her text thus bears within it a tension between appearances and reality.[55] Furthermore, autobiographical writing provides a way of situating oneself in history, in relation to history, as a mode of survival. Yet, as Butler wrote: "My account of myself is partial, haunted by that for which I can devise no definitive story. I cannot explain exactly why I have emerged in this way, and my efforts at narrative construction are always undergoing revision."[56] This perhaps explains why autobiographical writing, though not merely self-defense, usually contains a prominent inertia toward self-defense and a decidedly fictional quality. The subject wants to take control of a narrative (and a life) of which she is losing all control.

Consequently, the additive and revisionist qualities of Callejas's memoir reflect her desire to gain control of a life in shambles, simultaneously revealing a certain opacity of the subject to herself. She either cannot recognize or is not willing to *name* her ideological alignments as such. Instead, she prefers to take refuge in a self-fiction and to compartmentalize the aspects of her fissured subjectivity neatly. She admits as much: "In my mind, I managed to separate my private life from the darkness of the basement" (a reference to the torture chamber and evil acts that took place on the lower level of the Lo Curro mansion).[57]

Callejas's impulse toward rationalization shines through in many moments, particularly in her weak defense of Townley's complicity in the 1973 murder of a worker in Concepción. In March of that year, at Raúl Hasbún's request, Townley tried to foil the Allende government's blockage of a pirate television station set up by the rightist opposition, killing a man in the process.[58] (When compared to Dinges and Landau's investigation of the murder, Callejas's allegation that the man died not primarily because he was gagged and suffocated with chloroform but because he had a "bad cold" that exacerbated the chloroform's effects is eminently laughable.) In another breath, she explains away the Spanish diplomat Carmelo Soria's notorious 1976 murder, which occurred in the Lo Curro mansion, as an "isolated" case about which she knew nothing until several days after it happened. Shockingly, the Prats murder, her most shameful memory, is entirely absent from her memoir.

Although Callejas's text asserts repeatedly that she did not belong to DINA, either ideologically or emotionally, a slip of her pen tellingly contradicts her incessant denials. At a certain point, she recalls a dialogue in which one of the Cubans who helped carry out the Letelier murder asks Townley if he and

Callejas belong to the CIA, to which Townley replies (according to Callejas): "No, *we* work for DINA in Chile."[59] This inclusive *we*, carelessly materialized from Callejas's subconscious, rears its ugly head, undermining all efforts at textual control. Her fiction of mastery tries to conquer her shame but cannot do so completely or convincingly.

La larga noche: Fictional Strategies for Coping with Shame

> Quizás por eso he escrito este relato, maestro: exponiendo mi culpabilidad pretendo acallar mi conciencia. (Perhaps that is why I have written this story, professor: by narrating my guilt [or shame], I am trying to quiet my conscience.)
>
> Mariana Callejas, "Perdóneme, maestro Paz"

If Callejas's 1995 testimony offers a space in which to grapple with the memory of her crimes (at a fourteen-year remove) in decidedly linear terms, her fiction, especially the fascinating 1981 short-story collection *La larga noche*, written in the eye of the storm, allows us to glimpse the torment of a soul that on some level *knows* it is losing its ethical compass.

I am, of course, well aware of the difficulties that autobiographical readings of fiction imply, but in the specific case of *La larga noche* the autobiographical elements seem undeniable. Callejas's comment to the journalist Juan Cristóbal Peña in a 2010 interview corroborates my intuition: "[I] have no imagination," she says. "I have to write about what I know."[60]

Shot through with images of death, suicide, and pain, *La larga noche* exudes a palpable air of suffering. Shame and reactions to it, as we shall see, pervade many of the collection's twenty-seven stories. Although none of the texts refers specifically to the crimes in which Callejas participated, several of them do, in fact, contain elements that very strikingly correspond to reality. It hardly seems coincidental that Callejas's fictional world delves deeply into the psychological states of her characters. Not all of them are female, but readers of *La larga noche* can imagine that many of these characters—male, female, old, young, left, right—lend insight into Callejas's own states of mind in the years immediately following her most egregious complicities with the crimes of DINA. Self-published and probably born of a flurry of emotion, the book emerges from a personal need to speak but does so in a register that permits the accomplice to gain a certain level of abstraction with her own experience; this abstraction, or mediation via fictionalization, facilitates her utterance of shame. Furthermore, the publication's "scrappiness," that is, the less than professional material circumstances in which it was produced, lends it an air of urgency; this urgency also comes to the fore symbolically in a number of glaring typographical errors littered throughout the book's pages.

To get a sense of the ways in which shame and reactions to it permeate the collection, I want to focus briefly on four main categories into which I think many of the stories fit: (1) stories that make shame an overt theme; (2) stories that blur the boundaries separating identities or subject positions, which becomes relevant when we consider how Callejas constantly blurs the boundaries among her criminal, professional, and personal "selves"; (3) stories in which we see a surgical split within a person's subjectivity so as to separate the "I" that brings pain and shame from the more banal, normalized "I" of everyday life; and (4) stories that foreground escapism, perhaps as a means to survive. I give some examples to illustrate each of these categories in turn, recognizing that many stories I have decided to leave out might also be subsumed within them. On the one hand, I want to establish that shame is an important theme in the collection as a whole; on the other hand, I want to show how Callejas's book highlights a number of psychic and narrative reactions that attempt to mitigate shame or assuage cognitive anxiety.

Shame as Theme

Two stories in particular make shame an overt theme: "Mediodía del lunes" (Monday at Noon) and "Atajo" (Shortcut). The first of these stories tells of a "has-been" bureaucrat (a conservative) who is donning a white dress shirt and blue tie—a person who once lived a life of middle- to upper-middle-class comfort but who has recently fallen on hard times. The bureaucrat feels "repugnance" when he reflects on his "degraded" socioeconomic status and loathes the way in which his life has collapsed, bringing him to "rock bottom."[61] To make ends meet, he devises a strategy: he obliges his four-year-old daughter, against her will, to beg for coins in downtown Santiago. Doing so strikes him as a necessity but brings him shame. Passersby stare at him as his daughter hands over the coins she has collected—this moment blatantly thematizes the external gaze that becomes internalized and produces the blush of shame: "He takes the coins, ashamed, and rapidly hides them in his pocket. He feels that everyone is staring at him, that they all know. He blushes [enrojece] and tries to take distance from the girl, but she follows him, fearful and perplexed."[62] By the story's final paragraph, the ashamed father wants to flee both from himself and from the situation he has created—"to flee far away so as not to see himself in the portrait [he has painted], in the action [he has taken] and that has plunged him to the rock bottom of all rock bottoms."[63] He diverts his gaze because if he turns around, he knows that he will see his reflection in the

Fictions of Mastery

front window of a department store. And that reflection—that looking at himself in the mirror, so to speak—is entirely unbearable.

The motif of the unbearable mirror is repeated in "Atajo." This story focuses on a narrator named Marcial who has been offered a job opportunity that will allow him to leave behind a life of misery and poverty in a small town called Los Molles to make a better future for him and his family. Accepting the job offer, however, requires that he abandon his ailing father, with whom he has spent all his life to that point and who will assuredly die in the care of his loyal but mentally ill ranch-hand Cosme. Ashamed of his decision to forsake his father, Marcial tries to sneak out of town at dawn before anyone rises. As he prepares to leave, Rogelio Montes, a neighbor, catches him in the act and urges him to heed his father's metaphorical "call" to stay: the neighbor's literal "call," which might be read as a call to act ethically and not in one's own self-interest, audibly conjures the father's inaudible call, which interestingly reminds us of the Levinasian face. Marcial suffers pangs of conscience the night before he leaves: "I slept, tossing and turning with my conscience, and before dawn I left the house and saddled up quietly, but the old man [Rogelio] must have heard the squeaking of the wrought-iron gate, and he came out to tell me, 'You're leaving without saying good-bye to your father, Marcial.'"[64] Significantly, the story hinges not only on Marcial's decision to leave but also on his refusal to take with him a family-heirloom mirror that he and his wife received as a wedding gift. After some pressure, eventually he gives in to his father's request that he take the mirror along on the journey. Not far down the path, he stops and looks at himself in the mirror; in the distance he sees Cosme reflected there, as well as his father. The reader is uncertain whether these "faces" that interrogate Marcial from within the mirror and weigh on his conscience are real or figments of his imagination. Deeply frustrated by the unbearable image that haunts him, he throws the mirror to the ground, shattering it into a thousand pieces. But a shard gets lodged in his arm, and when he pulls it out, he bleeds profusely. This poignant moment, this chance occurrence, causes him to regret his initial decision and return to the father. In the end, the shame of looking in the mirror inspires a change of heart. The son repents so that, in his words, "[his father] will see that [he] is not a bad son, even though [making the right] decision sometimes comes a [bit too] late."[65]

Blurred Subject Positions

By now it is clear that Callejas dons a number of identities: the DINA agent/criminal, the writer, the mother, and the wife, among others. Sometimes these appear separate or isolated from one another; other times they overlap.

Perhaps the two most common theories that exist to explain how seemingly "normal" people can become killers or accomplices given the right circumstances are those of Robert Jay Lifton and Ervin Staub.[66] Both theories concern the effects that shameful acts have on the configuration of an accomplice's subjectivity or identity construct. According to Lifton's "doubling" theory, complicit subjects are able to compartmentalize their public and private lives neatly. For Lifton, the subject experiences a psychological break that, in Callejas's case, would allow her to isolate her existence as a wife, mother, and literary writer from that of her parallel life as a spy and a criminal. In contrast to Lifton's theory, Staub asserts that subjects cannot easily compartmentalize conflicting identities or personalities. Instead, he argues that complicit subjects accommodate their actions to shifting sets of moral or ethical values. In Staub's view, accomplices convince themselves that by committing a wrongful act they are actually contributing to a greater social good (e.g., Chile's salvation from the throes of Marxist socialism). The subject's "split" personalities meld such that the boundary separating them becomes porous. The complicit subject can therefore slip fluidly from one role into another without much mental disturbance.[67]

Whether or not Callejas could successfully compartmentalize different aspects of her life without much mental disturbance remains open to debate; to be honest, it seems unlikely. A story such as "Reflejo" (Reflection) speaks to the opposite impulse: it attests to the blurring of identities or subject positions that cause her mental angst. The story begins:

> At the moment of the crime we are one, the victim and the aggressor; I, the victim, falling to the ground in a slow, spiraling movement, watching the crazed spinning of the buildings at the corner, the sudden ceasing of the pedestrians' disorderly meanderings. . . . And I, the aggressor, a knife in my hand, right in the middle of downtown, perceiving nothing more than a bunch of red, shiny circles fluttering around the victim that pressure me, urge me, kill him. But at that moment I can't remember why, what he has done to me, how I got the knife, or what is implied by the shout of my name, or the victim's name, or everyone's name, or why a huge black man, a stranger smelling like sweat and desperation, has jumped on top of me.[68]

In the middle of a city, someone attempts murder for no good reason. A fight takes place between two people who have known each other all their lives and who have succumbed to violence in a moment of drunken ire. We never really find out whether the voice that speaks is that of the victim or the perpetrator. The reader is privy only to the moment of the crime itself, which is recounted in a surreal tone, like a movie in slow motion. The impulse to kill lies beyond the perpetrator's control, as if he were a victim of his circumstances acting on pure instinct. The "black man" adds an interesting element to the narrative insofar as he functions, again, as a kind of radical other, a Levinasian face personified that intervenes, interrogates, tries to stop the crime, and haunts the victim-perpetrator-narrator in the crime's aftermath. The black man catches the narrator off guard; his appearance on the scene constitutes a marked inversion of the civilization/barbarism dialectic (significantly, it is the black figure that functions as a force of good and marks the space of ethics in a violent, twisted world). Although the perpetrator feels that he is to some extent a victim, he remains aware of an ethical *outside* that interrogates his actions. The black man functions, then, as a metaphorical mirror—here, the mirror motif reappears—that reflects the narrator's behaviors back toward him and allows him to see them differently. While the perpetrator and the victim reflect each other and point toward the gray zones that violent situations sometimes generate, the presence of an ethical "other" that reflects both of those positions (the victim and the perpetrator) back on themselves serves as a reminder that blurring the lines too intensely might constitute an evasion of ethics.

Parsing Subjectivity

Although the lines separating identity constructs can become blurred, this does not mean that complicit subjects do not still attempt to delineate clear boundaries. If by the 1990s and 2000s, when she wrote *Siembra vientos*, Callejas appeared to be actively seeking ways to integrate and explain the tensions that persisted within her, in the 1980s, when she wrote *La larga noche*, we see her (perhaps logically) trying to compartmentalize conflicting aspects of her subjectivity. The clearest example of this dynamic comes in her short story "Un parque pequeño y alegre" (A Small and Happy Park), which forms the centerpiece of her book.

In that story, Callejas fictionalizes a car bombing that could very well be based on the murder of Prats or Letelier. The text deploys a curious, dual-narrative structure in which the banality of daily life becomes surgically quarantined from the description and contemplation of the crime. Where we find references to the crime itself, the descriptions always appear within parentheses: this detail may reflect a compartmentalization of Callejas's subjectivity that was already occurring at the time of the events. In these descriptions, the main characters, Cecilia and Max, rationalize their participation in the proposed car bombing. For example, Max claims not to be interested in working as an "operative" but prefers to work in more bureaucratic, supporting roles that do not require direct involvement in killings; he wants to help the government's cause because he believes it is the right thing to do but vows to stop short of becoming an actual assassin. Yet eventually he succumbs to peer pressure from his cronies in the secret police who compel him to act in the best interest of the fatherland; they assure him they will never again ask him to do such a terrible thing. For her part, Cecilia chalks up her involvement to her supportiveness for Max as well as to her youthful, adventurous spirit. A middle- to upper-class girl "uninterested in the country's political situation," Cecilia naïvely seeks an escape from the boring quagmire of her day-to-day existence. In short, rationalizations (e.g., youthful adventure, the good of the country, a one-time affair, pressure from superiors, an escape from boredom) all become "compelling" reasons to commit murder.

These rationalizations by two criminal minds contrast starkly with the alternating (nonparenthetical) narrative of the couple's everyday life. In this second narrative plane, Cecilia focuses on irrelevant details such as the couple's mutual love for poetry or the death of her cousin's cat. The split in the two narratives speaks not only to the way in which the criminal mind tries to compartmentalize and rationalize its actions but also to a wish for normalcy. It is almost as if the criminals would like to erase the sordid life in which they find themselves and become something other than what they are: they want to become regular, everyday people.

Consonant with the compartmentalization of subjectivity that we find in the story's narrative structure, the fictionalized rendering of the car bombing is separated (or departs) from what happened in real life. Unlike in the cases of Prats or Letelier, the car bomb in the story does not explode. Just as the crime is set to take place, the targeted victim's wife suddenly calls him back into the house to take an unexpected phone call. When this happens, the assassins abort the mission. Meanwhile, the targeted victim's child remains in the car, his fate uncertain. Readers are therefore left in limbo, wondering what is going to happen, while the couple stands in a park lamenting the corpse of a dead little bird that rests in the shadow of a statue of a "man with a mustache," a juxtaposition of images that eerily evokes death in the name of nationalism.[69] In this final moment, the couple again rationalizes that this little bird's life is not very important in the greater scheme of things because it is just one among "many, oh so many dead birds."[70]

While it is possible to interpret Callejas's fictionalized reversal of the crime as a literary maneuver whose goal is to forestall reality, stop time, or revert to an anterior, precriminal moment, it is also plausible to read the story as a literal rendering of the prehistory leading up to the Prats–Cuthbert assassination or, more accurately, as a conflation of what happened prior to the assassination and the moment of the assassination itself. In their journalistic account of the Prats murder, Jorge Escalante, Nancy Guzmán, Javier Rebolledo, and Pedro

Vega record a very relevant detail: several days before the actual crime, Townley had staked out Prats in a Buenos Aires park with the intention to kill him. He planned to shoot him with a pistol "but at the last minute decided not to [go through with it] because there was still daylight and people were still circulating in the park."[71] In Callejas's mind, perhaps the "small and happy park" of her story's title evokes this original park in which the Prats crime *did not take place*. We, of course, know that the actual crime occurred not near a park at all but rather in front of Prats's apartment on Malabia Street, in Buenos Aires. To revert to the "small and happy park," that is, to a time in which the couple had not yet become murderers, therefore becomes another strategy for compartmentalizing identity while concurrently playing with or compartmentalizing temporalities. Doing this constitutes a form of escapism.

Subjective splits can also happen when the subject gains perspective on herself by analyzing her existence from a distance of greater objectivity than that which she is normally capable of achieving. This dynamic manifests in another story, "Ariana," which provides the most intensely uncanny portrait of Callejas in the book. Here, a male narrator talks about how he broke up with a woman. He views the woman from the outside, and this perhaps can be read as another form of the mirror figuration through which Callejas gazes upon herself. The narrator describes the woman's life of privilege: her apartment in Providencia full of antiques, her beautiful, well-educated children, and her weekend trips to the beauty parlor. The woman's new husband, startlingly reminiscent of Townley, is described as a "functionary" with a "mustache."[72] The reader senses in the narrator's tone a negative judgment of the woman's unquestioning acceptance of the neoliberal status quo. "And how do I know all of this about you?" the narrator remarks. "All I have to do is look at you, poor thing, with your eyes full of forgetting and conformity."[73] The woman, normalized to her current life of comfort, denies knowing her former lover, who clearly represents freedom and the dreams of youth. (This detail interfaces well with other stories in the collection that reference revolution's high ideals yet ultimately dwell on its failures.) The conformist woman rejects her former lover outright. Is the man she rebuffs modeled on one of Callejas's former husbands, perhaps the one with whom she experienced the "socialist" life? The story is both a lament for what the woman left behind (freedom and dreams) and a melancholic reflection on her present-day conformity, which brings shame.

Escapism

For the ashamed accomplice seeking to flee from her present life, nostalgia can be one form of escape. "¿Te acuerdas, Angélica?" (Do You

Remember, Angélica?) provides a good example of the impulse to return to a happier time. The story is about a father, "un viejo idiota" (an old, mentally infirmed man), who denies that time has passed and who is still living a better, past life in his mind. His family was once wealthy, but illness and death have left him destitute. Nostalgia becomes a home in which to dwell and a defense mechanism for survival.

Escapism, however, does not always lead to a happy ending. Occasionally suicide is a more preferable form of escape, as in the case of "Sobre Meyer" (About Meyer), a brief story about an eighty-three-year-old war criminal who commits suicide in the boardinghouse where he lives.[74] The narrator, who also lives in the boardinghouse, eats dinner with Meyer every night but would never suspect by looking at him that he "exterminated a town in France."[75] Appearances deceive. Only a single vestige of Meyer's criminal past remains: in the drawer next to his hanging body, his friends find some news clippings that document his role in mass killings.

However, in spite of these different forms of escapism—nostalgia and suicide—*La larga noche*, as a whole, seems to assert that shame is nearly impossible to escape for the accomplice whose conscience cannot rest easy. The last story I will mention, "Heil, Peter," drives this point home. It features a male narrator who tells the story of his relationship with a man named Peter, a foreigner, a German, a Nazi who came to South America and lived in a house where a picture of his father and Adolf Hitler hung on the wall. Peter's fascist ideology and egotism bother the narrator to the point of making the two mortal enemies. One fateful night, the narrator decides to put Peter's haughty bravado to the test. They walk along the banks of a dirty, urban river that could very well be Santiago's Mapocho River when a staged tragedy occurs. A body is heard falling into the water at a distance. The narrator tells Peter he cannot swim and challenges Peter to jump into the river to save the drowning stranger. Peter, staying true to his egotistical character, accepts the challenge and, in a twist of fate, leaps to his death. The narrator is forced to live with the dirty secret for the rest of his days. Looking back, repentant and reflective, the narrator apostrophizes Peter's ghost: "The least I can do for you, [Peter], is live with the guilt [or shame] [*culpa*] forever, the secret guilt [or shame] I share with those who were my friends. . . . I think we are covering up for each other to avoid the memories of that night."[76] If at the story's onset we see a fictionalized Callejas rejecting the entire "fascist" persona that Peter embodies (implicitly lamenting her own biographical and irreversible association with that world), in the end, with candor, her fictionalized self admits her shame, weakness, and lack of ethics with a poignancy that the autobiographical Callejas of *Siembra vientos* cannot match.[77] In a turn of a phrase, Callejas disturbingly

Fictions of Mastery

captures the pacts of silence that have made truth and justice such embattled concepts in the context of Chile's post-Pinochet transition.

Jacques Derrida notes that the "secret" often remains inscribed in testimony and constitutes the hallmark of perjured discourse. When the self cannot tolerate itself, secrets remain. But, Derrida adds, even when secrets are kept, they "speak."[78] "[They] speak] to the other by keeping quiet, by keeping something quiet from him," and this silence often has a resounding quality.[79] Callejas's fiction thematizes her secret shame, which becomes a literary figuration through which to read, anachronistically, her autobiographical act. The accomplice bears witness to the shame she is reluctant to admit, for to do so would obliterate her subjectivity. As a result, her fictionalized self becomes one more bit of folklore, as mythical as the lore that has been spun around her in Chile as a cultural icon of complicity. To be anything more than a perjured subject offering a contrived narrative would imply a willingness to probe this secret shame, to recognize the true depth and breadth of her complicity out of responsibility toward her fellow citizens. Callejas, however—a fissured, compartmentalized, confused, fearful, anguished, evasive, and terribly narcissistic subject—is unwilling to be undone by her narrative. Consequently, she forestalls any chance at self-transformation, at social transformation, in short, any chance of becoming human.

Impossible Forgetting

There is a saying that people in Chile often use when a long cycle of impunity closes: *La justicia tarda, pero llega* (Justice takes time, but it comes). Unexpectedly, justice in the Prats case came first in Argentina on November 26, 2000, twenty-six years after the original crime. Enrique Arancibia Clavel, a civilian living in Argentina who had acted as a liaison and logistical support person for Townley, was sentenced to life in prison. However, because of a legal technicality, he would be released in July 2007 after serving just twelve years of his sentence, only to die shortly thereafter in his Buenos Aires apartment in enigmatic circumstances, his body riddled with stab wounds. Although other perpetrators affiliated with DINA, including Townley, were also named in the verdict, differing circumstances impeded their extradition to Argentina: Townley remained in the Federal Witness Protection Program in the United States, Pinochet had already been declared unfit to stand trial because of supposed dementia, and DINA agents such as Raúl Eduardo Iturriaga Neumann and Pedro Espinoza were already in prison for other crimes.

The Chilean justice system admittedly lagged behind the Argentine courts, but starting in 2003 Judge Alejandro Solís vigorously prosecuted the perpetrators in the Prats case. The list now included another name: Mariana Callejas Honores. Santiago's Ninth Appellate Court sentenced Callejas to two consecutive ten-year terms in 2009 for her role in the murders, but the Supreme Court overturned that ruling in 2010, letting her off with only five years of house arrest and no jail time.

In 2007, as I wandered through the stands of Santiago's International Book Fair, held every October at Estación Mapocho, Callejas's prosecution was already in progress. Aware of her situation, I was deeply shocked when I passed the kiosk of a publisher called Editorial Puerto de Palos and spotted on the table a shiny new book by Mariana Callejas, *Nuevos cuentos* (New Short Stories), which had been released that year.[80] How could any publisher in good conscience, I thought, disseminate the work of a criminal? And what did finding Callejas's book there say about how the voices of victims, perpetrators, and accomplices have all found resonance (to differing degrees) in the public space of Chile's transition? I was sickened to think that the forces of the marketplace can disturbingly equalize memory narratives. Texts by victims, perpetrators, and accomplices can lie right next to one another on a table for sale, with no hierarchies, warning signs, or distinguishing markers.

Callejas's latest stories merit no analysis here because they contain nothing of particular interest to my argument. They are largely apolitical and purposefully *de-ideologized*, a detail that can perhaps be read as an extension and intensification of the de-ideologizing mask that we saw emerging more than a decade earlier in her 1995 memoir. Still, the new book does contain an introduction worthy of comment: it speaks to the normalization of the accomplice figure and to a deadening of affect that the present-day-Callejas requires to survive.

The introduction to *Nuevos cuentos* reads like a mini-memoir and focuses almost exclusively on Callejas's identity as a writer: the award she won in her youth, the vibrancy of her literary workshops, the networks she formed with the crème de la crème of Chile's literary establishment, both right and left. Her political being therefore takes a back seat to her writerly identity, though at one point she does imply that she remains a pinochetista. She adds that this decision to be *consecuente* (faithful to her convictions) garnered her few accolades. It would have been much easier, she asserts, to have rejected Pinochet, as other "sympathizers" did, and reap the benefits that being a *concertacionista* brought.[81] Forgetting is now her path of least resistance: "In these memories that I now write, I have not wanted to refer to the country's political situation or to the events that marked me forever and gave birth to all sorts of legends [about me] in subsequent years. Suffice it to say that if I could, I would erase various chapters of my existence. But, is there anyone in the world who would not want to correct, amend, or forget some part of her life?"[82]

Depoliticizing her subjectivity becomes a form of escape. Her language is filled with clichés—quotes from Neruda about the passage of time and the loss of brighter days (*We, of that time, are no longer the same*), as well as a play on Patricio Aylwin's famous line about truth and justice "insofar as they are possible" (*en la medida de lo posible*): "I still have some life left to live, and I plan to take advantage of it insofar as it is possible."[83] Having trampled the human rights of others, she shamefully trivializes the very idea of human rights by defending her own "human right" to write. In so doing, she implicitly turns her back on the victims by turning the focus toward herself: "I have the Human Right to publish what I write, and I will continue to do so."[84]

Examined holistically, Callejas's case teaches us that the ashamed accomplice cannot rely on one singular fiction of mastery to get through life. Surviving with shame means adapting to changing circumstances to defend oneself adequately; it means devising different stories in self-defense. If in the 1980s Callejas deployed in her fiction an elaborate arsenal of strategies to cope with shame (e.g., externalizing shame via thematization, blurring subject positions, compartmentalizing subjectivity, escapism), by the mid-1990s, as I have shown, we see her shutting down, normalizing her subjectivity and de-ideologizing the self. By 2007, when she was prosecuted and facing prison, her use of this dynamic only intensified. To silence her past, to forget, to fall back on her public persona as a writer became, in 2007, her only recourse. She put up walls and succeeded, to some extent, in deadening the affect that so clearly still coursed through her veins in the 1970s and 1980s.

There is a chilling moment toward the end of Roberto Bolaño's *Nocturno de Chile* (2000; By Night in Chile, 2003) in which Mariana Callejas makes an appearance; Bolaño—not so cryptically—calls her María Canales. The novel, a deathbed confession by Sebastián Urrutia Lacroix, an ultra-right-wing Opus Dei priest who collaborated with the Pinochet regime as a teacher and literary critic, remains one of the most insightful fictional accounts to date of an agonizing, ashamed, and complicit voice.[85] In the novel's final pages, Urrutia goes to the home of María Canales, the infamous Lo Curro mansion, and engages in conversation with her.[86] He confesses that he knew, second-hand, about the killings that took place in the house's basement. Bolaño's prose foregrounds María Canales's evasiveness. She tells the priest that all she really wants to talk about is literature and complains that people keep insisting she talk about politics. Like the real-life Callejas, María Canales is withdrawn, ashamed, and given over to forgetting. The priest, too, is equally ashamed of his actions, haunted by a number of sordid episodes in his life.

The Lo Curro mansion in ruins. Photograph courtesy of the *La Nación* newspaper archive, Universidad Diego Portales, Chile.

As the conversation between the two progresses, a question arises that brings the priest profound discomfort. "Do you want to see the basement?" Canales asks.[87] Urrutia Lacroix suddenly becomes evasive, turns his head away, and closes his eyes. But Canales insists: "Do you want to see the basement?" For a woman who wishes nothing more than to forget, the question, which arises from an impulse located somewhere deep within her, startles the reader. Her insistence on *seeing the basement*, despite her desire to look away, speaks to the persistence of shame. It is as if the *joven envejecido* (aged youth)—Bolaño's literary figuration of the priest's conscience—were interrogating her too, taking her to task, calling out to her to act responsibly, as if another manifestation (personified) of the Levinasian face. Yet Canales is too weak. She desperately wants to avert her gaze but cannot. Bolaño ultimately shows that doing so is impossible for the accomplice who feels shame. The accomplice will always be haunted by her past.

More than forty years later, then, until her death, Callejas remained a haunted subject—her writing an ever-evolving conduit for the tensions between what is seeable and sayable vis-à-vis her own ethical quagmire.

2

Specters of Jaime Guzmán

(Pablo Longueira Montes, Sergio de Castro, Ignacio Santa Cruz)

A specter is haunting Chile, the specter of Jaime Guzmán: neoliberal Chile's founding ideologue; the "gray matter" of the dictatorship (as some have called him); principal author of the 1980 constitution that, despite modifications, continues to shackle the country and perpetuate endemic inequality: a man excoriated by the left and canonized by the right following his 1991 assassination at the hands of the ultraleftist group Frente Patriótico Manuel Rodríguez (Manuel Rodríguez Patriotic Front, FMPR); a staunchly Catholic man who, according to more than one source, grappled with a closeted homosexuality on which he may or may not have acted; by all accounts, one of the most influential architects of contemporary Chile, perhaps even more so than General Pinochet.

Of course, Guzmán's is not the only specter haunting Chile. Marx still floats in the air, as do Pinochet, Allende, Pablo Neruda, Eduardo Frei Montalva, the disappeared, and many other ghosts that demand to be conjured and subjected to further reckoning. In fact, so many specters hover over Chile that one might think of the country's entire transition to democracy and even its "posttransition," if and when that ever began, as thoroughly haunted. In a matter of speaking, the postdictatorial scene has become a veritable battleground for specters—ghosts whose force is actualized and measured through an ongoing war of memories waged by the living.

Periodically and insistently, political actors from all walks of life receive visits from ghosts. These actors spin tales—often publicly, and in writing—

around the dead with the goal of acknowledging, celebrating, vilifying, purging, or integrating them. On the left, Tomás Moulian's *Conversación interrumpida con Allende* (Interrupted Conversation with Allende, 1998) comes to mind as a beacon example of the kind of hauntology to which I am referring; in it, Moulian melancholically asks Allende's ghost where the left went wrong in its pursuit of revolutionary change and what, if anything, the fallen socialist president's memory might mean today.[1] On the right, we might recall the 2003 claim of the Unión Democrática Independiente (Democratic Independent Union, UDI) politician Pablo Longueira that his nightly prayers to his mentor, Jaime Guzmán, resulted in paranormal advice that, according to Longueira, helped him and his party to navigate troubling political times.

Taken together, these ghosts from across the ideological spectrum remind us of an important truth that Derrida posited in *Specters of Marx* (1994): that haunting "belongs to the structure of everyday hegemony."[2] The hegemony of global capital is shot through with ghostly returns, not only of the victims who became the collateral damage of the neoliberal order but also of the perpetrators and accomplices whose haunting presence in society feeds the very propagation of neoliberal hegemony. Derrida went on: "At a time when a new world disorder is attempting to install its neo-capitalism and neo-liberalism, no disavowal [by Marx's naysayers] has managed to rid itself of all of Marx's ghosts."[3] Neither, we might add, has any amount of disavowal through mass street protests or constitutional amendments managed to rid Chile of Jaime Guzmán's ghosts—I say *ghosts*, in the plural, because, like Marx for Derrida, Guzmán has several. And, as we shall see, he means different things to different people.

Derrida felt that Marx continued to haunt Europe and the world even after the fall of the Berlin Wall, the dissolution of the Soviet Union, and the so-called death of Marxism. He wrote motivated by an impetus to rescue Marx, to admonish us because our collective reckoning with Marx's legacy and contributions has not been complete enough. Moreover, Derrida urged a return to Marxist thought not simply as an intellectual pursuit but also—and even more important—as a political commitment for tackling deep-seated and perpetually entrenched issues of poverty and inequality that the capitalist world order has not managed to abate.

Informed by this logic, I want to suggest, in something of a reverse move, that it can also be useful to reckon with a ghost not to redeem it (as Derrida does with Marx) but instead to exorcise it, to purge it, to cast it away so that we can be free of its grip. This is the process in which Chileans who today favor writing a new constitution or taking other kinds of measures to mitigate neoliberalism's impact are currently engaged. They want to rid Chile of Guzmán's specter: a specter that undergirds the country's privatized pension system, its privatized education system, its debilitated to nonexistent labor unions, its rampant inequality, and other holdovers from the dictatorship. Their struggle, however, is ongoing, and, in the absence of deeper reforms, Jaime Guzmán's ghost will continue to maintain its grip on the nation, to insist on its presence. Even more concerning is that Guzmán's figure still garners fervent loyalty from certain political actors, businesspeople, and common citizens (mostly of the extreme right but also of the moderate right) whose acts of reckoning with Guzmán's paradoxical legacy—always partial—are carried out halfheartedly, instrumentally, or with great difficulty and angst.

Taking these ideas as a starting point, I want to show in this chapter how complicated it is for complicit figures of the right who are Guzmán's direct heirs and allies to grapple openly and honestly with his complex legacy, particularly his legacy on the question of human rights. As an important mouthpiece and thought-shaper for the regime, Guzmán offered intricate philosophical justifications to frame human rights violations as a necessary evil for placing Chile on a bright path toward its exceptional and "modern" future. Such contradictory justifications, years later, have left his heirs, particularly those of a younger generation (but also those of the "coup generation"), unsettled insofar as they, too, have been forced to reconcile discursively with what I call Guzmán's paradox: the acceptance of human rights violations as a necessary though perhaps regrettable price to be paid for the country's current "peace" and "prosperity."

A simple query motivates my reflection: Can the living conjure the dead in ways that avoid mythmaking and approximate something closer to what we might call a real avowal or a true reckoning? The answer seems clear: to do this is quite difficult for complicit subjects, including those of younger generations who try (unconvincingly) to disavow the foundational violence that undergirds today's neoliberal Chile without acknowledging and claiming that violence as *their own*, as part of their political heritage and the very constitution of their political subjectivities.

Reckoning is a tricky enterprise. When it comes to Guzmán, Belén Moncada Durruti affirms that, despite the writings that exist about him, something about his figure—the public man, the private man—continues to prove elusive and prone to distortion: "His figure and influence in Chile remain shrouded by a certain air of subjectivity, characteristic of personalities whose actions are considered controversial. . . . Guzmán's close ties to the military government have made his memory an enormously passionate matter, which makes objective analysis risky and difficult for anyone who has lived the last three decades of Chilean history."[4]

A survey of the growing bibliography on Guzmán confirms Moncada's intuition. Her own study, *Jaime Guzmán: Una democracia contrarrevolucionaria; El político, de 1964 a 1980* (Jaime Guzmán: A Counterrevolutionary Democracy;

The Politician, 1964–1980, 2006), one case in point, all but avoids Guzmán's relation to the fraught issue of human rights because, as the author asserts, "the majority of information that exists on the subject is held in reserve [*by whom, she does not say*]," and, as she claims, "[she has] not been able to access it."[5] If Moncada characterizes Guzmán as a Machiavellian politician rather than a gifted theoretician, Renato Cristi, in another fascinating book, *El pensamiento político de Jaime Guzmán: Una biografía intelectual* (Jaime Guzmán's Political Thought: An Intellectual Biography, 2011, first edition 2000), contradicts Moncada and argues instead that Guzmán should indeed be considered a theoretician insofar as his body of work is marked by "a notable unity and conceptual harmony."[6] Cristi characterizes Guzmán as a nationalist thinker who was influenced by the neoliberal ideas of the Austrian philosopher and economist Friedrich Hayek, as well as by the Chilean economists who trained with Milton Friedman at the University of Chicago. To lend credence to his thesis, he cites Guzmán's unwavering faithfulness to liberal ideas such as protecting individual rights over collective rights, the right to private property, and the undesirability of state interference in business.[7]

Much more subjective than the aforementioned authors, the historian Cristián Gazmuri, in *¿Quién era Jaime Guzmán?* (Who Was Jaime Guzmán?, 2013), assumes the role of a *memorialista* (memorialist or memoir writer—his term) who, informed by scant interviews with a few of Guzmán's family members, invokes his own personal perceptions and distant memories of Guzmán, whom he met while a law student at the Catholic University in the 1970s. These memories result in a fragmentary account of a figure whose presence in Gazmuri's life and times was decisive.[8] Prone to armchair psychoanalysis, Gazmuri argues that Guzmán, who was abandoned by his father at a young age because of divorce, spent the rest of his life suffering from the "syndrome of the absent father," seeking replacements in figures like General Francisco Franco and José Antonio Primo de Rivera, both of whom he greatly admired in his youth, as well as in right-wing Chilean president Jorge Alessandri and the dictator Augusto Pinochet, both of whom he fervently respected in later years.[9] Gazmuri's final chapter, "La leyenda" (The Legend), reinforces Moncada's assertion regarding the air of subjectivity that surrounds public memories of Guzmán. The historian reiterates how little we really know about Guzmán: his motivations, how he became who he was, his intimate life, or who actually masterminded the assassination plot that ultimately brought about his demise.[10] We are still not sure, for example, whether the assassin was acting for FMPR, Contreras, or Pinochet himself.

As is evident from the aforementioned authors' varied "uses" of Guzmán's figure, when one conjures a specter, it is with the intention of *doing* something to it—or with it. *Conjuration*, a kind of exorcism of a spirit that one convokes or evokes (either intentionally or unintentionally), can, on the one hand, be a means to upholding and validating that spirit, while on the other hand it can mean "exor-analyzing" the specter, that is, taking an objectifying distance from it with the intention of conjuring it away.[11] Derrida notes that conjuration, insofar as one performs an operation *on* the ghost, should be understood as a means to "neutraliz[e] a hegemony or overtur[n] some power" such that the ghost ideally no longer maintains a psychic hold on the haunted subject.[12] In the best-case scenario, through the act of conjuring one strives to take control of the ghost—even though, as we know, this is not always possible and even though the ghost, as in the cases I study, sometimes proves to be the more formidable opponent.

In what follows, I focus via cultural production on three different conjurations of Jaime Guzmán that permit me to draw a contrast between how the founding generation of UDI and its allies remember Guzmán and his ideas about human rights and how a younger generation (either of the center right or center left, though certainly less hard-line pinochetista in its political stance) is now starting to take steps toward a more thorough, though still incomplete, conjuring of this critical yet perpetually enigmatic figure.

Using a dynamic of point and counterpoint, I look first at a book—*Mi testimonio de fe: El servicio público, el sentido del dolor* (My Profession of Faith: Public Service and the Meaning of Pain, 2003), by Pablo Longueira Montes—founding UDI member, acolyte to Guzmán, longtime senator, short-lived 2013 presidential candidate, and Minister of the Economy under President Sebastián Piñera.[13] Longueira's book—a hagiography of Guzmán the victim and right-wing martyr—is, in a way, his own *conversación interrumpida*. It conjures Guzmán's specter and instrumentally manipulates the idea of human rights with the goal of ensuring a legacy not just for Guzmán's "good" name and "good" works but also for UDI and Longueira himself in a moment of intense political crisis.

The second cultural product I analyze, Carola Fuentes and Rafael Valdeavellano's documentary film *Chicago Boys* (2015), foregrounds the present-day, first-person narratives of five Chilean economists who trained with Milton Friedman at the University of Chicago and who played key roles in the Chilean neoliberal counterrevolution. Among the film's informants, I focus primarily on Sergio de Castro, one of Guzmán's major allies and the father of Chile's version of neoliberal "shock therapy." De Castro's testimony channels Guzmán's ghost by rationalizing the "human rights question" in a manner similar to Guzmán in the early 1970s. I argue that de Castro (and the other Chicago Boys featured in the film) embody the emergence of *homo neoliberal*—a term that the sociologists Kathya Araujo and Danilo Martucelli use to describe the "new" Chilean citizen who stakes his identity more on individualistic pursuits and the acquisition of material goods than on a concern for the collective or the rights of others. To become *homo neoliberal* for de Castro and the Chicago Boys serves (as it did for Guzmán) as a powerful memory lens, another fiction of mastery: it provides a reason for being, a schema through which to remember the past and justify the present. By highlighting de Castro's self-referential discourse, I show that for *homo neoliberal* to emerge, the speaking subject must depoliticize and normalize his subjectivity; he must refunctionalize his life and his speech to echo the principles of neoliberal rationality. In that sense, to channel, actualize, and promote Guzmán's specter, for de Castro, *is* to channel the neoliberal ethos.

In contrast to Longueira's instrumental conjuration and de Castro's subtler channeling of Guzmán's specter, the final part of this chapter analyzes an intriguing film called *El tío* (My Uncle, dir. Mateo Iribarren, 2013), which stars Jaime Guzmán's own nephew, Ignacio Santa Cruz, an openly gay actor who plumbs the familial and societal "myth" of Guzmán in ways that are, as we shall see, in some ways quite bold but in other ways quite self-serving.[14]

At stake in all these analyses (as in the previous chapter) is the concept of *avowal*, of reckoning, of speaking the truth and settling accounts. I want to ask: Through what means and to what ends do Longueira's text, de Castro's narrative, and Santa Cruz's filmic portrayal perform operations *on* or *with* Guzmán's ghost? What I hope to illustrate through these readings is that for any figure linked through pedigree to the political right—even when, as in Santa Cruz's case, that figure openly claims to be "of the left" and motivated by good intentions—it becomes exceedingly difficult (and usually undesirable) to carry out a true (dis)avowal that will lead to deep truth and real transformation (political, personal, narrative, or societal).[15] To do so would prove too unsetting or destabilizing to the "I" who speaks.

On some level, the materials I have chosen to juxtapose in this chapter may seem unorthodox. When we think of *intergenerational memories*, certain subject-specific memories tend to come to mind: memories of the children of the disappeared or of those who grew up in a context of political violence—or memories of even younger generations, those born well after the coup and who inherited the legacies of dictatorship. Rarely, however, do we think about the direct descendants (political or biological) of those who did the dirty work of radically restructuring the economy by any means necessary. My choice of Longueira, de Castro, and Santa Cruz—the first two figures *of* the right and *of* the dictatorship generation, the third a figure linked by blood ties to the right and (perhaps) seeking to break free from those ties—thus proposes a new optic on intergenerational memory from within the family tree of the dictatorship's heirs. These heirs, from the moment that the transition to democracy was first being designed in the mid-1980s until now, have been a powerful and moneyed force that has tried to quell the efforts of opposing radical agents for societal change. While, in Santa Cruz's case, it seems truly significant that one of Guzmán's blood descendants has taken real steps toward vetting his figure critically, in the end that same heir is ultimately unwilling to lay his uncle bare or burn him in effigy (so to speak) with the same zeal that students protesting in the streets today might do. Why? There seems to be *something* at stake—a familial loyalty, a material comfort, an inherited set of cultural norms—that, even for a self-proclaimed man of the "left," impedes a full, transformative reckoning that might lead to deep healing rather than partial healing or perpetual torment.

Yet, for a society to advance, reckoning cannot be partial. That *something*—implied but unsaid—the *secret*, must be confronted to break free of the ghost.

Guzmán's Paradox

Jaime Guzmán Errázuriz (1946–91) has gone down in history as the Pinochet regime's most influential civilian collaborator. As the author of key documents such as the dictatorship's 1974 "Declaration of Principles" and Pinochet's infamous 1977 speech on Chacarillas Hill, which advocated for "an authoritarian, protected, integrated, technophile democracy," Guzmán played a decisive role in creating and promoting the unique marriage of neoliberalism and authoritarianism that shaped Chile throughout the 1980s and beyond.[16] Even more important, as lead author of the 1980 constitution, he was responsible for designing and institutionalizing the so-called authoritarian enclaves (e.g., designated senators, the binomial electoral system) that cemented the Pinochet regime's legacy and haunted Chilean politics long after the 1990 transition to democracy.

Guzmán was born into a well-to-do family, and his early influences came from Catholic priests whom he met in the late 1950s and early 1960s while studying at Santiago's Sacred Hearts School. Father Osvaldo Lira, who had lived in Franco's Spain just a decade earlier, was one of Guzmán's teachers and introduced him to the thinking of the Spanish conservative ideologue José Antonio Primo de Rivera as well as to the corporatist ideas that underpinned the institutionalization of Franco's regime.[17] Such early influences resulted in a special mixture of conservative Catholicism and right-wing ideology that would lead Guzmán to reject the tenets of Liberation Theology that had taken root throughout Latin America in the 1960s. He joined the ultra-right-wing Catholic movement Fiducia while a university student, and by the early 1970s, with Allende in power, his extreme conservatism and skepticism toward democracy had inspired him to become a member of the "political council" of the ultra-right-wing paramilitary group Fatherland and Liberty, the same group to which Mariana Callejas and Michael Townley belonged (chapter 1).[18]

Guzmán's penchant for leadership emerged in the late 1960s during his years studying at the Catholic University Law School. Fearful of the Christian Democrats' promotion of agrarian reform (a political program for land redistribution that would later intensify significantly under Allende) and of the progressive radicalization of Chilean university culture (a dynamic from which not even the traditionalist Catholic University was exempt), Guzmán became responsible for the founding, in 1967, of the movement known as *gremialismo*, which forged significant inroads into the Catholic University's economics department, proved to be a powerful magnet for conservative youth, and rose to prominence as an opposing force to the now-famous "reform" of the Catholic University. Founded on a corporatist belief in the autonomy of institutions (in opposition to the socialist idea of institutions collectively serving the revolution and society), the gremialista (guild-based) movement would implacably oppose Popular Unity as well as the perceived "populist reformism" of the Christian Democrats. Steve J. Stern succinctly notes that as an opposing force to the politicized left and center of the late 1960s, the gremialistas, ironically, "promoted the politics of antipolitics."[19] "Professional, university, and trade associations [that] self-identified as 'guilds' (*gremios*) yearned for an organic society of nonpoliticized corporate groups, able to pursue their needs without turning into instruments of political ideology or party—and protected by [an] authoritarian government against the excesses of liberal democracy and professional politicians."[20] As a bastion of conservative values, the gremialista movement would later attract many individuals who, following the coup, became the most important civilian and economic advisors to the dictatorship as well as the most stalwart promoters of the Chicago-inspired neoliberal agenda.

As an adviser, speechwriter, and media presence during the dictatorship, Guzmán was one of the most vocal promoters of the idea that on September 11, 1973, Pinochet and the military had saved the country from the brink of civil war. His voice and personal writings thus mark a point of origin in a long genealogy of attempts by the right, since the coup, to separate the "laudable" neoliberalization of the economy (as well as the establishment of "peace" and "order") from the human rights violations on which that economic overhaul was founded.[21] Inspired by Hayek's idea of the "liberal dictator," Guzmán believed that authoritarian regimes could, paradoxically, increase people's freedom and degree of choice by overtly limiting other freedoms.[22] His argument, like Hayek's, was ultimately utilitarian in nature: it held that sometimes certain lives and freedoms had to be sacrificed to foster the greater good. According to such logic, a "state of exception" and the targeted killing of "subversives" was necessary for reestablishing a peaceful and orderly society. The notion that Chile in September 1973 teetered on the verge of "civil war" and that, in that scenario, the military saved the country from an impending Marxist dictatorship provided justification for mass human rights violations. As heirs to this utilitarian logic, hard-line pinochetistas still argue today that Pinochet should be remembered as a "good" Cold Warrior because he managed to eliminate the Marxist threat with far fewer deaths than occurred in Argentina, Guatemala, or other countries in the region.[23]

If one returns to Jaime Guzmán's own writings on the subject of human rights, penned around 1985 and compiled posthumously by the Jaime Guzmán Errázuriz Foundation in the collection *Escritos personales* (Personal Writings, 1992), one senses a certain irony in the conservative ideologue's instrumental argumentations precisely because the entire premise for his argument is to critique how others, specifically the Chilean left, instrumentalized the "theme" of human rights.[24] He begins by rejecting the binary idea that only two classes of human beings can exist: violators of human rights and those whose rights are violated.[25] Attenuating this Manichaean view to accommodate his own contradictory subjectivity, he engages instead in an "effort to transcend mere emotion and instead privilege reason," even though his attempts at rationality ultimately result in an argument riddled with contradictions that reads as a justification for his own ambiguous actions and positions with regard to human rights violations.[26]

Guzmán's impetus to write about human rights consequently stems from a profound discomfort with the paradoxical nature of his own position. He admits this explicitly.

> I live today a paradox: that I figure—according to certain detractors who have thrown it in my face—among those who would be considered "guilty" by association with a regime that has been condemned for violating human rights. And I affirm that this strikes me as a paradox because I possess testimonials of thanks from innumerable opponents of the current Government who are thankful for the gestures I have made on their behalf to the authorities with respect to human rights problems: people of all ideologies, including Communist Party militants whom I have helped in very difficult circumstances, because when it comes to human dignity, I recognize no political, racial, religious, or other barriers.[27]

In an attempt to resolve philosophically the "paradox" he lives, Guzmán affirms in his writings a *hierarchy of rights* that places the rights to property and to individual liberty—both liberal ideas consonant with his economic beliefs—above "natural rights," a concept on which he does not elaborate but whose existence and importance he nevertheless acknowledges. He rejects the idea that protecting the individual from abuses by the state should hold in all cases and advocates instead for a much more limited definition of rights. In that vein, certain "social aspirations" (his phrase) such as health, housing, and education should *not* count as human rights for the simple reason that because of differing economic conditions in societies around the world, poorer countries cannot guarantee access to these things in the same way that richer countries do.[28] Harking back to what he learned as a student of *franquismo*, he acknowledges that certain historical circumstances necessitate "states of emergency" and "states of exception" and that these states may, in turn, lead to a suspension of rights.[29] Because, for Guzmán, "communism" or "terrorism" represent more significant threats to humanity's well-being than dictatorship, he arrives at a paradoxical conclusion: *not* to violate certain human rights under certain exceptional circumstances would, in reality, amount to an even graver violation of human rights *by omission*. This logic, concretely applied, allows him to spin his argument toward the agrarian reform of the late 1960s and early 1970s to assert that it flagrantly violated the "human right" to property (a patently liberal idea), and this, in turn, permits Guzmán to justify the military's intervention of September 11, 1973, and its salvation of the country from an "objective situation of civil war."[30]

Beyond his philosophical rationale, in a very practical sense, an air of mystery clouds the issue of whether Guzmán ever actually intervened to protect political prisoners from harm after the coup. Carlos Huneeus remarks that while "some of [Guzmán's] friends in the opposition said that he made several gestures [on behalf of prisoners] . . . [t]hese gestures . . . cannot be confirmed. If indeed Guzmán did make them, he did so very discreetly to avoid damaging his relationship with Pinochet. A review of the correspondence housed at the Jaime Guzmán Errázuriz Foundation, [Huneeus adds], reveals nothing to support this claim."[31]

In contrast to Huneeus's argument, Cristián Gazmuri provides a short list of names of people whom Guzmán may well have helped to liberate: Jaime Solar, Osvaldo Andrade, Ángel Parra, Roberto Celedón, and "various others."[32] But wherever the truth on this matter lies, Gazmuri is likely correct in asserting that Guzmán was a man whose beliefs encapsulated a kind of "ductile morality" (*una ductilidad moral*) necessary to navigate the murky political waters in which he found himself immersed.[33] Unwilling to give up on his life's work of promoting corporatist neoliberalism or to renege on his unwavering ideological convictions, which clearly favored institutions, authority, and "protected democracy" above natural rights, Guzmán made a "pact with the devil" that

General Augusto Pinochet Ugarte (*right*) and Jaime Guzmán Errázuriz. Photograph courtesy of the *La Nación* newspaper archive, Universidad Diego Portales, Chile.

turned him into a walking contradiction. His public discourse clearly reflects this pact and can be read as an instrumental attempt to resolve (unsuccessfully) the contradictions in which he found himself mired.

Regarding his intervention on behalf of prisoners, Guzmán himself commented, "A basic sense of discretion always compels me to hold my labors [helping political prisoners] in reserve. This is because [those labors] are born of motivations that are basically *moral*, not *political*."[34] In stating this, the founder of UDI commits a logical flaw by attempting to separate morality from politics. Such a rhetorical move recalls Adolf Eichmann's self-defensive argument in his 1961 trial, in which he famously claimed to be "guilty before God, not the law." Giorgio Agamben, in his smart deconstruction of Eichmann's argument, asserts that the law is always already inscribed within the realm of ethics: as a result, one cannot be guilty in the eyes of God but innocent with respect to the law and humanity because God (who emblematizes the realm of ethics) supersedes humanity and institutions in the hierarchy of being.[35] Guzmán's reasoning, similarly examined, suffers a similar fate to Eichmann's if we accept the premise that politics, like the law, has to be more than a pragmatic game and, as such, is also always already inscribed within the realm of ethics.

Whether Guzmán intervened on behalf of prisoners will probably remain something of a mystery that historians will struggle to unravel. Still, one fact is undeniable: Guzmán's pro-regime public discourse occasionally put both political prisoners and those who defended them at risk, sometimes setting off very specific and damaging consequences. Steve J. Stern recalls an important example of this: a moment in June 1976 in which five lawyers, all defenders of human rights, sent a thirteen-page public letter on human rights violations to delegates of the Organization of American States who had gathered in Santiago for the OAS General Assembly.[36] In that moment, Pinochet seemed eager to host the OAS meeting in Chile so that he could put his best face forward and show the world that human rights were indeed being respected in his country. Incensed by the traitorous letter, whose authors included two prominent and highly respected centrists, Eugenio Velasco Letelier and Fernando Castillo Velasco, among others, Guzmán appeared on the National Television Network's (TVN) evening news program *60 Minutos* (Sixty Minutes, June 10, 1976) and spoke out vehemently against the jurists: "What becomes . . . unacceptable is that when in our country an international organism is meeting, and the whole nation has united to show a truth of our homeland [that] has been disfigured and slandered abroad [namely that human rights are *not* being violated in Chile] . . . a group of people of Chilean nationality rises up to try to sully our homeland and join with the foreign plot."[37] In this unforgettable moment, Guzmán showed his true stripes. As a result of the backlash he unleashed, the government soon issued an order to silence the human rights defenders' letter. Within six weeks, both Castillo and Velasco were arrested and forcibly sent into exile.

Guzmán was ever a strategist and a pragmatist. And this at least partially explains both the malleability of his ideas and the evolution of his public position vis-à-vis the regime over time. His strategic decision in the mid-1980s to repudiate Contreras and publicly distance himself from Pinochet proved politically expeditious as he worked to found a new political party—even though, at bottom, he remained loyal to Pinochet until the end and managed to look beyond the profound discomfort he assuredly felt about the blood that indelibly stained the regime's hands. As part of his long-term strategy to guarantee the survival of the dictatorship's economic project, he surgically and methodically encouraged the regime to embrace the idea of a civil-military alliance that would serve as more than just a stopgap for repairing the dire and "chaotic" situation that plagued Chile in 1973. Instead, he yearned for that alliance to have long-lasting historical projection and profound societal impact for years to come.[38] To that end, he believed that as soon as the regime's legacy had been memorialized in the 1980 constitution, Chile would be best served to move toward an impersonal brand of authoritarianism disconnected in the popular imagination from the dictator's figurehead.[39] UDI, the party he founded in 1983, would function as the primary conduit for achieving that goal: perpetuating pinochetismo without Pinochet. The dictatorship's project would linger, while Pinochet, Guzmán hoped, would recede quietly into the annals of history.

With this in mind, it perhaps becomes possible to read the entire history of the right in Chile since the early 1980s as an attempt to honor Pinochet's work while also seeking to break free from the dictator's specter, which was no longer politically or tactically expedient for the civilians who would carry on his legacy. The now commonplace gesture of mentally parsing Pinochet the violent dictator from his neoliberal counterrevolution thus began with Guzmán.[40] And after Guzmán, many other politicians and figures of the right have similarly tried to disavow Pinochet the criminal while hypocritically celebrating his economic transformation of the country.

In short, Guzmán encapsulates the paradoxical specter with which the right must live and grapple. While adherents of the hard-line right—admittedly ever fewer in number—cling to Guzmán's paradoxical logic on human rights, reproducing it almost verbatim, a newer, center-right position has since emerged that distinguishes Chilean modernization from the dictatorship's violence more markedly by arguing that economic liberalization could, in theory, have occurred without the dictatorship's crimes. Proponents of this thesis, such as the former center-right president Sebastián Piñera (2010–14), who made arguments to that effect around the time of the fortieth anniversary of the coup (2013), hold that while neoliberal modernization is undeniably good and beneficial for the country, the dictatorship's human rights violations were a regrettable occurrence to be blamed on specific, situated historical actors.[41] This line of argumentation serves the political right electorally and in terms of its public image by delinking it from the baggage of authoritarianism. Contradicting Piñera's thesis, the political scientist Hassam Akram forcefully argues that separating neoliberalism from dictatorial violence, as the progressive right tries to do today, is wholly "untenable."[42] He convincingly proves that neoliberalism needed dictatorship to penetrate deeply into the social fabric, while Pinochet likewise needed neoliberalism to consolidate his power. Akram carefully illustrates that the Chicago Boys and Pinochet shared a perfect marriage of convenience. On the one hand, the Chicago Boys gave Pinochet a reason for being, a telos and a historical legacy that differentiated him from his more moderate, "populist" peers (Christian Democratic soldiers who favored a more measured approach to economic matters and who might have posed a threat to his power); on the other hand, Pinochet gave the Chicago Boys the heavy hand they needed to force neoliberalism on the population with no questions asked.

If today the center right tries to separate Pinochet the murderer from Pinochet the economic reformer, it engages in a self-appeasing fiction of mastery or act of wishful thinking. As inheritors of Guzmán's paradox, the center right fails to acknowledge the historical fact that Chile's current social and economic order was founded on thousands of cadavers and tortured bodies. Jaime Guzmán, who also failed to recognize that fact openly and with all its ethical weight, was a bounded subject shaped by his carefully honed and guarded discourse. It comes as no surprise, then, that his heirs, reluctant to disavow Guzmán's ghost entirely, have become equally bounded subjects, trapped by the paradoxes of their own beliefs.

Avowal, or Its Lack? Pablo Longueira's Hagiography of Jaime Guzmán

In his 1981 inaugural lecture at the Catholic University of Louvain, Michel Foucault defined *avowal* as "a verbal act through which the subject affirms who he is, binds himself to this truth, places himself in a relationship of dependence with regard to another, and modifies at the same time his relationship to himself."[43] Interested in the connection between avowal and other notions such as truth, justice, and responsibility, Foucault identified a Western tradition of avowal that runs from the ancient Greeks to the Christian tradition and to confessional discourse and modern criminal law. In this regard—and this will become relevant as I analyze Pablo Longueira's text—one might think of a "profession of faith" (*un testimonio de fe*), a speech genre that dates from the sixteenth century in the Roman Catholic tradition and refers to a declaration by an individual before God and the Church community, as an instance of avowal in which one dedicates oneself to God and the greater community in belief or service. It is thus underscored by a commitment to morality and ethics.

To avow, however, is not simply to speak what one believes to be true but to do so in a way that is selfless and for another—a notion that interfaces with Judith Butler's concept of "accounting" as I explained it in chapter 1. One of Foucault's central ideas on the topic was that "what separates avowal from a [simple] declaration . . . [is] a certain *cost* of enunciation."[44] When one avows, one submits to a higher power (call it God, the law, one's fellow humanity, or some other instance of authority) vis-à-vis which one is willing to assume the cost of speaking the truth. Where there is no price to be paid, no real avowal occurs. In other words, if one is unwilling to speak the whole truth, to assume the consequences of one's words, to submit to the judgment of forces beyond the self, to be interpellated by counterarguments and positions, avowal cannot lead to transformation. Furthermore, because avowal is always inscribed in a power relation—that is, one speaks *to* another and one must thus be willing to be judged *by* another—it carries with it an implicit disposition to be punished. Consequently, avowal should be understood as a radical act in the sense that it harbors the potential to modify power relations among individuals.[45]

Given the connotations (i.e., truth, justice, responsibility) that Foucault attached to the notion of avowal, it is likely already clear that Pablo Longueira's *Mi testimonio de fe* fails as a true avowal. It reads as a self-interested, self-aggrandizing account masked as altruism, selflessness, and being-for-another. To appreciate this dynamic, however, one must go beyond the text and inquire about the conditions in which the book was published. Context is key to the discussion.

Longueira's book appeared in 2003, a moment in which UDI's public image had been severely tarnished by the "Spiniak Case," a scandal linking two UDI senators of pinochetista stock, Jovino Novoa and Carlos Bombal, among others, to a pedophilia, child pornography, and child prostitution ring run by a bisexual business magnate, Claudio Spiniak.[46] Pía Guzmán, a congresswoman from the moderate right-wing party Renovación Nacional (National Renovation, RN), basing her accusations on information acquired from people she had met at a shelter for sexually abused youth, publicly declared that the two UDI senators had formed part of Spiniak's inner circle. In light of these accusations, the senators were charged with "illicit association," a charge of which they were eventually exonerated, though not without first having their names dragged through the mud in a media circus that brought profound political consequences for the parties of the political right and UDI in particular. Spiniak went to prison for ten years, and Pía Guzmán faded into the woodwork when RN refused to renew her congressional seat in 2005.

As president of UDI when the scandal broke out, Longueira spent nearly all his time and energy trying to save his party—Catholic, conservative, homophobic—from degradation and political destruction. In general, the scandal left the right divided and eroded possibilities for a united front against the Concertación in the approaching 2005 presidential election, in which Joaquín Lavín, former mayor of Santiago and an UDI stalwart, eventually lost in the first round to the RN candidate, Sebastián Piñera. Longueira decried the "sinister montage" and witch hunt that Pía Guzmán had unleashed on UDI and published *Mi testimonio de fe* in self-defense, in an attempt to counteract the bad press that was raining down on what had become, until that point, one of the country's strongest political parties in electoral terms.[47] Longueira explains in his "Prologue" that the book was written in haste, in response to the urgent demands of the moment. His goals are clear: (1) to prove that UDI, as an influencer of public opinion and a supposed bastion of morality, remained above the fray in the realm of Chilean politics; and (2) to prove that Chileans should rally around Lavín's candidacy.

Incessantly quoting the Bible, papal encyclicals, and homilies by bishops and cardinals and invoking Thomas More, the "patron saint of politicians"—who appears on the book's cover alongside Jaime Guzmán, Miguel Kast, and Jesus Christ—Longueira constructed a hagiographic account of UDI founder Jaime Guzmán, lauding him as an "apostle" of Chilean political institutionality, and of Miguel Kast, whom he likewise touted as an "apostle" of the Chilean economy, praising Kast for the role he had played in designing neoliberal Chile.[48] Taken in tandem, the two men's lives and work form the backbone of Longueira's self-validating discourse, which simultaneously functions as an homage and as a pseudo-philosophical justification of UDI's magnanimous and purportedly selfless contributions to Chilean political life and to improving the lot of the poor. *Mi testimonio de fe* is therefore, at its core, a political hagiography inspired by the specters of two central figures (Guzmán and Kast) whose influence, especially Guzmán's, proved decisive for Longueira's initial conversion to politics. The book must therefore be read not only as a hagiography or martyrology—Kast died of cancer and Guzmán was murdered—but also as a conversion narrative reminiscent of texts by St. Paul, St. Augustine, and many others. Longueira opened the door to such a reading when he wrote: "I was like so many young people in this country. [I did not even have] an iota of political ambition . . . [until] a unique and exceptional man, Jaime Guzmán, changed the lives of so many of us and made us want to abandon our professions and dedicate our lives to public service."[49]

A riff on and deformation of the genre known as *testimonio*, *Mi testimonio de fe*—oddly reminiscent of well-known books such as Rigoberta Menchú's *Yo me llamo Rigoberta Menchú y así me nació la conciencia* (1982; English translation, *I, Rigoberta Menchú: An Indian Woman in Guatemala*, 1984)[50]—curiously mimics certain formal aspects that we find in testimonies by subaltern subjects: (1) a desire to denounce an urgent and unjust situation; (2) a metonymic quality to the voice that speaks, that is, an acknowledgment that the "I" who bears witness does so in the name of a larger group or community experience (in this case, UDI, several of whose high-profile members also anthologize writings in Longueira's book that validate the author's own canonization of Guzmán and Kast); (3) a desire to document and provide details to support truth claims; and (4) a hope that one's act of witnessing will create real change in the world. Understood in purely formal terms, the use of the word *testimonio* in the book's title seems apt. Yet we soon discover that the term wholly deceives because testimonio, in theoretical terms, cannot and should not be delinked from subaltern subjects, the downtrodden, and the victims of social and political injustice. What we have then, in this case, is something entirely different from *testimonio*: a pamphleteering hybrid of autobiography and hagiography penned from a position of power and wealth.

Moreover, Longueira's book, lacking in transparency, silences important realities, such as the role that the Kast family played in aiding and abetting the 1973 assassination of seventy rural inhabitants of Paine who supported Allende's agrarian reform efforts. The complicities of the Kast clan have been well documented and described in a recent book by the journalist Javier Rebolledo, *A la sombra de los cuervos: Los cómplices civiles con la dictadura* (In the Shadow of the Ravens: The Dictatorship's Civilian Accomplices, 2015) but are, of course, never mentioned by Longueira.[51] To the contrary, in reconstructing the Kast family's fiction of origin, Longueira wrote that "Miguel Kast Rist was born in Germany in 1948 and, for family reasons [*por razones familiares*], moved to Buin as a child" (58). Longueira's phrase *por razones familiares* sheepishly masks the detail that Michael Kast, Miguel's father, was a virulent opponent of communism as well as a Nazi officer who sought refuge in Chile after World War II. The family's beliefs and ambitions are therefore, in point of fact, founded on a sordid Nazi past.

Mi testimonio de fe repeats certain ideas ad nauseam: UDI's will to serve the people, love of one's neighbor, and the party's philosophical inspiration in Liberation Theology's concept of a "preferential option for the poor." None of this is very surprising if we recall that UDI has historically operated by sinking resources into increasing its base support among young people (through a network of youth organizations) and among the poor (through clientelism and deep penetration into underserved and marginal neighborhoods). From a philosophical perspective, the book defends neoliberalism, inspired by Guzmán, as a system to be praised for creating equal opportunities and allowing individuals to exercise free choice; strangely, it defines *ethics* as a marriage of trickle-down economics and charity (or humanitarianism) packaged rhetorically in Catholic doctrine.

Longueira's text constructs a defense of neoliberalism that skirts contradictions in logic by clinging to chains of reasoning that for him prove thoroughly convincing. A case in point: in his sketch of Miguel Kast's life, the author points to a tension that existed in Kast as a young man between "serving other people and the country or serving [him]self by trying to make money in great quantity."[52] Studying with Milton Friedman at the University of Chicago provided an unexpected and decisive framework within which Kast could resolve this tension intellectually. Under Friedman's tutelage, Kast discovered that making money in great quantity can ideally, and by extension, open doors to help other people: "I know that because I have been given much, I [also] have to give much [to others], and give it to those who need it most."[53] This defense of wealth leaves no room for questions about structural inequities, the causes of poverty, the dissolution of community, or the myriad ways in which people's human rights are violated under a system that economizes everything, including the individual's *bios*.[54]

Among the many topics Longueira develops in more than three hundred pages of prose, his treatment of human rights is perhaps most attention grabbing. Roughly six months before the publication of *Mi testimonio de fe*, on the eve of the thirtieth anniversary of the coup (2003), Longueira took the lead on what he calls "the most significant event with regard to human rights that has taken place [in Chile] in the last decade": namely the publication of a document titled "La Paz Ahora" (Peace Now), in which UDI details a series of meetings that it held with a group of eight families of victims from Pisagua, a town in northern Chile where many were killed during the dictatorship's early years.[55] Summarized succinctly, the centerpiece of UDI's proposal to the families was to aid them in seeking the truth regarding their deceased loved ones' whereabouts and to assist them in securing monetary reparations to compensate for their losses. Any gesture toward real justice, punishment, or accountability for perpetrators and accomplices was markedly absent from UDI's proposal, which critics chided as highly instrumental and yet another ploy to position the party for electoral advantage in a moment of crisis and loss of face. In an article published just shortly after the report's release, Juan Carlos Gómez Leyton scoffed that UDI's proposal "[would] go down in the annals of history as the biggest act of cynicism and hypocrisy in the history of Chilean society."[56] He went on to note that the pinochetista party's sudden change of heart regarding people it had once classified as humanoids "should be understood as part of a rational and calculated political strategy to establish conditions of governability for an eventual Joaquín Lavín government."[57] He further likened UDI's hypocrisy to what he called "the syndrome of the abusive father": a father who punishes, consoles, and makes peace offerings but never asks forgiveness.[58]

At its core, Longueira's book inherits and promotes the salvationist memory script that I signaled in Guzmán's writings and that, despite minor attenuations, has long characterized UDI's public discourse. Consequently, one can read *Mi testimonio de fe* as inscribed in a longer genealogy of instrumental uses and abuses of human rights that can be tracked back to Longueira's martyred hero and mentor. This instrumentality shines through when Longueira, eager to lay debates about human rights to rest once and for all—because, as he says, the "average Chilean in the street . . . is supersaturated by the topic"—applauds

General Augusto Pinochet Ugarte (*right*) and Pablo Longueira Montes. Photograph courtesy of the *La Nación* newspaper archive, Universidad Diego Portales, Chile.

UDI's meeting with eight families of Pisagua as a true space of "peace," "forgiveness," and mutual tears.[59] In personal terms, he denies having known anything about the military's crimes at Pisagua at the time they occurred; nevertheless moved, he magnanimously responds (in 2003) to the pleas of family members who, exhausted from years of being bandied about like political pawns (he implies, by the Concertación), were left with no other option than to seek help from UDI.[60] To lend credence to his argument, he quotes extensively from a statement by one of the victims' sons, Demetrio Sampson Trujillo: "One cannot measure pain in qualitative or quantitative terms; one can only say that *we all lost*. For that reason, today we don't just make demands, we also offer our commitment to a true never again. This little coming together of UDI and our families, so unjustly criticized, is a small step toward ending a permanent cycle of pain in our families and toward healing societal wounds that, perhaps, cannot be totally healed. . . . Today, we are not only proud of the step we have taken, but also of our parents and spouses who left us a great legacy: they faced everything courageously and honestly."[61]

Several points are worth noting here. First, Longueira uses Demetrio Sampson's statement to erase the division between victims and perpetrators by implying that, in a sense, "we were all victims." Second, he frames the statement by admiring the courage of families that were willing to overcome fear and "take the step" (*dar el paso*) that could change the tenor of human rights discussions in Chile forever. (Ironically, this phrase, *dar el paso*, which appears in other well-known testimonies, including that of the socialist militant turned collaborator Luz Arce Sandoval, and that usually implies a selfless and courageous avowal and dedication to the truth, is here twisted toward self-serving ends and thus divested of its ethical weight.)[62] Third, Longueira uses Sampson's statement as proof that reconciliation provides the key to healing in Chilean society thirty years after the coup. He argues that other victims' families have no right to get in the way of their peers who, correctly (in his opinion), are "willing to sacrifice some things, such as 'the whole truth,' so that they can find their loved ones."[63] Advocacy for such trade-offs peppers the "Peace Now" document, which, in the spirit of the South African truth commission, argues in favor of shortening trials (*agilizar los procesos*) and reducing or eliminating punishments for perpetrators and accomplices who might be willing to come forward with valuable information.[64]

As in the previous chapter's analysis of Mariana Callejas, then, in Longueira's book we find a similar compartmentalization of subjectivity whose goal is to de-ideologize the "I." The image of the "I" that the author sells to the reader is that of an apolitical youth who, in the spirit of rejecting *ideologismos* (a pejorative term connoting blind ideological belief), opts for "ideas" over ideology—we sense the irony—all in the interest of promoting the common good.[65] The separation of the self from ideology is just one of many intentional splits that the book crafts and posits: politics are separated from ethics, the dictatorship's political project is separated from its human rights violations, and UDI's altruistic mission of promoting social justice is separated from the neoliberal project's dark underbelly. Through it all, pain becomes the primary trope Longueira uses to write himself and the UDI into a *genealogy of victimhood*—"we were all victims"—that would claim that Guzmán, Kast, and everyone else who has ever belonged to UDI has suffered greatly for the good of the country and for love of his or her neighbor.

Incensed by the many manipulations of subjectivity and fact that pervade Longueira's book, perhaps Patricio Fernández said it best in a July 17, 2013, editorial piece published in *The Clinic*: "There comes a moment in which words full of good intentions and understanding of one's neighbor become perverse."[66] Pure self-defense, Longueira's performance of avowal ultimately fails because it resists all gestures toward self-critique, refuses to entertain counterarguments, and is wholly unwilling to assume the *cost* of truth-telling.

More than a decade after the publication of *Mi testimonio de fe*, Longueira today finds himself—like many other politicians and businesspeople of the right and the left—embroiled in political scandal. When personal emails between Longueira and Patricio Contesse, Chief Executive Officer of Sociedad Química

Minera (Soquimich or SQM), a Chilean chemical company with multinational interests in mining, fishing, and many other industries, came to light in 2016, Longueira's world began to crumble around him. The emails suggested that Longueira had incorporated into a 2010 mining royalty law (which Congress eventually approved and that potentially brought millions of dollars in tax benefits to SQM) specific language that Contesse had supplied to him. On top of this scandal, the former senator and his entourage are also now suspected of issuing "ideologically false invoices" (*boletas ideológicamente falsas*) to cover up 730 million pesos in questionable campaign contributions. With his reputation tarnished and likely encouraged to step down by members of his own coalition, who began to see him as a political liability, on March 9, 2016, Pablo Longueira, one of the most emblematic faces of UDI, resigned from the party he helped found: "I have resolved to renounce my militancy and solicit it again only when the courts confirm that I have not committed any crime. . . . I will devote all my will and all my energy to defending my honor and my innocence. I will compile a complete history of my legislative work to prove that never, never have I favored any person, institution, or company improperly."[67]

In light of these recent developments, readers of Longueira's 2003 book sense tremendous hypocrisy given that his defense of UDI's good name is partially fueled by the contrast he draws between his own political party's uprightness and his political opponents' corruption and financial crimes. One of the book's opening sections, "Compromiso con Chile" (Commitment to Chile), denounces the involvement of then-President Ricardo Lagos and several Concertación congressmen in the "Caso Coimas" or "MOP-Gate" (Bribery Case, Ministerio de Obras Públicas-Gate), a 2003 scandal, akin in many ways to the scandals of today, in which the country's Ministry of Public Works was used as a vehicle to line the pockets of contractors for services never rendered. Reacting to this corruption, Longueira solicited an audience with Lagos to demand legislation aimed at achieving "greater transparency in financing political activities, especially campaigns."[68] That same year, he also took the lead in pushing through Congress thirteen laws that would more rigorously regulate political contributions and state funds. Ironically, his 2003 bid for transparency may ultimately be what spells his political death.

Homo Neoliberal

Guzmán's paradox haunts not only the discourse of his acolytes, such as Pablo Longueira, but also the memories of his closest allies, including Sergio de Castro Spikula (1930–), who today, like other figures of the right, grapple with and seek to "resolve" in their own ways the fraught conflict of a modernization project founded upon unspeakable acts of violence.

De Castro, a professor of economics at the Catholic University and Dean of the Economics School from 1965 to 1968, became a powerful thought leader and a highly influential figure within the Pinochet regime.[69] Having studied at the University of Chicago in 1956 under the tutelage of free-market crusaders such as Arnold Harberger and Milton Friedman, following the September 11, 1973, coup this first-generation Chicago Boy stood at the ready to eviscerate the Chilean welfare state and impose an alternative economic model rooted in a pure, unbridled belief in neoliberalism. As the principal author of the regime's economic policy known as "El ladrillo" (The brick), which provided a calculated counteroffensive to Allende's deprivatization initiatives, de Castro played a central role in selling the merits of the free market to Pinochet as a panacea for the country's dire economic situation.

Though Pinochet was at first unsure of the economic direction his regime would take on economic policy, he eventually listened carefully to de Castro, who assured the General that neoliberalizing the economy would safeguard his legacy and guarantee the regime a positive image for history. Also moved by Milton Friedman's decisive March 1975 visit to Chile, in which the free-marketeering professor reinforced for the dictator the need for capitalist "shock therapy," Pinochet quickly took a leap of faith and promoted de Castro from an advisory role to the key position of Minister of the Economy. De Castro would serve in that capacity until Pinochet named him Minister of Housing in 1977, taking advantage of his time in both posts to spearhead the divestiture of myriad state-owned businesses, the privatization of strategic industries, and the slashing of public spending. "The state," de Castro and the Chicago Boys thought, "[had to] give way to the market; populism [had to] be replaced by expertise[;] and ideological conflict [had to be replaced] by economic competition. Only by shrinking government and streamlining enterprise . . . could Chile become a developed nation. And only economic growth could cure poverty—even if that meant extra hardship while waiting for the *chorreo*, or trickle-down, to occur."[70] All the while, de Castro and his technocratic cohort felt they were acting in the interest of the common good and seemed willing to ignore the blood staining the regime's hands as a price to be paid for modernizing the country.[71] Their discourse of "self-sacrifice" resonated perfectly with that of the military crusaders who had "saved" the nation from the toxic grip of Marxist ideology and who now, to protect their epic story, also needed to free the economy from the grip of socialist policies.

To a certain extent, Pinochet's alliance with de Castro was a relationship of convenience, much like de Castro's alliance with Jaime Guzmán and the gremialistas. Guzmán and de Castro had met in the hallowed halls of the Catholic University in the mid-1960s. The two were immediately drawn to each other by certain natural affinities: their staunchly Catholic beliefs, their conservative and "traditionalist" backgrounds, their skepticism with regard to democracy, their hatred of socialism, and their adherence to authoritarianism as the best way to correct a chaotic situation. Shortly after the 1965 birth of the gremialista movement, de Castro took notice of Miguel Kast, Guzmán's prized pupil, and saw in him a vehicle to penetrate the movement with his ideas about the free market. Five years later, with Allende in power, the gremialistas and the Chicago-trained economists would regularly hold closed-door meetings whose objective was to gestate an "alternative economic plan" to combat Allende's peaceful road to socialism; Jaime Guzmán would occasionally attend those meetings.[72] Five years after that, with de Castro having risen to a position of notoriety within the Pinochet regime, his relationship with Guzmán would grow stronger than ever before. Motivated less by a concern with formal politics than with crafting "revolutionary" economic theory, de Castro saw in Guzmán a vehicle for institutionalizing politically his bold ideas about the economy. By marrying his own neoliberal prowess to Guzmán's political savvy and Pinochet's ruthlessness, de Castro seized an opportunity to secure a victory for economic freedom, even at the expense of individual liberties and human rights. After Guzmán's murder, in 1991, de Castro would continue to push his neoliberal ideas, serving as economic advisor to UDI and helping the party to market a public image of itself as the one most responsible for Chile's "economic miracle" and modernizing transformation.[73]

How does de Castro today look back on his life and grapple with Guzmán's paradox? Carola Fuentes and Rafael Valdeavellano's documentary film *Chicago Boys* (2015) provides important insight for answering this question. The film foregrounds the voices of five Chicago Boys (Sergio de Castro, Ernesto Fontaine, Carlos Massad, Rolf Lüders, and Ricardo Ffrench-Davis), slating de Castro in the role of key informant. On one level, the film traces the history of the Chicago Boys' formative years. However, its primary goal is not historical. Instead, it seeks to highlight how Pinochet's closest economic advisers, in the here and now, rationalize their involvements with the regime and understand the legacy of their work vis-à-vis the regime's human rights violations. To that end, the first voice we hear in the film, that of Arnold Harberger, de Castro's teacher, begins implicitly with the idea of shame: "[People] blame me," he says, "for having created . . . [*He stops himself midsentence.*] They attribute a role to me that I find to be an exaggeration." Tellingly, Harberger's statement is imbued with silence, an ellipsis, a reluctance to admit to the unspeakable source of his (the accomplice's) shame. This silencing of unspeakable violence, in general, extends to the voices of the film's other informants, who prefer to hold themselves up to the light as economic heroes rather than admit that they are contradictory, conflicted, or morally responsible human beings.

The Chicago Boys' retelling of their beginnings sounds like a Horatio Alger story. When Arnold Harberger first arrived in Chile in 1955, offering de Castro and others an opportunity to study in Chicago, the young men jumped at the chance to better their lot in life and escape their "Third World" destiny. Ernesto Fontaine remarks that when he first met Professor Harberger, he immediately took notice of Harberger's handsome yellow shirt, coveting it as an object that could be obtained only in the "First World." Fontaine adds that such a beautiful shirt is something one would never see in this "shitty country of ours." Several other Chicago Boys muse about how "poor" they were when they first went to study in the United States (in reality, most of them came from middle- or upper-class families) and about how life in the United States opened their eyes to other realities and stoked their desire to wage a capitalist counterrevolution in Chile. The Chicago Boys' foundational fiction therefore hinges on a vision of the self that is staked on material wealth. Possessing a beautiful yellow shirt metonymically defines the identity to which these self-made, enterprising men aspire.

From early on, the Chicago Boys began to think of themselves as apolitical beings. Doing so was indeed necessary for the emergence of *homo neoliberal* as an identity construct. To that end, de Castro observes, "In Chicago, we never spoke about politics; we never tried to poison . . . the minds of the [other Chileans] who went to study there." To be born as the "Chicago Boys," as neoliberal subjects par excellence, required that these men forsake their political subjectivities and embrace their role as free marketeers with an almost religious fervor. Though each of these men came from a political party of the right or center, their newfound belief in the market supplanted politics and became a cure-all for every kind of social ill. They would thus redefine themselves as a "mafia"—as fighters in a crusade to divest Chile of ideology and turn it into a neoliberal paradise. As part of this process of transforming into an *economic hero*, de Castro, for example, speaking in the present, denies having ever crafted a specific (political) plan for the military. He wants his interviewers to believe that the Chicago Boys came together to draft their economic theory, "El ladrillo," as a mere "intellectual exercise," without ever considering a specific methodology for its implementation. To contradict this claim, the filmmakers include footage of a private meeting held in the mid-1970s in which de Castro is heard telling other members of the military regime that to achieve its ends the government will have to use a "heavy hand" (*mano dura*). He then begins to formulate a follow-up idea: that the government must tread carefully lest its heavy-handedness get "out of hand." Unable to complete his thought because of the blush of shame that is about to wash over his face, his voice tapers off until it becomes inaudible.

The sociologists Kathya Araujo and Danilo Martucelli argue that redefining the Chilean citizen as *homo neoliberal*—neoliberal man—was one of the Pinochet regime's main objectives after its economic program had been consolidated in the mid-1970s.[74] To revolutionize Chilean society meant not only overhauling the economy in formal terms but also redefining citizenship. It meant conquering hearts and minds. UDI politician Joaquín Lavín, in his well-known book *Chile: Revolución silenciosa* (Chile: A Silent Revolution, 1987), spoke to this objective directly when he observed, "Over the last decade [1977–87], Chile has experienced profound change, transformations that are modifying the ways in which new generations of Chileans live, think, study, work, and rest, the way they dress, the food they buy, the way they spend their free time, the cities in which they prefer to live, the majors they choose in school. . . . Everything is changing."[75] Employing a different kind of analytic language, Araujo and Martucelli argue that the dictatorship's project of creating *homo neoliberal* hinged on four main priorities that included: (1) using widespread repression to generate fear, to quell collective mobilization and protest, and to strategically orient citizens toward individualistic, rather than collective pursuits; (2) using public discourse and other methods to foment traditional moral values and make family and religion (not political parties, unions, or collectives) the nodal points for Chilean social interaction; (3) generating a dynamic of competition and individualistic pursuit at all levels of Chilean society; and (4) instilling a pro-market mentality that would convince people that they should become masters of their own destiny, without relying on the state for support.[76] Although Araujo and Martucelli, writing in the wake of the 2011 student protests, claim that Chileans today are socially minded and valiantly resist the impetus to become *homo neoliberal*, they are also mindful that the dictatorship's utopian vision for society involved creating a depoliticized citizen-consumer whose every activity and thought would be oriented toward the market.[77]

When we consider the narratives that de Castro and the other Chicago Boys offer in the film, it is clear that to frame themselves as *homo neoliberal* constitutes a powerful fiction of mastery that allows them to preserve a heroic vision of the self and alleviate the anxieties that derive from Guzmán's paradox. In later sequences of the film, for example, pressed by the filmmakers to account for his complicity, de Castro make statements such as the following:

1. I never knew of anyone who had been killed or mistreated.
2. When people would talk about those kinds of things [i.e., human rights violations], I thought they were absolute lies.
3. Many times I attended meetings of the World Bank or the International Monetary Fund, and I had friends in the [United States] State Department. And they would say to me, "Look, in Chile there is repression and torture and this and that," and frankly I didn't believe them.

Unconvinced by these statements, Fuentes intervenes and asks de Castro if, upon returning to Chile from any such meetings, he ever asked Pinochet if the rumors he was hearing were true. De Castro predictably denies ever having spoken of the matter with Pinochet. He adds: "[I never asked him] because I was involved in the economic thing [*yo estaba en la cosa económica*], and I had my own problems. Why would I want to go looking for other kinds of problems?" He adopts a don't ask, don't tell mentality, hiding behind his comfortable role as an economist.

Chicago Boys does an excellent job of forcing de Castro and others to face the fact that transforming Chile economically came at an immense human cost. The filmmakers' questions sometimes make the men uncomfortable and compel them to see what they wholeheartedly resist admitting to discursively: that economic change of such enormous magnitude and rapidity would never have been possible in Chile without the "heavy hand" of dictatorship. The viewer senses the informants' discomfort and can therefore appreciate their complicity all the more palpably. Still, the Chicago Boys recoil into themselves, willing to accept torture, killing, disappearance, and exile as necessary prices to be paid for Chile's prosperity. Rolf Lüders speaks directly to this: "And if you ask me, do I justify human rights violations [I say], 'No, I find them awful,'" . . . but . . . but . . . [*He stumbles over his words, wanting to formulate his next thought carefully*] but it has seemed to me that it would not have been possible to make the change that was made in Chile without an authoritarian regime."

In a sense, Lüders, like de Castro and the other Chicago Boys, remains frozen in time. He clings to a heroic-crusader discourse to justify his existence. But patently heroic memories such as those of Longueira and the Chicago Boys—memories that, for the most part, deny any moral responsibility for human rights violations—are no longer tolerable to most Chileans today. Times have clearly changed, and salvationist lines of discourse that made "sense" and found significant degrees of resonance in a Cold War context or in the early years of the transition have ceased to be convincing to most people. Such memories, however, linger obstinately on the scene as holdovers—like specters from another time. In contrast, younger generations with ties to the right, as I show in the next two sections, grapple with the conflicted legacy of pinochetismo not through the construction of heroic narratives but through more nuanced confrontations with Guzmán's paradox.

The Traitor and the Hero

Jorge Luis Borges's story "Theme of the Traitor and the Hero" (1944), like Longueira's *Mi testimonio de fe*, Sergio de Castro's testimony, and Ignacio Santa Cruz's portrayal of his uncle in *El tío*, which I analyze now, brings us face-to-face with the difficulty of avowal.[78] In Borges's story, Fergus Kilpatrick, a revolutionary "hero" fighting to liberate Ireland from British domination, turns out, in reality, to be a traitor to the revolutionary cause. Throughout the narrative, which in true Borgesian style emphasizes the artifice and convention that configure all storytelling, the traitor-hero's great-grandson conducts a thorough investigation of his great-grandfather's treacherous past. He combs through archives, comes to understand the decidedly fictional nature of his source material, yet ultimately believes that his research has led him to uncover a bitter, silenced truth that underlies the Irish nation-state's foundational fiction. Somewhat predictably, however, Ryan, the great-grandson, resolves to protect long-standing national lore, as well as his family's reputation, by censoring that truth. Borges thus leaves us wondering if it is ever really possible to tell a family story, a personal story, or a nation's history in a way that is anything other than fictional.

Mateo Iribarren's film *El tío*, which stars Jaime Guzmán's nephew Ignacio Santa Cruz (also the film's executive producer), actualizes Borges's story by placing center stage Santa Cruz's process of reckoning with his uncle's specter, a process whose principal dynamic is to explore the blurred lines separating fact from fiction, history from myth. The film is a bold undertaking. Its protagonist, "Ignacio," an actor by trade, sets out to *become* Guzmán, to play the role of his uncle so fully and authentically that he might come to discover something deeper about the specter that since childhood has haunted him, his family, and the nation he calls home.

In fact, Guzmán's ghost possesses Santa Cruz so thoroughly it seems unhealthy. An example: Ignacio's attempts to dress, speak, and even think like Guzmán consume every fiber of his being—so much so that his boyfriend Julio breaks up with him, unable to tolerate it when Ignacio channels his uncle's voice in bed after sex. Willing to suffer just about any consequence for the sake of his craft, Santa Cruz persists in his quest to become Jaime Guzmán, hoping

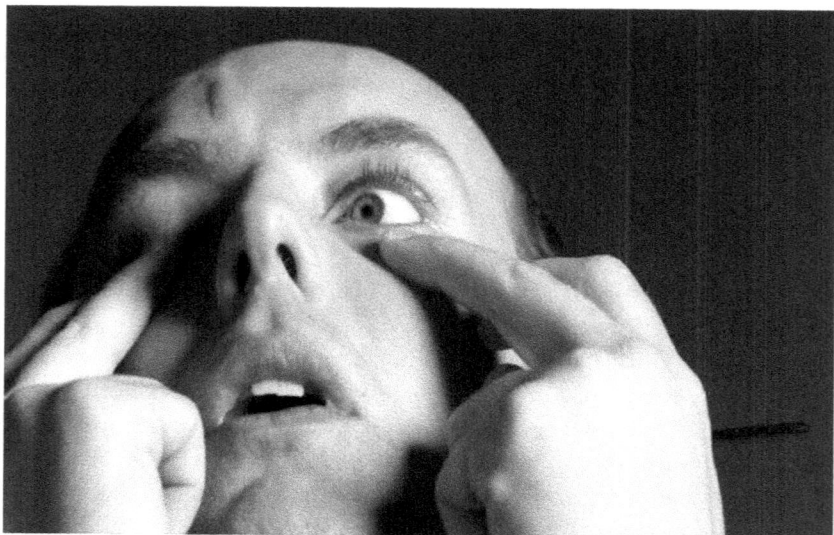

Ignacio Santa Cruz becomes Jaime Guzmán (*El tío*).

to make peace with the ghost. He lets his uncle in so that he can cast him away or, at the very least, gain a healthy distance from him.

Metacinematic gestures permeate *El tío* from start to finish. More than a film about Guzmán, what the viewer really sees is a film about the making of a play called *Guzmán*—a work directed by Iribarren and starring Santa Cruz that actually existed and enjoyed a short run in Santiago in 2011. Life, theater, and cinema therefore illuminate one another in a clever game of mise en abyme. This tactic proves fruitful because, on the one hand, it allows Santa Cruz to explore the fine line separating myth from reality, while, on the other hand, it helps him to maintain a safe (mediated, or Brechtian) distance from his controversial uncle. Paradoxically, just as Santa Cruz brings Guzmán up close, he also recasts him as "art" or performance and, in that way, manages to keep the figure (perhaps unwittingly) at a convenient arm's length.

Making the play (and the film) turns out to be anything but easy. Santa Cruz is met with scorn by just about every actor he asks to take part in his project. No one dares touch a figure as controversial as Guzmán. In a humorous sequence toward the beginning of *El tío*, Ignacio goes to Iribarren's apartment and confesses his desire to make a play about his uncle. He finds the bohemian Iribarren, a well-known writer and actor, drinking off a hangover after having just spent the night with a woman. Dumbfounded by Ignacio's request that he write the play, Iribarren reacts viscerally and with disgust at the very thought of Guzmán. He tells Santa Cruz to get lost: "Get out of here, you freaking fascist. I don't know what makes me want to throw up more . . . my hangover or Guzmán. . . . You know who can help you make your play, man? Longueira!" After significant hemming and hawing, Iribarren agrees to write and eventually direct the play, mainly because no one else will do it. He sees a challenge in the task. Peering down at his Salvador Allende T-shirt, he mutters sheepishly, "My mother is going to kill me for this."

How to portray Guzmán becomes a nagging dilemma for Santa Cruz, torn as he is between family loyalty and a commitment to verisimilitude. Ignacio, in effect, acts as a collaborator to Iribarren as he drafts the script—a detail that likely echoes what took place in real life in the cases of both the play and the film. An early exchange between Ignacio and Iribarren summarizes quite accurately the happy medium the nephew seeks to reach regarding Guzmán's persona.

IGNACIO SANTA CRUZ: I don't want to do anything to extol him or whitewash his image.
MATEO IRIBARREN: Well, to manage that you'd have to have been born into some other family.
IGNACIO SANTA CRUZ: But I don't want to crucify him either.

In a similar vein, during a later sequence that takes place in a bar, Santa Cruz challenges Iribarren's directorial prerogative to portray Ignacio's grandfather, Jorge Guzmán, in a less than idealized light.

IGNACIO SANTA CRUZ: Don't you think it might be offensive to the family to represent my grandfather like that? [*Note*: It is said that Jaime Guzmán's mother, Carmen Errázuriz, who came from a well-to-do family, kicked her husband, Jorge Guzmán, a man of lesser social pedigree, out of the house when Jaime was only thirteen years old.]
MATEO IRIBARREN: But your grandmother destroyed your grandfather. She turned him into a vagrant and an alcoholic. Am I right, or am I wrong?
IGNACIO SANTA CRUZ: You're right. But perhaps it wasn't exactly like that [*tal vez no fue tan, tan así*].
MATEO IRIBARREN: Well then, how was it, man?
IGNACIO SANTA CRUZ: I don't know.
MATEO IRIBARREN: Look, it's really tough to deal with subjects like this, so if you're going to object to every little thing I suggest because it didn't happen exactly in that way, then we're in bad shape, my friend.
IGNACIO SANTA CRUZ: Fine, but we have to strike a happy medium.

A happy medium. *El tío*, though critical of Guzmán in many ways, ultimately opts for a *poetics of ambiguity* regarding certain aspects of Guzmán's historical figure, both public and private. For example, regarding the public nature of the UDI founder's position vis-à-vis human rights violations, which I discussed earlier, *El tío*, in a manner similar to that found in other sources on Guzmán, raises the pesky question of whether Chile's neoliberal ideologue may have intervened on behalf of prisoners, while at the same time affirming that there is no real proof that he did. Improvising creatively on the lore surrounding Guzmán, the film includes an "acted" scene—part of the film-in-progress—in which Guzmán demands that Manuel Conteras, head of DINA, liberate a prisoner who, in a previous, gut-wrenching sequence, we have seen raped on screen for more than two full minutes. Contreras leads Guzmán into a dark basement where he discovers a secret cell hidden behind a wall. There he finds the tortured woman naked and trembling. Moved to help her in some way, Guzmán magnanimously offers her his overcoat. This gesture catches the viewer off guard because it is deeply out of sync with the commonly held public image of Guzmán as an accomplice (passive or active) to human rights violations. The imagined cinematic sequence, like the film as a whole, therefore *humanizes* the figure and leaves the viewer asking if a humanitarian scene like this could have taken place in reality at any point in time.[79] It therefore tests the hypothesis, without refuting it, that Guzmán was a compassionate, good Samaritan who simply became misguided by ideology. Ambiguity pervades the sequence insofar as the film poses this paradox through rehearsal and acting rather than definitive affirmation.

A second manifestation of the poetics of ambiguity concerns Guzmán's sexual orientation. Throughout *El tío*, different characters opine as to whether Guzmán was gay, leaving open to speculation questions such as whether he could have had an intimate relationship with former president Jorge Alessandri, an allegation that has run through the gossip mill in Chile at different points in time.[80] (It is worth noting, too, that rumors have also floated in Chile regarding a possible homoerotic relationship between Guzmán and his "disciple" Longueira, an issue that the film chooses patently to ignore. Fragments of several letters that Guzmán allegedly wrote to Longueira in the mid to late 1980s, in which Jaime addresses Pablo as "Mi Hitler Criollo" [My Creole Hitler], have circulated on the internet, though the authenticity of those letters has never been definitively confirmed.) Curiously, when in the opening sequence we see Ignacio having sex with his boyfriend while old television debates featuring Guzmán play in the background, we not only sense a stark contrast between the conservative, homophobic, public discourse that Guzmán embodied but also wonder if Santa Cruz might be acting out a situation (as Guzmán) that could have played out many times throughout Guzmán's life. While both UDI and Guzmán's sister Rosario, a writer and journalist, have publicly advocated for an asexualized image of Guzmán as a figure who sublimated his libido in the interest of public service, Santa Cruz's portrayal suggests, conversely, that Guzmán was likely gay even though he may never have acted on his impulses. To that end, Santa Cruz states in an interview with *Caras* magazine that his uncle was gay "in orientation, but not in practice."[81] In that same interview, he points to an additional paradoxical aspect of Guzmán's persona that both he and Iribarren try to capture in the film: "[We suggest] that the most traditional Chilean figure of the last sixty years [Jaime Guzmán] was essentially a liberal at heart [*un liberal del alma*], and that despite this inner liberalism, he created the harshest and most conservative thing we have in our country, the Constitution."[82] Guzmán's sexuality, like his stance on human rights, is therefore offered as key to reading him as a conflicted, tormented, paradoxical, and ambiguous historical character. Santa Cruz's ambiguous play on the term *liberal* (i.e., sexually liberal though morally conservative, while also economically [neo]liberal) functions as a cipher for understanding his and Iribarren's overall ambiguous approach to the character.

Secrecy, like ambiguity, pervades *El tío*. The figure of the secret that hovers around Guzmán's homosexuality becomes metonymic of a larger air of secrecy hovering over Chile—of other ghosts or silenced realities whose unresolved presence frustrates a deeper public reckoning with Chile's recent history. Understood metaphorically, the idea of the secret urges us to reflect on the silences that pervade Guzmán's family, the right, the military, the Concertación, and the Nueva Mayoría, even if those secrets are never mentioned directly in the film. In this sense, too, Guzmán's assassination, which is in fact one of the film's main thematic focal points, thus becomes hyperemblematic of the pacts between left and right that found the transition.

Regarding Guzmán's assassination, Iribarren and Santa Cruz also leave questions lingering: Was Guzmán's assassination an act entirely conceived of and executed by an ultraleftist insurgent group, or did Pinochet and/or Contreras have something to do with it? Was Guzmán's assassination advantageous to the right because, after his death, it could paint its fallen hero as a martyr for modern Chile (as the left had done with Allende)? Or, in another sense, was it advantageous to the left because Chile was finally rid of a reviled emblem of the dictatorship? The consolidation of such unresolved secrets or pacts ensures that truth remains veiled while the hypermasculine, homonormative, neoliberal order of today's Chile goes undisturbed. Attuned to this logic, Santa Cruz's interrogation of Guzmán's sexuality, like that of his uncle's unresolved death, becomes a strategy to lay bare (*partially*) certain unspoken pacts. By questioning the historical narrative surrounding major themes relevant to Guzmán's life (e.g., his homosexuality and his assassination), it is as if the director and main actor were also interrogating all the realities and specters that the transition has been unwilling to admit. In another sense, as Fernando Blanco might suggest, to reflect on the paradox of Guzmán's homosexuality allows us to discover "the imaginary matrix that hides the direction of social desire in [Chile's] postdemocracy"—a desire for higher degrees of equality, recognition of rights, and deepening of democracy—but that is covered over by the emplotments of publicly circulated and legitimized memory narratives.[83]

Ignacio Santa Cruz hails from a generation that grew up under dictatorship and that inherited Pinochet's legacy without being directly responsible for the coup or the situation that led to it. Like other younger artists who treat the country's conflicted memory in their work, he manages to take a certain distance from his object of inquiry—in this case his uncle—that allows him to treat that object creatively and subject it to deeper deconstructive analysis. To do this, acting and performativity become devices for trying on and testing questions and subject positions whose answers may prove uncomfortable if addressed more directly. I therefore find the film's multiple gestures toward performativity (e.g., mise en abyme, the use of black-and-white sequences, metacinematic elements) compelling because in *El tío* we see a younger generation *rehearsing* the past, bringing it up close and channeling it so as to gain a better grip on it and, perhaps, ultimately take a healthy distance from it. In certain of the film's sequences, for example, we see actors exploring questions such as: What was it like to experience the trembling and shock of torture? Or what was it like to *be* Contreras, Pinochet, or Guzmán? While older actors, when presented with the opportunity, vigorously resist playing these roles, younger actors embrace the challenge readily. Performance and acting therefore function as strategies for incorporating memory and establishing vicarious contact with a past that both is and is not one's own.

Unlike for Longueira, for Santa Cruz the cost of making *El tío* is palpable. Everyone in his family except for his mother ostracized him, and he was thoroughly chided by his uncle's political allies who did everything in their power to refute the work and to block the film's distribution. On the day *El tío* was set to debut (Thursday, October 17, 2013), the Jaime Guzmán Foundation, headed by prominent UDI members such as Jovino Novoa, Hernán Larraín, and Andrés Chadwick, published a special insert in two major newspapers, *El Mercurio* and *La Tercera*, titled "Ante una película infamante" (A Reaction to a Dishonorable Film). The authors characterized the film as a "cowardly attempt" to "morally assassinate" their martyred hero: "In this film, for reasons unknown to us, [Jaime Guzmán's] ideas, intentions, life, and death appear so deformed that Guzmán becomes entirely unrecognizable. The film makes it easy to discharge onto him . . . all of the frustration, hatred, and lies that his adversaries seek to sow."[34] In addition to publishing this insert, UDI also tried to squeeze the production company, Santa Cruz Producciones, financially and to ensure that the film would never air on television. To make matters worse, the Banco de Estado, the only public bank in Chile, which had given initial seed funding for the project, reacted vindictively by withholding funds from *all* Chilean filmmaking for a period of one year.

Yet, despite these costs and the boldness of Santa Cruz's personal and artistic endeavor, one still wonders if his deconstructive portrayal of Jaime Guzmán is bold enough. In the film's final sequence, FMPR assassins shoot Guzmán in front of the Catholic University's Campus Oriente (Eastern Campus), the very place where Guzmán died. The "acted" scene fades from black and white to color (which supposedly represents extracinematic "reality"), and we see all the film's actors, still dressed in their costumes, peering through the university's front gate toward the car where "Guzmán" (that is, Santa Cruz) lies bleeding. Contrary to the viewer's expectation, Mateo Iribarren approaches the car and calls out, "Ignacio, Ignacio!" Guzmán dies, and Ignacio Santa Cruz dies with him in a perfect fusion of art and life.

How are we to read this ending? Is the character Ignacio's death more than just a perfect portrayal of his Uncle Jaime or a fulfillment of his wish to *become* Guzmán? Might it also be that this death symbolizes, too, the metaphorical death(s) that Santa Cruz has experienced day in and day out because he was born, for better or for worse, Jaime Guzmán's nephew? Does the death scene lay a specter to rest? Or is the process of confronting that specter, conversely, too much for Santa Cruz, so overwhelming in fact that it spells his demise?

Beyond the film, it is clear that Guzmán's ghost still haunts both Santa Cruz and the nation. For Santa Cruz, the film provides an opportunity to explore and raise questions, but secrets remain. We find no wholly satisfactory answers—and seemingly no future either, no working beyond. Ambiguity reigns. Myth lingers. And perhaps it would be asking too much to expect anything more. While Santa Cruz's (dis)avowal is certainly much more radical and honest than Longueira's or de Castro's, he still falls short of a complete avowal because he wants to protect something about his uncle's legacy: the neoliberal ethos.

Intrigued by the boldness of *El tío* but unsatisfied by Santa Cruz's unwillingness to take a firmer stand in the film regarding his uncle's legacy, I put the question to him point blank in an interview I conducted in September 2015: "Is Chile," I asked, "better off today because a man named Jaime Guzmán existed? Or would it have been better if Guzmán had never played a role in shaping the direction the country would take?" Taken aback by the directness of my question, Santa Cruz paused. And after a moment, he muttered: "It's difficult to answer you because Jaime Guzmán is my uncle, and he always will be."[85] He went on to assert that the 1980 Constitution made Chile economically competitive both regionally and in the world, giving it an edge with respect to other Latin American countries; however, he continued, "that constitution was inscribed on a foundation of hundreds of cadavers."[86] Santa Cruz also acknowledged that neoliberalism has benefited only a few—perhaps including him. Dangerously, the well-worn discourse of Chilean exceptionalism—that is, of Chile as "economic tiger" or the "jaguar of Latin America"—lurks behind his words.

In the final assessment, Santa Cruz is indeed willing to disavow certain aspects of his uncle's character (e.g., *indirect* complicity with human rights violations, unwillingness to embrace his homosexuality fully), but his disavowal falls short. Like those who mentally compartmentalize Pinochet the criminal from Pinochet the savior of the economy, Santa Cruz compartmentalizes his uncle in ways that are convenient and advantageous to his own identity as a neoliberal who, perhaps like his uncle, though much more openly so, understands himself to be "liberal at heart" (*un liberal del alma*).

Spectral Returns

No matter what we do, specters return. They won't let us go. Their methods are not always predictable, and exactly where and when they will make their presence felt is not always clear. They haunt us—continually.

Avery Gordon, in *Ghostly Matters: Haunting and the Sociological Imagination* (1997), reminds us that "if we want to study social life well, and if in addition we want to contribute, in however small a measure, to changing it, we must learn how to identify hauntings and reckon with ghosts, must learn how to make contact with what is without doubt often painful, difficult, and unsettling."[87] The ghosts of conquest, colonialism, imperialism, socialism, neoliberalism, and other constructs continue to vex Chile as a "social totality."[88] These phantasms mediate relationships among individuals and institutions, social structures and subjects, histories and biographies in ways that are often messy and difficult to sort out.[89] Part of the critic's job, as Gordon suggests, is to lay bare these hauntings by identifying the motivations, underpinnings, and discursive constructions that shape narratives about violence and why it happens. This, in a sense, is what I have tried to do in this chapter. Additionally, I have wanted to emphasize that complicit subjects, as we saw in the case of

Mariana Callejas (chapter 1), are haunted subjects who find it nearly impossible to own up to the past in ways that are truthful, deeply nuanced, and open to the interests of another. By now it should be clear that subjects of the hard-line right (and even the center right), those who find themselves distastefully trapped in Guzmán's paradox, generally speak, write, and act out of self-interest. Their texts are either shameless and not vulnerable at all (as in the cases of Longueira and de Castro) or ashamed, on some level, though perhaps not vulnerable enough (as in the case of Santa Cruz).

❦

To conclude my reflection on the haunted Chilean right, I want to cite briefly two more spectral returns that have occurred since the 2013 premier of *El tío*.

The first of these came in an "open letter" penned by the journalist Rosario Guzmán (Jaime Guzmán's sister and Ignacio Santa Cruz's mother) that appeared in *La Tercera* newspaper on March 27, 2016, just days before the twenty-fifth anniversary of her brother's April 1, 1991, assassination.[90] The letter constitutes another attempt by one of Guzmán's family members to make peace with Jaime's vexed ghost. At the same time, it is an attempt by the author to make peace with herself.

The second spectral return came in the form of a short editorial piece titled "Lenguaje odioso, retroceso de convivencia" (Hateful Language, [and a] Setback for Coexistence) that Pablo Longueira published in *Diario Financiero* on May 9, 2016, just weeks after Rosario Guzmán's "open letter" and exactly two months after the forfeiture of his militancy in UDI.[91] I will say something about each of these hauntings in turn, beginning with the case of Rosario Guzmán.

Fed up with the post-fortieth-anniversary climate (2013) in which former president Sebastián Piñera implied that Jaime Guzmán and others were "passive accomplices" to the Pinochet regime, Rosario Guzmán used her open letter to vindicate her brother's role in history, claiming that he is misunderstood because today we live in a world very different from that of September 1973. Her letter is not a hagiography but an attempt (in a broad sense like her son's) to humanize the accomplice so that people can place him in his proper historical "context" and judge him through the correct lens. She asserts that if her brother were alive today his thinking about "protected democracy" (outside the Cold War context) would assuredly be quite different. Like *El tío* and Longueira's book, Rosario Guzmán's letter wants to set the historical record straight: it serves as an invitation for readers to see the grays in history and to recognize, as Guzmán himself so often affirmed, that ambiguity is a key to interpretation. Much in keeping with arguments she made many years earlier in her own hagiographic account, *Mi hermano Jaime* (My Brother Jaime, 1991), she seems to suggest that a "person" can be separated from "the ideas that that person espoused."[92] Here again we see complicity leading to a compartmentalization of subjectivity.

In the tradition of several open letters that have appeared in different moments of Chile's transition, Rosario Guzmán's letter is a *j'accuse* whose main goal is to denounce Contreras and Pinochet for the role that they, according to her, played in killing Guzmán.[93] In this sense, she validates her son's position on the assassination as he portrays it in his film and the surrounding interviews. Echoing to a T Santa Cruz's conspiracy theory, Rosario Guzmán provides hearsay evidence aimed at dispelling twenty-five years of "confabulation to prevent solving the crime." To gain credibility and objectivity in her readers' eyes, she declares that she is an apolitical subject whose only motivation is to speak the truth: "I am not of the right or the left. I declare myself to be a Christian humanist, independent, and apolitical." Yet her intervention is most certainly self-interested, a fact that becomes evident a bit later in the document when she expresses her desire to "cause the least harm possible to others and repair insofar as it is possible [*en la medida de lo posible*] [her own] errors and past inconsistencies." In that moment, she lets the reader glimpse her secret shame. Moreover, beyond her goal of accusing Pinochet and Contreras of complicity in her brother's murder, she clearly has a bone to pick with UDI, which she claims finds itself in the "intensive care unit" due to rampant corruption scandals that have destroyed its public image. She seems annoyed by young rising stars in the party, such as congressman Jaime Bellolio, who, in an attempt to save face for UDI, publicly takes distance from Guzmán, in her opinion out of political convenience.[94] Such behavior, which she finds abhorrent, also extends to the UDI leader Hernán Larraín, who, she claims, shamefully tolerates disrespectful insubordination by the younger rank and file.

Aside from complaining about the right's political decline in the present and wanting to set the historical record straight regarding a number of lingering secrets, Rosario Guzmán's "open letter" harbors one more ulterior motive. It asks her brother's forgiveness and understanding for the "fit of madness" that overcame her son Ignacio in making *El tío*. She avers to Jaime's specter that she and the rest of the Guzmán clan implored Ignacio not to make the film. Yet, despite their pleas, he did so anyway—and this led to a combination of both hatred and praise descending on him and the family. She hopes that "those who condemned [her] son without knowing his motivations, and [her] for sticking by his side with a mother's unconditional love, might one day understand." Ultimately, she sees good in the film because her son's "humanized"

Evidence of a homeless person living in the shadow of a memorial to Jaime Guzmán located in Santiago's Vitacura neighborhood. The memorial was vandalized during the September 11, 2016, commemoration of the coup. Photograph by Michael J. Lazzara.

version of Guzmán, which grapples with his "angels and demons" (in other words, his paradox), managed to make some people hate him just a little less.[95]

The second haunting return—much more concerning in many ways than Rosario Guzmán's letter—is Pablo Longueira's brief editorial column "Lenguaje odioso, retroceso de convivencia." Incensed by the corruption charges levied against him and awaiting his day in court, in the column Longueira waxes poetically about what has become of Chile, its civic life, and the peaceful coexistence that once existed among his countrymen. How could it be, he wonders, that Chile has reached such a debased and "deteriorated" state of affairs? For Longueira, the current situation of protest, street action, and political witch hunts eerily reminds him of the climate he perceived in his "apolitical" youth, before he discovered his call to "public service": the bitter war of words that raged in Chile around the time of Popular Unity. He admonishes that by 1973 this war of words had become so entrenched in the country's social fabric that any possibility for "civic friendship" had broken down; consequently, institutional life was eventually destroyed by a military coup. Sensing that rhetoric in the country in 2016 was reaching a similarly frenetic fever pitch, Longueira jabs: "I don't have to explain why I am writing this today. Some may agree more and some less, but we all share the idea that the tone and language of politics has not only become vulgar but is also contributing to creating a climate of hatred and polarization that will not have a good outcome [*nada de bueno traerá*]." Although he acknowledges that the country today finds itself far from the breakdown of institutionality that occurred on September 11, 1973, he also feels that citizens (students, indigenous peoples, and even middle-class Chileans railing against the neoliberal model) would be wise to tread cautiously lest today's polarization intensify and spin out of control.

While one might read Longueira's editorial piece as a simple, inconsequential expression of ire by a condemned man, on another level his words are profoundly disturbing: a figure of the right, historically linked to pinochetismo, launches a veiled threat that people should watch out because today's polarized and hate-ridden climate "*nada de bueno traerá.*" Is Longueira insinuating that, given the right circumstances, another coup could happen? Is he flexing his (now greatly weakened) political muscles to influence his cronies not to discard the possibility of a return to dictatorship? Should we read his editorial column as a modern-day, rhetorical *boinazo* staged by a debilitated member of UDI?[96] Perhaps to suggest these things is to read a bit too much into Longueira's text. But minimally we should recognize that his rhetoric of hatred and his warning of "bad" future consequences are stoking the very fires he hopes to abate.

Though Chilean democracy is sufficiently consolidated such that another coup, at least in the short term, seems quite unlikely, it remains concerning that the pinochetista right, threatened by a climate of social protest and persecution for past crimes, continues to launch veiled threats against the population. Such veiled threats beg asking whether actors like Longueira are firmly committed to democracy at all costs or whether democracy, from their perspective, should have limits when those holding political and economic power feel threatened.

Clearly, then, specters remain, and people will manipulate them in any way necessary to "save face" and protect their turf. The battle over memory rages on as actors of different stripes, unwilling to assume the cost that avowal demands, persevere in their quest for political and moral legitimacy; they performatively actualize and interpret ghosts without really engaging in true reckoning.

❦

If Pablo Longueira's *Mi testimonio de fe* represents an instrumental and hagiographic representation of Guzmán that falls short of true avowal, the case of *El tío* illustrates that intergenerational memory, too, for the right is vexed: it is characterized by a tension between a desire to let go of certain complicated aspects of the past (e.g., Pinochet, human rights violations, the Cold War) and an entrenched loyalty to the economic project his regime promoted.

UDI presents an interesting case in point. Examined closely, the party today finds itself caught between an "old guard" (*los coroneles*) unwilling to relinquish power (even to save itself from political destruction) and a "new guard" whose discourse is more progressive but that is still reluctant to turn its back on its benevolent fathers completely. Deputy Jaime Bellolio—born in 1980, trained at the University of Chicago, a member of the Jaime Guzmán Foundation, but a man also willing to challenge the "old guard" in his public discourse— perhaps most succinctly epitomizes the generational tension to which I am referring. Whether Bellolio's words are born of pure political expediency or reflect a genuinely felt need for reform remains open to debate. His discourse, however, broadly conceived, emphasizes a need for UDI to adapt to the new Chile, lest the party disappear.[97] Perhaps predictably, this willingness to cast off or downplay some of his party's foundational memory scripts has been met with disapproval by several founding fathers within Chilean gremialismo.

In a recent interview, Bellolio claimed that Chile today is caught between two historical cycles: an old cycle (linked to the Cold War) and a new cycle (linked to change) that has not been fully born. Both Ignacio Santa Cruz, who claims to be of the left but who cannot escape his familial links to the right and his neoliberal beliefs, and Bellolio, who sees a need for a change of political image but also harbors loyalties to Guzmán's economic model, embody the conflict between these two historical moments. On the one hand, these figures channel the incessant hauntings of the specters that engendered them (biologically or politically) and that, to a certain extent, determine their words; on the other hand, they express a desire to forge a new voice that confronts those ghosts to conjure them away because doing so is crucial to their survival.

3

Boundedness and Vulnerability

(Hugo Zambelli)

The bystander is one of the most difficult figures to locate and assess within the universe of postdictatorial cultural production. This is because bystanders tend not to write or speak publicly; they generally prefer to remain anonymous. Neither victims nor perpetrators—although they arguably share characteristics with each—bystanders are those who watched from the sidelines, who saw and heard about human rights violations, either directly or indirectly, and later remained silent about them, out of fear, apathy, or self-interest.

In many cases, bystanders stood at a far remove from the horror such that they could do little or nothing to stop it; in such situations, it might seem reasonable to think that they bear diminished responsibility for their failure to speak or act. However, in other cases bystanders may have had real opportunities to intervene yet still chose to remain silent. Although their hands may not have been directly stained with blood, they became, in the words of the Holocaust scholar Raul Hilberg, "helpers, gainers, [or] onlookers": that is, people who in ways large or small aided the perpetrators directly, stood to gain something (perhaps economically), or acted as mere spectators to deplorable deeds and lacked the conviction to speak out.[1]

In postconflict societies engaged in pursuing justice, bystanders usually do not pay a legal price for their complicity. Legal prosecutions tend to focus on the clear perpetrators and avoid bystanders. Sometimes bystanders do serve as witnesses in court even when they are not directly accused of any crime. Nevertheless, exemption from legal responsibility does not absolve bystanders of moral responsibility or of an obligation to say what they know. Victoria J. Barnett argues that history should indeed judge bystanders and that in some cases they should be held morally responsible for their failure to act. Barnett bases her reasoning on a belief that "individuals [in a society] are socially and politically accountable" to their fellow citizens by virtue of the fact that they live in community with one another.[2] While she does not go so far as to issue a blanket condemnation of all bystanders or to stretch the figure of the bystander beyond recognizable limits—that is, to lapse into a logic that would claim that everyone living under dictatorship was, in a sense, a bystander—she reasonably encourages us to evaluate bystander complicity on a case-by-case basis, in accordance with the intentions, behaviors, and reactions of real people in real-life situations.[3]

If we survey the universe of Chilean postdictatorial literature, the bystander figure crops up more frequently in fiction than it does in nonfictional genres. This may be because it is easier to imagine the bystander creatively (or theoretically) than to find someone actually willing to admit publicly that he or she was one. Young novelists like Alejandro Zambra and Nona Fernández, several of whose books look back on the Pinochet years, have stood at the forefront of this reflection. Zambra's *Formas de volver a casa* (2011; English translation, *Ways of Going Home*, 2012), for example, narrates the dictatorship from the standpoint of what he calls *personajes secundarios* (secondary characters): the adults who secretly sympathized with the regime but pretended to be apolitical or the children who inherited their parents' ideological positions and were later obliged to take a stand either for or against those positions. In Nona Fernández's novel *Space Invaders* (2013), another good example, a young bystander named Estrella matures to adulthood and eventually comes to discover that years earlier her father killed several communist militants, a detail of which as a child she was only vaguely aware. These fictional characters, now adults, feel guilt or shame for having actively or tacitly supported violence or for having looked the other way. Their fears, loyalties, or gut instincts to self-protect trump any contrary impulse to render themselves vulnerable or to risk speaking out in the interest of truth, justice, or the greater social good.

While we can therefore point to several examples of bystander complicity within the realm of recent Chilean fiction, I want to draw attention in this chapter to one of the only Chilean nonfiction books to focus specifically on the bystander figure: Diamela Eltit's *Puño y letra: Juicio oral* (In My Own Handwriting: An Oral Trial, 2005).[4] Reminiscent of the court-reporting genre, whose most famous contemporary example is probably Hannah Arendt's *Eichmann in Jerusalem* (1963), Eltit's project selectively records her experience in Argentina witnessing the public trial of Enrique Arancibia Clavel, a civilian liaison to

DINA in Buenos Aires, who was convicted on grounds of illicit association and aggravated murder for the 1974 car-bomb killings of Carlos Prats, the commander in chief of the army who preceded Pinochet and remained loyal to Allende until the end, and his wife, Sofía Cuthbert.[5] Eltit's creative text consists of a montage of documents (oral arguments, testimonies, depositions, and personal essays) that she, as author and documentarian, selected and organized to give readers a feel for the trial and its idiosyncrasies.[6] Within this selection, one might logically expect Arancibia's testimony to play the central role. Unexpectedly, though, Eltit chooses to avoid the trial's main protagonist altogether and zeroes in instead on an entirely secondary or marginal character: Hugo Alberto Zambelli, a hairstylist turned dancer and musical-theater actor, Arancibia's former boyfriend, a mere bystander to the crime, a man who for twenty-seven years likely *knew* things but never talked. Decades after the Prats-Cuthbert murders and forced by the court to avow his past knowledge, Zambelli boldly lied on the stand to protect himself and his former lover. His contrived and perjured deposition, which spins the reader into a convoluted and confusing web of lies, constitutes the majority of the book; Eltit reproduces the deposition verbatim in a form that on the written page looks like a theatrical script. A "Presentation" and an essay by Eltit titled "1974," which respectively open and close the book, frame Zambelli's falsified deposition and relate the moment of the Prats crime to Eltit's subjective experience as a citizen who lived through (and resisted) the Pinochet dictatorship. The book is therefore as much about Eltit as it is about the lack of justice in the postdictatorship period and the vital (and, in this case, theatrical) lies that a bystander tells to save face.

Throughout *Puño y letra*, the *boundedness* of Zambelli's "truth" is striking. For that reason, it allows us to draw close parallels between the bystander witness's discourse and that of other types of accomplices I have studied thus far. If the complicities of figures such as Mariana Callejas, Pablo Longueira, Sergio de Castro, and Hugo Zambelli admittedly differ greatly, all these figures (material accomplices, economic or ideological accomplices, and bystander witnesses) curiously resort to similar narrative tactics when fashioning their memories. Their strategies, as I have shown in previous chapters, include evasiveness, denial, euphemisms, justifications, and fragmenting subjectivity, among others. Barnett speaks to this point as well for the case of the Holocaust: "It is interesting to note how similar the characteristics of bystander and perpetrator behavior are in much of the literature—and how apologists for both groups tend to offer the same excuses for their behavior. It was typical of both groups, for example, to make an ethical distinction between the public and private realms, or to use subservience to authority as grounds for exonerating individuals of responsibility."[7] In Zambelli's case, it is also clear that fear played a major role. We never really find out *what* or *how much* Zambelli actually knew about the

Boundedness and Vulnerability

Prats-Cuthbert crime, though the intimacy of his connection to Arancibia remains unquestionable. He nevertheless appears implicated, in a tangential way, in a massive web of complicities whose ultimate point of origin was the Chilean dictatorial state, a web that included not only DINA but also functionaries of the Chilean Embassy in Buenos Aires, the pilots who flew documents back and forth between Chile and Argentina during the planning of the crime, and the Bank of Chile, which served as a conduit for information and funding, among many other actors and entities. Likely ashamed of his position (however marginal) within that matrix, Zambelli recoiled into the privatized fantasy of his life as an actor to avoid admitting responsibility, as if to say ad nauseam, "I was just a simple musical theater actor whose only mistake was getting involved with the wrong guy."

Judith Butler, in *Precarious Life: The Powers of Violence and Mourning* (2004), suggests that as humans we are all vulnerable—although the degree to which we feel our vulnerability differs greatly depending on our economic means, our race, our position in the world order, or the amount of power we possess, among other factors. As inherently vulnerable beings whose safety can easily become jeopardized or taken away under the right circumstances, we constantly try to mitigate our risk of vulnerability by building up walls to protect ourselves. This, in turn, means closing ourselves off to others; it means an unwillingness to become "disarmed" by truly seeing the other's face or recognizing his or her plight.[8] Butler adds, "Under certain social and political conditions, especially those in which violence is a way of life and the means to secure self-defense are limited" (such as authoritarian regimes), vulnerability "becomes highly exacerbated."[9] In these situations, individuals are faced with a choice: they can acknowledge a shared condition of vulnerability and act in solidarity with one another, or they can deny vulnerability "through a fantasy of mastery ([or] an institutionalized fantasy of mastery)" that creates a façade of protection but also serves to further "fuel the instruments of war."[10] Though it is undeniable that every human being is on some level inherently vulnerable—and perhaps the bystander experiences this vulnerability in particularly salient ways—the struggle at the heart of ethics involves resisting the urge to kill or *deny* the other in the interest of self-preservation.[11] In Zambelli's case, this dilemma is poignant: he was a lowly man, a minor actor who, because he felt vulnerable, chose to ignore the other's pain and protect himself—even make himself seem to be something much grander than he was. Shamefully, he reneged on his responsibility to history and greater society even years later, long after the conditions of his relative safety had changed.

In this chapter, I use the work of Diamela Eltit, a feminist writer, as a conduit for deepening my reflection on the need for vulnerability in avowal. By reading Eltit with (or alongside) Judith Butler and other feminist critics, I want to add layers to my argument that rendering oneself vulnerable—opening oneself up to being impacted and moved to action by another's pain—is vital for the health of postdictatorial societies full of individually motivated, bounded subjects. Such bounded subjects, as I have shown in different ways in chapters 1 and 2, generally prefer to shirk the truth or shield themselves behind fictions of mastery rather than render themselves vulnerable and assume their responsibility before the other, society, and history.

Becoming *unbounded* serves as an invitation to both individual and societal change. It goes far beyond mere sympathy or empathy and implies a commitment to really see another's pain and act in another's interest rather than one's own. It also implies a commitment to working toward greater equality of social and economic rights for all people. A notion of the subject based on vulnerability, as feminist scholarship suggests, works against a philosophy of the "autonomous and sovereign subject that . . . thinks of itself as closed and self-sufficient"; in other words, it works against a philosophy that is founded upon the idea of the liberal, individualized subject and that operates fundamentally by seeking ways to mitigate risk to the subject and its well-being.[12] A model of subjectivity based on vulnerability, by contrast, "allows an ontology of linkage and dependence to come to the fore," serving to remind us that we are all, first and foremost, relational beings called to value and exercise responsibility for one another's lives.[13] Extending this logic to the realm of narrative, we might say that by telling the truth, one makes oneself *linguistically vulnerable,* and this can serve as an important first step toward what Judith Butler calls "corporeal vulnerability," toward breaking down the walls and inequities that divide us as human beings and that cause us to value certain lives and rights—*our own*—more than those of others.[14] If we act in any other way, Butler holds, we remain, on some level, complicit with violence.

Butler's idea of *boundedness* thus inspires my analysis of Zambelli's performance of invulnerability: "When we think about who we 'are' and seek to represent ourselves we cannot represent ourselves as merely bounded beings, for the primary others who are past for me not only live on in the fiber of the boundary that contains me (one meaning of 'incorporation'), but they also haunt the way I am, as it were, periodically undone and open to becoming unbounded."[15] This observation provides a lens for understanding how and why Eltit deconstructs Zambelli's performance of perjury. Reminiscent of my earlier analysis of the haunted accomplice (chapter 2), Butler's reference to the bounded subject as *haunted* suggests that postconflict societies and the individuals who inhabit them are constantly afflicted by ghosts: by those they exclude, by those against whom they discriminate (implicitly or explicitly), or by those to whom they have done or continue to do violence. As a haunted subject, the bounded subject thus finds himself faced with an option: Will he let himself become undone by the ghosts that float untamed in dictatorship's aftermath, or will he put up walls to keep those ghosts at bay and resist a true reckoning at all costs?

In *Puño y letra*, the Prats daughters (their pain), as well Eltit's own authorial voice (her pain), embody the call to become vulnerable. From the margins of the courtroom scene, these key actors critically and morally intervene in the bystander's bounded discourse. Their call to vulnerability—which can be read as concrete instantiations of the unpersonified Levinasian face—operates on us as readers (as well as metaphorically on Zambelli, in a retroactive sense) and allows us to see how the bystander, driven by effusive theatricality, epitomizes the bounded neoliberal subject who arrogantly engages in willful ignorance of the other's plight to preserve his way of life.

The courtroom scene provides the perfect backdrop or "stage" for Eltit's reflection on the bystander's theatrical performance of complicity. On the witness stand, Zambelli shores up his discourse, lapses into fantasies about his life as an actor, and fails to acknowledge the other's pain. The context of procedural justice, which Eltit understands to be an inherently limited scene for truth production, spotlights now a witness with something to hide resists the Levinasian call to ethical response. Eltit's book, in this sense, urges us to think about what *becoming vulnerable* might really mean in the neoliberal, postdictatorial moment. It advocates for a model of vulnerability that goes beyond the simple act of candor in truth-telling and that also comes to include features such as the mitigation of neoliberal structures and the search for ways to combat racism, sexual discrimination, gender bias, and profound socioeconomic inequities.

What would it look like if accomplices who constantly tell half truths to save themselves from shame or judicial reprisal were to let themselves become undone by the other's call to avow and act ethically? In short, Eltit creatively rewrites the Prats trial to question its proceedings, reveal its faults and lacks, and open up potential spaces for reflection not only about the limits of truth and the boundedness of the accomplice's testimony in general but also about the limits of the law and the very nature of *justice*—in a broad sense—in the postdictatorship period. Her call to become vulnerable emanates from those very limits.

The Limits of Truth, Justice, and the Law

If we think about Chile's long transition to democracy as a continuum on which greater degrees of truth and justice have become possible over time, it seems plausible to affirm that, having already passed through numerous political attempts by the various Concertación and post-Concertación governments to "repair" or "reconcile" with the past (attempts, I should add, that have met with varying degrees of success and public satisfaction), we now find ourselves situated squarely within the phase of justice-seeking.

The search for truth and justice in Chile has a long history that dates from 1973. Starting almost immediately after the coup, valiant lawyers from the Vicariate of Solidarity risked their lives to take on cases involving political prisoners and the disappeared at a time when attaining justice seemed a near impossibility. An Amnesty Law, penned by the regime in 1978 and still existing today, has made securing justice an uphill battle ever since.

After 1990, in a tutelary democracy in which the military continued to loom large on the scene, the imperative to achieve justice took a back seat to establishing truth. As a first step toward truth, President Patricio Aylwin (1990–94) convened the National Commission on Truth and Reconciliation (or Rettig Commission, 1990), whose final report detailed the regime's human rights violations but did so without naming the perpetrators or accomplices directly and without giving sufficient treatment to the reality of torture as a state policy under Pinochet. The report's shortcomings left the human rights community and certain sectors of the citizenry incensed and feeling that the government had responded only partially to its ethical obligation to address the past openly and honestly.

Almost a decade later, the Rettig Commission's incomplete work lingered in the public imagination and necessitated further attempts to establish truth. These included, on the one hand, the Mesa de Diálogo (Dialogue Roundtable, 1999–2000), convened during the Eduardo Frei Ruiz-Tagle administration (1994–2000) and completed during Ricardo Lagos's administration (2000–2006)—another instance of trading justice for truth (albeit, again, incomplete truth)—and, on the other hand, the National Commission on Political Imprisonment and Torture (2003–5) whose *Informe Valech* (Valech Report, 2004), based on more than thirty thousand torture victims' testimonies, became a milestone document that, at last, raised public awareness about torture as a reprehensible and widespread state policy advocated by the Pinochet regime.

Through it all, we have occasionally seen public apologies by perpetrators—I am thinking particularly of the mea culpas by different branches of the armed forces that made the news around the time of the thirtieth anniversary of the coup, in 2003. Yet the military—as was abundantly evident in the case of the Mesa de Diálogo—has consistently been less than forthcoming with the truth about the disappeared and far from contrite in accepting responsibility for its crimes. Moreover, the memory narrative of Pinochet as a "savior" who rescued the Chilean people from the throes of Marxism, though much less prevalent than it once was, still exists today among hard-line pinochetistas and persists as well in certain conservative pockets of Chilean society.[16]

Truth has therefore been slow in coming—but then again, so has justice. To be fair, the possibilities for prosecuting human rights violators in Chile are far greater today than they were in the early 1990s, when President Aylwin issued his famous call for truth and justice *en la medida de lo posible* (insofar as they were possible). Augusto Pinochet's surprising detention in London (1998) contributed in no small measure to the prosecution of dictators and human rights violators not only in Chile but also in transnational contexts, as did the tireless work of lawyers and judges who dedicated decades of their lives to advancing prosecutions and who managed, with admirable success and in spite of legal and political obstacles, to put many perpetrators behind bars.[17] Cath Collins speaks to this point when she notes that even when "political channels were unresponsive" and "judicial channels continued to respond negatively" to calls for justice, "small groups of lawyers managed to keep claims alive. This continuity of accountability pressure, with the concomitant accumulation of cases and legal know-how, eventually proved a useful launching pad for renewed accountability pressure in the more favorable circumstances prevailing since 1998."[18] The declassification of CIA documents for certain emblematic cases (including those of Orlando Letelier, Bernardo Leighton, and Carlos Prats) also contributed to opening doors to prosecutions.

As a result—and though much remains to be done—legal justice is undeniably advancing, while the rule of law is becoming an ever-stronger anchor for the long-desired consolidation of democracy. Nevertheless, it remains essential to recognize that the possibilities for legal justice also very much hinge on the political will to see justice done in any given moment, a will that undeniably varies in tandem with the desires, motivations, and dictates of successive governments or of different political actors. In that regard, Collins adds that certain "countervailing forces" still impede justice: "These include certain transitional arrangements that have persisted in[to] the modern period, with the amnesty statute constituting the most obvious example. [Likewise,] political—legislative and executive—attitudes in Chile to accountability breakthroughs have also been ambivalent. The executive [has] appeared at times relieved to let the courts assume the burden of controversial decision-making, and at other times ready to intervene to slow the pace of judicialization."[19]

Despite advances, then, certain concerns remain—and these are not minor. For example, the idea of "letting the courts do their work," a phrase frequently bandied about by politicians in the media as a signal to the citizenry that the country's democratic institutions are functioning properly, can be read, on the flip side, as a conduit toward *olvido* (forgetting)—the ever-so-familiar "turning the page" or "looking to the future" that has functioned as a leitmotif in various moments of Chile's transition; it can also function as a convenient escape mechanism to avoid confronting traumatic and incendiary issues. When memory—real memory, deep memory, difficult memory, memory that reveals and recognizes both the victims' faces and the faces of political and economic injustice—is too politically contentious to tackle head on, relegating "justice" to the courts seems an easy fix for politicians who find it more convenient or expedient to pass the buck than to assume responsibility for the past. These same actors are reluctant to admit complicity—covert or overt—with Pinochet's neoliberal project.

The tug of war surrounding the justice question is therefore constant. We repeatedly hear the legitimate frustrations of victims and families who believe that justice has been too selective, too lenient, or much too slow in coming and who become frustrated when they hear calls by the military or the government to *agilizar los procesos* (speed the trials along) so as to bring rapid closure to the judicial phase of postdictatorial justice-seeking. We also regularly hear complaints from victims, their families, and concerned citizens when political actors advocate for avoiding trials or for lightening the severity or conditions of perpetrators' incarceration.[20]

Truth and justice insofar as they are possible: this has therefore been the logic of Chile's transition to democracy. But legal justice—always partial, always selective—is also insufficient unto itself. To limit the idea of justice to the legal realm closes off possibilities of asking deeper questions about what might ideally constitute *justice* in postdictatorial times. I am referring to a kind of justice that not only reckons with the naked face of past violence but also is accompanied by a politics committed to mitigating social inequities and endemic discriminatory practices—that is, a notion of justice that also concerns itself with present violence and that understands present forms of violence to be connected in important ways to or, in some cases, to derive from past forms of violence.

Our definition of justice in the neoliberal, postdictatorial moment must therefore be broader: it has to imply not only owning up to the past in truthful ways (*dar la cara*) but also a commitment to building alternative, collective futures. If we accept this imperative, then, relevant questions arise: What can the law do to repair the past and promote personal or collective healing, and what lies beyond its reach? Or, put differently, what might be the *limits of law* in the aftermath of state-sponsored violence?

A sweep of the critical literature on this subject reveals a common refrain: the concern of judicial proceedings is not primarily to produce *truth* (although this is certainly part of its objective) but to produce *judgment*, to bring closure to a grievance and mete out a punishment tantamount to the crime.[21] To be sure, trials serve many positive functions: they create a credible, public record of crimes that were for years covered up; they generate documentation that can assist researchers in understanding the past; they provide a venue in which victims can tell their stories and confront those who harmed them; and they demonstrate a commitment by the government and society to making amends.[22] But, as Nancy L. Rosenblum points out, "formal judicial proceedings are often inadequate from the standpoint of victims, which is why individuals, groups, and whole communities [may] look outside the law for relief."[23] Procedural justice may produce insufficient documentation for gaining a complete picture of history and, at bottom, is not always specifically addressed to the victims' affective or psychological needs. Procedural justice, relatively limited in scope, therefore responds to broader society's need to see justice done and bring "closure" to a traumatic historical period; it provides reassurance that democracy and the rule of law are functioning properly. It follows, then, that even though legal remedy is undeniably of vital importance, trials and convictions alone may not be enough to acknowledge the losses of the victimized and the aggrieved. After a verdict is reached in court, something remains unresolved.[24]

The idea of the *remainder* derives from the Freudian language that, in general, has saturated postdictatorial thought. Evoking Freud's classic distinction between mourning and melancholy, Idelber Avelar argues that the task of mourning, even when it brings some semblance of "closure" that permits the mourner to escape melancholic malaise, always leaves behind a remainder that the living continue to mourn indefinitely.[25] Even if the mourner manages to displace his libido onto a surrogate object (e.g., a symbol of the lost loved one or a verdict in court), even if the mourner can reckon with the dead and bury his remains, "mourning is never simply completed."[26] It leaves something behind, unfinished. Institutional vehicles for healing trauma (e.g., truth commissions, public apologies, monetary reparations, public memorials) as well as noninstitutional vehicles (therapy, academic work, art, or literature) can play important roles in assuaging the impact of this remainder in ways both practical and affective. Yet the remainder will continue to be palpable until greater degrees of truth, justice, and reparation are achieved on a societal level.

❦

Responding to the always unfinished nature of truth and (social) justice, Eltit's *Puño y letra* hinges on a fundamental gap between the law and literature as epistemological modalities for dealing with traumatic memory. On the one hand, the law evokes the language of facts, of the finite, the concrete, and the circumscribed, while, on the other hand, literature connotes the subjective, the infinite, the wound that lingers, the affective, the space in which our shared responsibilities to one another come to the fore. Shoshana Felman, too, speaks to this difference.

> A trial and a literary text do not aim at the same kind of conclusion, nor do they strive toward the same kind of effect. A trial is presumed to be a search for truth, but, technically, it is a search for a decision, and thus, in essence, it seeks not simply truth but a finality, a force of resolution. A literary text is, [by contrast], a search for meaning, for expression, for heightened significance, and for symbolic understanding.[27]

A literary or symbolic approach permits Eltit to advocate effectively for the unheeded political demands of society's "losers": the Prats daughters, workers, students, anonymous victims who suffered in 1973 and still pay a price today. Her book hinges on a distinction between *procedural justice* and *radical justice*— between the mechanical production of a guilty verdict against Arancibia and the traumas and inequities, both individual and societal, that remain salient in the trial's aftermath and that consequently demand further acknowledgment and reckoning. For Eltit, radical (social) justice is always unfinished: it implies working toward an honest, critical vision of history. But, above all, radical justice is political in the sense that it seeks to reactivate the possibilities for leftist politics in the present in ways that go beyond the "spectacle" of consensus-based politics as it has been practiced during the transition.

In the textual analysis that follows, I start by briefly sketching the Arancibia case. From there, I attempt to show how Eltit encodes within *Puño y letra* a demand for vulnerability and radical justice. She does this precisely by exploring three remainders that linger (unresolved) after the gavel has come down: *truth*, *pain*, and *impunity*.

What repercussions derive from these three remainders of procedural, post-dictatorial justice—truth, pain, and impunity—that Eltit signals? First, Eltit demands complete truth and calls for unbounded testimony by highlighting Zambelli's act of perjury. Second, she advances an imperative to acknowledge the affective dimensions of trauma and memory, that is, to address both victims' ongoing pain as well as the essential unrecoverability (and/or un-sayability) of the original traumatic moment. To acknowledge these things might be taken as a first step toward becoming vulnerable. Third, even though Arancibia was convicted in the end, Eltit still understands justice to be partial; angered by the impunity that lingers all around her, she shifts the reader's focus toward a wider, more metaphorical type of impunity: that of every complicit body that participated in and/or benefited from the dictatorship's neoliberal project and that has failed to pay a price for that complicity. She urges continued work toward "complete justice" (a radical form of social justice) and "complete truth"—despite their impossibility.

The Case

A Chilean citizen, former cadet, and member of a military family, Enrique Arancibia Clavel decided to abandon his formal military education to study engineering. Yet, dressed in civilian clothes, he would stay connected to Pinochet's military apparatus for a long time thereafter. From the late 1960s, the *dinamitero* (dynamite-guy), as he was known, became affiliated with right-wing nationalist groups, using his engineering skills to plant bombs against leftist targets after Salvador Allende's 1970 election. Accused of violating the Ley de Seguridad del Estado (State Security Law), he fled to Argentina in 1971 to avoid punishment; while there, under the false name Felipe Alemparte (among others) and posing as an employee of the Banco del Estado (State Bank), he soon became a key functionary in DINA's "Exterior" (international) Department. Working closely with Michael Townley and Mariana Callejas, Arancibia aided and abetted the Prats murder as a cog in the wheel of Operation Condor's villainy. In 1978, with Pope John Paul I's intervention, he became a bargaining chip in negotiations to resolve the Beagle Channel conflict, was pardoned with regard to accusations of espionage, and was granted Argentine citizenship.[28] Much to the Prats daughters' dismay, he opened a restaurant and lived in impunity until 1996, at which time the court renewed the case against him. When Arancibia's case was reopened, Argentine judge María Servini de Cubría also called for the extradition of seven other DINA agents, along with Pinochet.[29] However, the Chilean judicial system opted not to uphold the extradition, which resulted in Arancibia taking the fall for the entire conspiracy. Sentenced to life in prison in 2000 for illicit association and aggravated murder, seven short years later he would be set free on a legal technicality. Soon thereafter he would be found dead in his Buenos Aires apartment, the victim of a supposed crime of passion committed by one of his gay suitors.

As of March 2003, a Chilean version of the Prats case aimed to prosecute other DINA agents. After seven years of litigation, Chile's Supreme Court, in July 2010, upheld a 2009 resolution issued by Judge Alejandro Solís and the Ninth Court of Appeals that convicted nine military officers and civilian employees of DINA for their roles as intellectual authors or direct accomplices to the assassination. Manuel Contreras, the former head of DINA, who was already in prison for other human rights crimes, received a seventeen-year sentence, plus three additional years for conspiring to commit a terrorist act. His second-in-command, Pedro Espinoza Bravo, suffered a similar fate. Raúl Eduardo Iturriaga Neumann, Christoph Willikie Flöl, José Zara Holger, and Juan Morales Salgado all received fifteen-year sentences. And in their roles as accomplices, civilian agents Jorge Iturriaga and Mariana Callejas each received a five-year sentence, while Subofficial Reginaldo Valdés got a prison term of 1,081 days. After that, in a shocking move, the Supreme Court contested the appellate court's decision and significantly lightened both Espinoza's and Contreras's sentences. In Contreras's case, for example, a double life sentence was reduced to only seventeen years, an occurrence that called into question the Chilean judiciary's commitment to punishing perpetrators to the full extent of the law.

Responding to the verdict, the Chilean army issued a statement in July 2010 repudiating all those involved in the Prats-Cuthbert assassination. This move reflected the army's by then well-established "modernizing" politics, which sought to whitewash its public image and delink it from past human rights abuses.[30] Faithful to those politics, which many people interpreted as instrumental, the army expressed its solidarity with and sympathy for the Prats daughters as well as its commitment to upholding certain core values—truth and justice—that Chilean society holds dear.

The Remainders

Truth

Immersed in his own fiction, he uses his eyes to instill fear, to inhibit, to cut through every word that incessantly incriminates and incriminates him.

Diamela Eltit

Textualmente (textually): this word functions as a section heading within Diamela Eltit's *Puño y letra* and crops up several times in the book's general lexicon. To reproduce language *textually* is to be faithful to displaying its truth (or lack thereof)—a veritable obsession for Eltit, whose project, at least in part, seems to be about the status of truth in testimony and about the kinds of truths that a trial can produce.

The book's geography is eclectic. As I have mentioned, in addition to Eltit's own first-person account of the trial's theatricality and another autobiographical essay titled "1974," Hugo Zambelli's deposition forms the centerpiece of the project. The book also includes a letter that Pinochet wrote to Prats, in which the former expresses his undying friendship and gratitude to the man he was about to have killed, as well as a series of closing statements by two of Arancibia's prosecutors. Intentionally, Eltit makes us privy only to certain aspects of the trial record, thereby emphasizing the subjective, fragmented, constructed, pastiche-like character of her account, and of memory in general. In effect, the book's structure—incomplete and selective—echoes the idea of a *pulverized memory* (dubious, traumatized, and partial) set up by the author's epigraph, which connects the public construction of memory and justice to a private, individualized scene of suffering: "To my mother and her pulverized memory."

Eltit's transcription of Zambelli's deposition points out tensions among what *can be proved*, what *has been proved*, and *that which exceeds proof*—tensions that concern the very goals of testimony. By drawing out these tensions, Eltit seems to be asking important questions about the finality of the testimonial act: Is testimony's primary goal to *prove* the facts of the case or to *transmit* the "unspeakable" and affective components of memory—or both? Does the aim of testimony change in accordance with the intended audience, venue, context, or purpose of the speech act?

The prosecuting attorneys' closing statements are fascinating illustrations of these tensions and questions, and this is probably why Eltit also includes them in her book. Doctor Guillermo Jorge's first intervention, for example, consists in a lexicon absolutely obsessed with phrases like *se ha probado* (it has been proved) and *claramente* (clearly), which appear dozens of times in the text. The lawyers cite documents, cross-reference testimonies, show graphics, make claims, reiterate, and carefully construct a reasoned, logical line of argumentation that goes something like this: (1) DINA existed, DINA functioned hierarchically, DINA had an Exterior Department, this department performed very specific functions in Argentina; (2) Operation Condor existed; (3) the accused participated in these operations; (4) the accused acted specifically in the assassination plot to kill Prats and his wife. These facts are the ones that *matter* for the court; other details (the emotional toll, the real psychological detriment of the traumas suffered) stand *in excess of* the trial.

When reading these rather tedious chains of reasoning, one wonders why it is necessary for the lawyers to expend such copious amounts of energy establishing the existence of DINA—a reality that seems to have long been proved beyond any reasonable doubt and that was widely known since the time of the coup; it is equally intriguing to see the lawyers confirming certain chains of causality that strike readers as perfectly intuitive. But as José Zalaquett, a prominent human rights attorney and a member of the Rettig Commission, once said, it may be true that "everyone knows that Pinochet was responsible for thousands of killings, torture, and disappearances, but that doesn't mean you don't have to prove it in court."[31] The legal venue, in this case, *requires* a certain kind of testimony that hinges on specific factual information and well-argued chains of logic.[32] To obtain such facts demands that the lawyers engage in particular lines of questioning whose scope is thus limited to and determined by the finality that the trial seeks.

Eltit includes the lawyers' closing statements in *Puño y letra* because she wants us to take note of their constructed nature; she wants to signal to readers that even after the prosecutors have laid out the "facts" to the best of their ability, the overall narrative still contains gaps, silences, and speculation. The lawyers' repeated use of phrases like *a mi juicio* (in my judgment) indicates that they are engaged in a process of subjective crafting of the real (positioned to the court as objectivity); in other words, she highlights that in every moment the attorneys are framing facts in narrative form, which is by nature always a selective and speculative activity. Consider, as an example, the following passage in which the verbal formula *puede ser* (maybe)—an indication of the unknown, the unknowable, or the irrelevant—strikes a fundamental tension with what has been definitively "proved": "Arancibia Clavel provided the contacts and, as Doctor Carrió pointed out today, *it could be* that the Federal Police or other local organizations supported the person responsible for overseeing the operation. In other words, *there may have been*, aside from this central chain of command, other support networks, *maybe* of an international character like the CIA, *maybe* some para-police group. . . . But *what we have proven* in the case *is* that the decision to place the bomb came from the upper echelons of the Chilean military hierarchy."[33]

The passage is significant because it gives evidence that the trial's structure and language produce a very specific kind of truth (geared toward a verdict and an indictment) but that they do not exhaust our inquiry into the past. Facts (that which *is* or *has been* proved) remain permeated by speculation. The figure of the *secret* lingers. In line with this idea, at another point during the closing statements the prosecutors allude to the forever unknowable secrets that the military continues to guard, veiled behind its long-standing pact of silence: "In other words, *there are no public documents* that can be used to find out what they [the military or DINA] did. [Those documents] are *secret*, and they are [therefore] not available to the Court. And, on another hand, a *pact of confidentiality* [*un compromiso de confidencialidad*] exists. The members of this organization are committed to keeping *secrets*. And the Chilean and Argentine judicial systems have no provisions for giving incentives to break that pact."[34]

Beyond the truths that evade or exceed the lawyers' intentions or abilities to lay bare the truth, testimony's greatest moment of crisis in *Puño y letra*, of course, comes with the interrogation of the witness: Hugo Zambelli, a bounded character obviously fearful of self-incrimination and full of delusions of grandeur exacerbated by his status as a second-rate theater actor.[35] Like Arancibia (the defendant), Zambelli (the bystander) is submerged in his own fantasies and fictions of the self, and in this sense he constitutes a prime example of how anonymous bodies, by virtue of living within a state of exception, become marked by power and altered irreparably. Attuned to the contrived and "acted" nature of Zambelli's deposition, Eltit transcribes it on the page in a manner that evokes a theatrical script. As the drama unfolds, the witness's interrogators constantly remind him that he is under oath, yet, true to his character and his bounded performance of perjury, he interjects that his life "was always based on theater, theater, theater."[36]

The reader gets lost in Zambelli's contradictions and shares the court's extreme frustration with his lies. In one moment, for example, the court questions a discrepancy between Zambelli's testimony and an answer he gave to a very simple question in a prior deposition: When was the last time you saw Arancibia? The interchange exemplifies the verbal webs that Zambelli spins and the ways in which he evades direct expression of the truth.

PRESIDENT: In 1989, you testified to Dr. Blondi that the last time you saw Arancibia had been the twenty-second or twenty-third of December of the previous year at La Rueda restaurant.

ZAMBELLI: Of this year?

PRESIDENT: No, of 1988. [That would be the case] if you testified to it in 1989.

ZAMBELLI: No. To what date in 1988 are you referring?

PRESIDENT: To the twenty-second or twenty-third of the previous year at La Rueda restaurant. That's what you said in 1989. So, we are talking about 1988.

ZAMBELLI: No. No.

PRESIDENT: No, what?

ZAMBELLI: No. No. You're saying that I saw him again in 1988 at La Rueda restaurant?

PRESIDENT: That's what you testified.

ZAMBELLI: That's not how it was.

PRESIDENT: That's not how it was?

JUDGE: So, why did you testify to that, Zambelli?

ZAMBELLI: In 1988, I didn't even remember that man. It's impossible because I never wanted to see him again.

JUDGE: So why was this in your previous testimony?

ZAMBELLI: I give you my word of honor. I don't know.

DEFENSE: Excuse me. Could it be that you had seen him?

ZAMBELLI: It could be. Now I understand the question, Doctor. It could have been that I saw him at La Rueda but that we were no longer together or anything like that. I saw him because I went there for dinner with some friends.

PRESIDENT: Zambelli, the question was this: When was the last time you saw Arancibia? . . . The last time you saw him! No one is asking you if you spoke. When was the last time you saw him?

ZAMBELLI: I saw him two or three times in the street. But the part about La Rueda . . . I'm sorry . . . I'm sorry. Oh yes, now I remember. It was that I entered and saw Mr. Arancibia at a table with people I didn't know. And I was with other people.

PRESIDENT: And was it then that you remembered it was December 22 or 23, 1988?

ZAMBELLI: Yes, yes. Surely, I would have remembered. Surely. Yes. Yes. But I didn't go with him. I thought you were asking me if I had gone with him.

PROSECUTOR: Zambelli, back then when you were questioned on those occasions by different judges, did you have the [overall] picture clearer or less clear than you do now?

ZAMBELLI: What I remember . . .

PROSECUTOR: Wait, wait. I'm referring to this: You testified thirteen years ago in 1987. Then you testified again eleven years ago in 1989. The facts that you remembered or the facts about which we are now asking, did you have them clearer then, now, or are they the same?

ZAMBELLI: I'm not sure I have it all clear.

PROSECUTOR: Does the passage of time make you lose your memory? Do you preserve your memory?

ZAMBELLI: No. . . . There are things I have quite clear. There are things that I have quite clear.

PROSECUTOR: And at that time, were they just as clear? Or less clear?

ZAMBELLI: I don't know. I don't know.

At certain points, the prosecutors wonder altogether about the usefulness of the witness's declarations. They become perturbed and aggressive in the face of his performance of perjury; they yell at Zambelli—";Que haga memoria!," ";Escúcheme!," ";Trate de ser claro porque si no va a tener problemas!" (Remember! Listen to me! Try to be clear, because if you're not clear with us you're going to have problems!).[37] Dates and details clash with Zambelli's prior declarations such that the law is left at a veritable impasse. One of the

Boundedness and Vulnerability

lawyers, exasperated, tells the judge: "I don't have the slightest idea whether he was lying back then or whether he is lying now. But I am going to ask you [the judge] to extract passages from [Zambelli's] declarations and have him investigated for the crime of perjury [*el delito de falso testimonio*] because there are so many discrepancies. [Zambelli] was so sure of what he was saying before, just as he is now. [Yet the details he gives are contradictory], so I don't know how to continue with this interrogation."[38]

Lies . . . truth . . . the tension between them pervades the juridical scene. Moreover, the theatrical polysemia of Zambelli's phrasing contributes to the spectacular nature of his performance. He consistently repeats ambiguous linguistic formulae such as "le mentiría si le digo" (I'd be lying if I were to tell you) that not only permit him to wiggle his way out of particular lines of questioning but also poetically capture (from Eltit's vantage point) the tense and twisted relationship between lies (*le mentiría*) and truth (*le digo*) that characterize the bystander figure's discourse.[39] In the end, his sworn act of truth-telling amounts to a performance of perjury, in the Derridean sense; it betrays the good-faith "pact of truth" that testimony usually presupposes between the witness and the listener.[40] Zambelli appeals to his audience to legitimate his word—¡créanme!, ¡palabra de honor!, ¡te doy mi palabra de hombre! (Believe me! Word of honor! I give you my word as a man!).[41] Yet in the end he cannot save himself from the judgment of rational minds: the attorneys' and the reader's. All the while, he remains dutifully ensconced in his bounded fantasy of avowal, fully aware of what he knows but is choosing not to tell. His playful evasiveness makes readers sense that he relishes the mockery he makes of truth, the lawyers, and the whole judicial process: "I want to tell you something, Doctor. During the first declaration they took, the first one, the first one after Arancibia was nabbed, I was in a really bad state. And now, all [that you are saying] is confusing me. It really confuses me because within my heart I know the real truth [*porque yo desde adentro de mi corazón, sé cómo es la cosa*]."[42]

Quite likely, Zambelli first learned to make himself invulnerable—to hide the truth, to stay shielded from the horror, to tune out the other's pain—as an inhabitant of the convulsive 1970s. Learned patterns of behavior from those times of state-sponsored violence now carry over into the democratic present and continue to permeate the bystander subject's cowardly, bounded discourse. A "peon" like Arancibia, "a secondary body that became enmeshed in a plot much larger than him" (Eltit's words), Zambelli is a product of a long history of "choices and actions that have made [him who he] is."[43] Faithful to those choices, he now buys into "the illusion that he is in control" and commits wholeheartedly to that role in court.[44] Moreover, the character's direct association (as an actor) with the culture of spectacle invites us to reflect on the spectacular nature of self-interested memory narratives that have been a constant on the postdictatorial scene; in other words, Zambelli's perjured voice compels us to recognize the spectacle that memory sometimes becomes in neoliberal times.

The witness stand affords Zambelli an opportunity to sell his version of events. It also gives him a potential spotlight in which to shine and be heard by others. In this sense, we can think of him, to recall Elizabeth Jelin's often cited concept, as a kind of "memory entrepreneur": one "who seek[s] social recognition and political legitimacy of *one* ([his] own) interpretation or narrative of the past."[45] As a memory entrepreneur—and, by extension, as an *entrepreneur of the self*—he channels a desire "to maintain a certain kind of subjectivity [that is] privileged in capitalist socioeconomic systems, namely, that of the proto-typical, arrogantly self-sufficient, independent, invulnerable master subject."[46] He is risk averse, protective of himself at the expense of others.

The feminist scholar Erinn C. Gilson points out that entrepreneurial subjectivity is founded precisely on an aversion to vulnerability.

> By definition, entrepreneurial subjectivity is vulnerability averse; an enterprise protects itself from conditions of vulnerability rather than seeking to avow, experience, or respond sensitively to them. The *modus operandi* of entrepreneurial subjectivity is control, both over the self and . . . over the effects others may have on the self. . . . Entrepreneurial subjectivity thus masks the unavoidable vulnerability that characterizes life, covering it over with an illusory ideal of self-made individuality. By entrenching this solely negative view of and an attitude of aversion to vulnerability, entrepreneurial subjectivity facilitates repudiation of responsibility for vulnerability both by fostering disavowal of vulnerability instead of reckoning with it as a fundamental condition we cannot evade and by devaluing those who are vulnerable to harm as deficient and weak.[47]

To be sure, Zambelli's position within the matrix of vulnerability never ceases to be complex. Although, as I have explained, he shamefully shields himself behind a mask of boundedness and invulnerability (false power), his actual lack of power makes us see that he is on some level also a vulnerable body. We should not forget that Zambelli is gay (as was Arancibia)—a detail that Eltit understands, first and foremost, to be a legitimate choice that lies beyond question. But, at the same time, she also understands that Zambelli's and Arancibia's homosexuality renders them particularly vulnerable to becoming tabloid fodder for the media, which they did in fact become at the time of the trial. The media capitalized on the couple's intimate relationship to exploit them, to construct a sordid tale of complicity and violence that ultimately did violence to them as well: Arancibia, a gay, civilian underling, an outcast from the "military family," took the fall while Pinochet and the upper echelons of the military remained untouchable. In such a scenario, Eltit perceives an injustice, notwithstanding (*and without forgiving*) Zambelli's act of perjury and Arancibia's culpability.

It is significant that the couple's homosexuality is almost entirely silenced in *Puño y letra* and only fleetingly referenced in Zambelli's own testimony.

> JUDGE: Has Arancibia Clavel been important in your love life [*su vida sentimental*]?
> ZAMBELLI: Yes, señora. As a person, he was always good to me.

We learn nothing more of their life together. Eltit provides no further details because she wishes to leave homosexuality (as a signifier) open to multiple valences and interpretations within her work. The details she provides, however, allow readers to sense connections between sexuality and neoliberal spectacle, as well as between the military's hypermasculine order and the inadmissible homosexuality of one of its civilian accomplices. If the neoliberal media exploits the characters' homosexuality to position them in a sordid and violent plot, Zambelli remains hyper-guarded about his relationship with Arancibia to protect both himself and his former lover. To speak of his own sexuality overtly, or even at all, might be perceived as a public affront to a man (Arancibia) whose reputation he wants desperately to protect and who years ago worked hard to carve out a place for himself within the "military family" (*la familia militar*). So as not to complicate matters for Arancibia or himself, Zambelli's boundedness therefore extends not only to a generalized evasion of truth but also to a feigned normalization of his sexuality. Put differently, he is neither *truthful* nor *true to himself*. His adopted role as an innocent, neutral bystander, in some sense, requires it.

Finally, as an entrepreneurial subject whose silencing of violence and difference evokes the neoliberalized order we currently inhabit, Zambelli serves as a mirror that Eltit holds up so that readers can take a good, hard look at themselves. In the case of the Holocaust, it has often been observed that those who lived beside the concentration camps or even at a great distance from them covered up the real horror or simply refused to see it—out of fear, or perhaps because acknowledging the other's pain was just too unsettling.[48] In a somewhat parallel fashion, Zambelli is a subject whose life is marked by an inseverable linkage to unsayable horror but who prefers not to see, who prefers not to draw attention to himself (even though he fails in his enterprise). Instead, he conforms, covers up, looks away, and lacks the candor to be his authentic self.

He clings to a role (or to multiple roles) that protect(s) him (and Arancibia) from harm. Understood in this way, Zambelli's character aptly dramatizes the position of potential readers (perhaps Chilean readers, military people, civilian accomplices, businesspeople, or even some US readers) who might prefer to maintain a safe distance from Prats's and Cuthbert's pulverized bodies, from the military's crimes, from US complicity in promoting war abroad, from the true impact of the dictatorship's economic legacy, or from the dictatorship's pulverizing memory in general. In other words, Zambelli's presence in the text forces us to ask about *our* role—explicit or implicit—in upholding Pinochet and the neoliberal transformation of Chile. What are *we* willing to confess? What shapes *our* vision? What are *we* trying to protect? What are *we* unwilling to give up? Who do *we* pretend to be to avoid disturbing the status quo? In what kinds of theatrical performances of invulnerability are we all engaged?

By holding the bystander figure up to public scrutiny, Eltit brilliantly incites the need for a society-wide (and global) examination of conscience whereby *justice* would imply an honest reckoning not only for those involved in particular scenarios of violence but also for all Chileans—and, by extension, for all of us.

Pain

> They—the women—are the ones who show their faces.
> Diamela Eltit

After the trial, the pain of victims and average citizens, though perhaps mitigated, also remains. In her introduction, Eltit specifically mentions the Prats daughters and the Arancibia sisters, who continue to suffer, overwhelmed by the intensity of the juridical drama and the protracted uncertainty that derives from many years of waiting. These women, abandoned by the Chilean military, in whose ranks their brother or father once served (though on different sides of the ideological spectrum), are, for Eltit, the only people valiant enough to "show their faces" on the public stage.[49] The Prats daughters, likened to Antigone, and the Arancibia sisters, likened by Eltit to Federico García Lorca's female characters, offer a metaphor for women's central, *public* role in the political struggle for truth and memory during the dictatorship and transition. The Prats daughters metonymically evoke the mothers and wives of the disappeared who deployed their gendered roles to act radically against the dictatorship in very public ways. Like Antigone, they challenged the authority of the state and its institutions. In contrast, the Arancibia sisters, reluctant to reveal their intimacy, emblematize a very different model of the feminine. Like the sisters in García Lorca's *La casa de Bernarda Alba* (The House of

Bernarda Alba, 1945), they cling to a much more traditional and dutiful supporting role: by virtue of their presence, they seek to humanize the accused and ultimately protect him from harm.

The Prats daughters' suffering particularly moves Eltit. While she notes that Arancibia's trial cannot hope to restore for them the essential truth of their parents' untimely death but instead offers "algo parecido a la verdad" (something that seems like truth), she also acknowledges the importance of their valiant and unwavering fight for justice.[50] There they stand, affixed at the margins. Still, despite their symbolic marginalization, their forceful presence interpellates the reader, Zambelli, and the entire courtroom scene. Eltit's evocation of the Prats daughters is shot through (secretly) with compelling images that haunt historical memory but today go unspoken: Sofía, Angélica, and Cecilia Prats-Cuthbert landing at Ezeiza airport after hearing their parents were dead; the daughters' identification of their parents' cadavers at the morgue; the sisters boarding a plane to return their parents' remains to Santiago; the memorial Mass held at Iglesia Las Condes; the burial at Santiago's General Cemetery; their interminable pacing through the halls of justice.[51]

While in Eltit's text the Prats daughters represent the victims' pain, they embody but one call to vulnerability. A second call to become vulnerable—and perhaps one of the most fascinating aspects of *Puño y letra*—is Eltit's own subjective presence in her writing. Her voice—at once poignantly individual, vulnerable, in solidarity with, and inclusive of a collective *we* who suffered under dictatorship—stands in defiant counterpoint to Zambelli's bounded discourse. Although it is true that Eltit's authorial voice had already spoken in previous testimonial works such as *El padre mío* (My Father, 1989) and *El infarto del alma* (Soul's Infarct, 1993), in *Puño y letra* her personal suffering as an "inhabitant of the Chilean dictatorship" comes across as much more salient, palpable, and emotionally revealing than in any of the aforementioned works.[52]

In her essay "1974," which closes *Puño y letra*, Eltit presents herself as a common citizen-victim whose life, memory, and thought were forever altered by living a state of exception. The year 1974 functions as a detonator, a link between her personal trauma and the Prats crime. Witnessing Arancibia's trial drags up repressed fears and rancor, stored in some remote corner of her confused and convulsive memory. According to Eltit, 1974, the most intense year of political violence, was a "pedagogical" year in which Chilean bodies—her own included—were reeducated, cowed, neutralized, muted, or displaced under authoritarian rule.[53] The author's first-person narration touches the reader as it struggles with the age-old question of how to express the inexpressible—perhaps the central question theorists and commentators of trauma narratives have grappled with in postviolence critical writing. In that vein, Eltit refers to

1974 as "that inexpressible year": 1974, the year in which the subjugation of Chileans to dictatorial rule, as well as their isolation from the outside world, became so pronounced that citizens were blinded (or chose to remain blind) to unspeakable crimes being committed just on the other side of the Andes mountains, or perhaps much closer to home—as if the Prats assassination were a perfect mirror image of the *exception*-ally infirmed Chilean interior.[54]

Eltit remembers her close friend Carlos, exiled to Paris. She remembers poor day laborers forced to rebuild a new and glorious *patria* for a pittance wage. Anonymous bodies. Many of those *obreros* (workers) were the same subjects who shortly before had taken to the streets to defend Allende and fight for change. Eltit notes that the dictatorship refunctionalized their insurrectional bodies, turning them into slave-like beings on whose backs Pinochet would soon erect the new, neoliberal state. Such memories resonate with Eltit; they evoke for her a shame and pain that linger still today. In fact, her narrative becomes so introspective at times that she steps back from her position as a highly regarded writer and speaks instead from a moving, intimate place: that of a common Chilean woman (or simply a human being) who still harbors deep questions and deep wounds: "My chronic body, from that year forward, could no longer be cured. I carry the scar that hides a moral wound that irreversibly tore through my soul. In that year, 1974, we had to forget the rituals that characterized our past as thinkers. [We had] to forget that the streets belonged to us. . . . To forget the aesthetics according to which we [used to] organize ourselves [politically]. To forget every millimeter of rebellion. . . . It seems impossible, doesn't it?"[55]

This comment becomes even more striking if we recall Eltit's unwavering commitment to Popular Unity and her valiant dedication to denouncing the Pinochet regime publicly during its most dangerous years. Eltit's participation, from 1979 to 1985, in Colectivo de Acciones de Arte (Art Action Collective, CADA)—lauded by critics and remembered as one of the most significant neo-avant-garde artistic interventions to emerge on the dictatorial scene—as well as her rebellious literary writings from those years, are called into question by her cutting self-examination.[56] Despite the overt and very vocal ways in which she and her colleagues from CADA protested against unspeakable state violence, her words give the impression that, on some level, she feels she could have done more to resist the refunctionalization of her political body. While it is very true that she used her body as a site of rebellion against the dictatorship's violence, she also recognizes that that same body was, in another sense, reprogrammed to live in a state of exception and wounded *irreversibly* to its core, compelled to un-think and un-dream. She boldly argues that in the ultraviolent year of 1974, those who before were the thinkers and dreamers of a more just society were forced to forget the depth of their rebellions, the depth of their commitments, and to become depoliticized subjects who, in some sense, became normalized within the neoliberal code of the "new Chile." Implicitly, Eltit suggests that her rebellious drive and hunger for change have never returned with the same intensity that they had prior to the 1973 coup. (This revelation, I reiterate, is raw and shocking; it speaks to the honesty of her voice as well as to the profound depth of her political commitments.) Life continues, and so does intense political activism, but trauma remains irrevocably inscribed, always present, not only as the loss of comrades but also as a *moral loss* (as she says), a political loss, the loss of possibility for radical social transformation (for real justice) that the dictatorship and transition governments relegated to oblivion through manifold amnesiac operations.

But there, in the midst of it all, the original, *unsayable* crime persists—in spite of the court cases and in spite of any and all attempts to access it, drag it up, or reckon with it. There, in the midst of it all, symbolically, stands the most unreconstructable remainder of the dictatorship's darkest days: the symbolically charged, entirely mutilated bodies of Carlos Prats and Sofía Cuthbert.

Implicitly engaging long-standing debates on human beings' ability to express or represent trauma, Eltit merely alludes to the disaster's infinite pain, without describing it outright. Her wager is that pain's real face defies description, and, by extension, its unsayability becomes an ethical imperative not to forget, to think critically: "Only modesty impedes me from describing the effects that the bomb had on Sofía Cuthbert."[57] For Eltit, those mutilated, emblematic bodies conjure the ruinous marks of the disaster: the moral wound, the shame of conformity, the guilt of not seeing or not wanting to see.

And, in fact, the bitter truth is that we know much more about Prats and Cuthbert than about thousands of anonymous bodies destroyed by the dictatorship, those excluded from the media-driven *farándula* (showbiz) of memory. Significantly, Eltit begins "1974" by mentioning two names in passing: Santiago Avilés, a painter; and Nicolás Flores, a textile apprentice. Both were detained in that year during a raid on the Quinta Bella shantytown. In her opinion, these are the kinds of anonymous subjects whose memories have been eclipsed by emblematic and grandiose figures like Prats and Cuthbert. What would it mean to gaze intensely upon these forgotten figures and evoke *their* silenced memory? Indeed, there are so many victims whose names persist in anonymity, just as there are so many accomplices whose anonymity stands as an affront to radical justice and as an inevitable font of shame, not only for them but also for all of us. In a 2005 essay on how the Chilean media tend to erase the density of memory and turn past traumas into a momentary fad or a banal sound bite, Eltit registers a lament that reminds us of what *Puño y letra* does *not* show:

"that to this very day we know so little, so very little about each and every one of those anonymous lives, and much less about their deaths."[58] We also know so little about those who caused the harm.

The gavel has come down. The Prats case is history. Justice, in a matter of speaking, has been done. But what of Avilés, Flores, or even Zambelli?

Impunity

That's what perturbs me: the juridical asymmetry. Judicial failure. There is Arancibia Clavel, responsible for what he's responsible for. Nevertheless, what gets left out is flagrant. The others are not there. His bosses. . . . The "real" military men are missing. They are absent bodies, but nevertheless crucial for configuring the definitive scene.

Diamela Eltit

More than a book about Prats and Cuthbert or their deaths, *Puño y letra* is about marginal, anonymous bodies: underlings and common citizens whose existence, in different ways, was sculpted and permanently altered by the experience of living a state of exception. Arancibia was a "cog in the wheel" of Chile's repressive state apparatus and Zambelli the pathetic, residual by-product of (or bystander to) that association. Eltit gets us thinking about how postdictatorial justice is meted out symbolically. Most of the time when justice is possible, high-level military officers take the fall, while the underlings get off scot-free claiming due obedience or ignorance. In this rather exceptional case, a lackey takes the fall (Arancibia) while the upper echelons of power remain untouched.[59] Nevertheless, while this may be the harsh reality of the political and juridical scene, neither Eltit nor the prosecuting attorneys let Pinochet go unjudged. *Puño y letra* provides persuasive evidence for accusing Pinochet as the ultimate criminal and mastermind behind the Prats-Cuthbert assassination. This is significant, because even though Pinochet's decrepit body had been declared unfit to stand trial in 2000, Eltit's text offers an alternative forum for proving him guilty beyond reasonable doubt. Where the law butts up against its limits, literature stands in as a surrogate.

As I think about bodies in impunity as remainders of the law, a case comes to mind that emblematizes the fragility of Chilean justice and brings into relief the brazen defiance of certain military officials when it comes to owning up to past crimes: that of retired army General Eduardo Iturriaga Neumann, one of DINA's most notorious criminals, convicted in 2007 of the kidnapping and disappearance of MIR activist Luis Dagoberto San Martín; he also played a supporting role in the Prats-Cuthbert assassination. Between June and early August 2007, Chileans were shocked when Iturriaga Neumann spent fifty-two days as a fugitive, in protest of a jail sentence that the Supreme Court had issued.

Before fleeing, he sent a public video statement to the media in which he affirmed his innocence and complained that a travesty of justice had been committed against him and five hundred of his fellow military men. "I openly rebel against this arbitrary, biased, unconstitutional, and illegal conviction," he ranted. "I don't accept it! How can we keep accepting this? Not me! No more!"[60] The image of Iturriaga Neumann raising his voice on television, making a mockery of Chile's judicial system, was disconcerting. A full-blown investigation ensued. Fifty-two days later, he was found living under a false name in a Viña del Mar apartment. The case sparked reactions across the board, most of which centered on the Concertación coalition's delight that "democracy was functioning properly" and that "no Chilean is above the law." A handful of right-wing politicians defended Iturriaga, which elicited outrage in other political sectors.

There he was, Ricardo Iturriaga Neumann, fifty-two days a fugitive of the law—another theatrical body performing a fantasy of innocence, a fiction of mastery evoked from the depths of his being. Eltit's reading of Arancibia (and Zambelli) seemed once again to apply: "Deliberate. Ridiculously theatrical. Yes, he knows that from this moment forward he will be observed, and he enjoys it. It's apparent that he greatly enjoys the twisted protagonism he has acquired. He poses his pose without reserve."[61]

Iturriaga is now in jail, but not without final bows to his adoring fans. Upon his capture, he headed toward the police car that would whisk him to his destiny. A television reporter greeted him: "Good morning, Mr. Iturriaga. How do you feel this morning?" With a smile, he replied: "Very well. Happy!"

And with that, the curtain came down.

Becoming Vulnerable

> The shopkeeper whose shop was on the corner was happy—happy with the wide assortment of his merchandise, with prices, happy with the way his shelves were arranged, with the clients' neutrality, with the superficial peace that enveloped his street corner. . . . Neutral, we maintain(ed) an unchanging expression as we move(d) through public space.
>
> Diamela Eltit

The image of the shopkeeper—another bystander (nameless, unlike Zambelli)—crops up subtly in *Puño y letra* and permits the reader to establish connections between political learning that occurred in 1974 while living a "state of exception" and the perpetuation of that learning as foundational for the neoliberal order that Chile is living today. Fearful inhabitants of dictatorship learned to look the other way—and did so all the more readily, as in the case of the shopkeeper, when there was something to gain by doing so or when their personal peace and well-being remained undisturbed. Eltit calls attention to the false tranquility that characterizes the shopkeeper's world: the neoliberal subject par excellence looks out for himself, ignores the violence happening around him, and learns to become neutral. *Homo politicus* becomes *homo neoliberalis*: gradually, a political body becomes addicted to the new socioeconomic order.

It is curious that Eltit refers to the shopkeeper in a book that is fundamentally about the Prats crime and about the limits of truth and justice. Clearly, most of the book focuses on a *remote past* and on the difficulty of bringing resolution to a crime that had occurred decades ago. How does the shopkeeper, another bystander who seemingly had nothing to do with the Prats crime, connect to Zambelli? What does the political learning of "neutrality" that originated under dictatorship have to do with the perjured testimony of a bystander in the here and now?

Eltit introduces the shopkeeper, symbolic of the neoliberal subject, into her book to inspire us to connect how the act of looking the other way *in the past* resonates (and persists) in the act of looking the other way *in the present*. The shopkeeper—the person who benefited economically from the elimination of the "other" and from the establishment of the neoliberal order—is now a generalized figure in posttransitional Chile. Eltit evokes this figure to critique the neoliberal moment and shine light on its foundational violence, to show us how the bounded (or invulnerable) subject was born and began to close off (gradually) to the pain and plight of others, shielded behind a false façade of protection and material comfort. In this sense, she does not write about the Prats trial simply to produce a historical document that makes a statement about how procedural justice plays out. Instead, she very specifically wants to use procedural justice (or its lack) as a pretext for talking about the lack of *social justice* that today prevails in Chilean society.

We always rewrite and revisit the past as a function of the present. For that reason, the question of justice cannot simply be reduced to collecting facts and meting out sentences to a group of the most brazen perpetrators. Symbolic justice is important, but the "idea of justice," as Amartya Sen argues, has to be broader: it has to move beyond the realm of the law (of the courts and legislation) and take as its point of departure a more capacious notion of freedom and socioeconomic equality.[62] The idea of justice must be not simply responsive or reactionary but rather a set of values that guides our way of life and helps us to live democratically and in solidarity with one another.

The Pinochet dictatorship is often thought of as an "exception": a "counter-revolutionary" response to a set of burgeoning revolutionary impulses that erupted dramatically and acutely in the midst of the Cold War. Though this reading is possible and, to some extent, accurate, it is also, admittedly, incomplete. To look at the 1973–90 period as an isolated instance of "exception" to a long-standing democratic tradition betrays a deeper examination of the social and political forces (e.g., racism, classism, economic disparity, ideological entrenchment), which date from the founding of the nation-state (or earlier) and that made the dictatorship possible in the first place.

If the Pinochet regime demands to be contextualized in a wider historical view, it should also be understood as a historical period whose effects touch the present in very palpable ways. Authoritarian practices as well as political and economic beliefs that originated with Pinochet continue to function in ways covert or overt. Since the return to democracy, many of the attitudes born during the Pinochet years have remained entrenched and untouched, while the market and the almighty dollar have created a society of "citizen-consumers."[63] For many, the neoliberalization of Chile has been a blessing (e.g., the shopkeeper), while for others, such as Diamela Eltit or students protesting today in the streets, it has brought dire consequences that urgently call for a radical reformulation of thought and political action. (Eltit, of course, identifies with a radicalized sector of the Chilean left that is critical of more orthodox leftist positions and is certainly critical of institutionalized leftist politics as they have been practiced throughout the transition.) Furthermore, discrimination continues against the Mapuche nation in the Chilean south, while unemployment, workers' rights, overcrowded prisons, and poverty remain issues that Chilean society urgently needs to address. Forging a viable historical memory, one that does not avoid the real face of the past, means embracing and addressing these realities as part of a move toward radical justice.

What would it mean to harness the political promise of a long-forgotten moment, the Popular Unity period, and bring it to bear on the present? It is a question not of restoring a lost moment integrally *as it was* but rather of asking what that lost era can teach us about achieving justice—real (social) justice—in a new context where the rules of the game have clearly changed.

In a sense, Eltit's entire political, ethical, and aesthetic project is about urging us *not* to be Hugo Zambelli: *not* to be fearful, bounded bystanders blinded by our own delusions, desires, comfortable worlds, and self-interested memories. Instead, her work challenges us to become vulnerable: to ask how we *should* live—how *we can* live—in relation to a crime that, on many levels, has not ceased to take place.

4

Framing the Accomplice

(Jorgelino Vergara)

More than forty years after the September 11, 1973, military coup, the public archive on the Pinochet regime continues to evolve and expand. New details come to light, or old details that were once shielded from the public eye (or that simply remained buried) gain traction in ways that make it possible for a society to see and hear what it previously could not. At times, these new details can spark a maelstrom or burgeon into a veritable phenomenon. Such was the case with Jorgelino Vergara, a man whom Chileans came to know as "El Mocito" (the young butler), a figure whose pathetic story of complicity added unforeseen dimensions to the memory "boom" that led up to and included the fortieth anniversary "memory season" (September 2013).[1]

In previous chapters, I focused almost exclusively on the ways in which accomplices refer to their experiences using their own words; this was clearly the case in my analyses of Mariana Callejas (chapter 1) and Pablo Longueira and Sergio de Castro (chapter 2). While my analysis of Hugo Zambelli's perjured discourse (chapter 3) also foregrounded the dynamics of the witness's first-person testimony, it simultaneously posited the importance of how the literary writer Diamela Eltit deconstructs and frames the accomplice's act of witnessing. Eltit's purposeful representational strategies, as I showed, highlighted the boundedness of the accomplice's words and signaled her personal, unfulfilled wish that Zambelli make himself vulnerable in the interest of justice and meaningful societal transformation.

In this chapter, I would like to delve more intensely into framings like Eltit's to ask how others—specifically journalists and filmmakers—have represented the accomplice-figure and to what ends. I, of course, do this without losing sight of the autobiographical aspects of the accomplice figure's discourse, which constitute the backbone of this study. To tackle the issue of "framing the accomplice," I take Jorgelino Vergara as my central example and concentrate on the four years (2010–14) leading up to the fortieth anniversary of the coup, a time in which complicity began to enter Chile's public narrative about the dictatorship in interesting and unexpected ways. My goal is to assess the textual (or what we might call *representational*) negotiations that happen around a figure like Vergara whose *responsibility* for his actions, both from his own perspective and from that of others, has become a source of contentious debate.

How did Chileans, forty years after the coup, configure a public archive around "El Mocito," a lackey in the apparatus of the dictatorial state, an entirely marginal figure (poor and impoverished) who carried out appalling tasks from a servile position in the regime's hierarchy? What languages made it possible for Chileans to think about, debate, or even consume voyeuristically this character whose life experience fits squarely within the "gray zone" of complicity with dictatorial power?[2] And what political and ethical consequences stem from these languages or representational choices?

The Fortieth Anniversary of the Coup: Memory's Expanded Field of Vision

The events of September 2013 felt palpably different from earlier commemorations of the coup. By that time, a constellation of circumstances had ripened the environment for a media frenzy in which new voices and figures linked to the country's traumatic past would appear. These circumstances included the repoliticization of the citizenry in the wake of the 2011 student movement and other social movements (for, among others, indigenous rights and sexual rights); advances in human rights prosecutions by the courts; the sustained presence of *memory* as a guiding ethos for human rights organizations, academics, and activists; and the final months of the presidency of Sebastián Piñera, a figure who symbolized neoliberal rule and whose very presence on the scene evoked the specter of the Chicago Boys.

By September 2013, the idea of a *military-civilian dictatorship* (*una dicta-dura cívico-militar*) had gradually seeped into common parlance. Widely circulated publications like the satirical weekly *The Clinic*, among others, regularly called attention to the role civilians played in upholding the Pinochet regime. A case in point: on September 3, 2013, *The Clinic Online* ran a piece titled "Los cien rostros de la dictadura" (One Hundred Faces of the Dictatorship), which included photographs and brief biographical sketches not only of military personnel but also of government ministers, artists, actors, businesspeople, and journalists whose actions or omissions had contributed to the consolidation and propagation of Pinochet's political and economic project.[3] Publications of this nature reminded readers that the cast of characters that created the dictatorship and profited from it was broad and, even more important, that the cast included civilians, many of whom continued to hold positions of power in Chilean society.

Given this expanded field of vision, in which the dictatorship was now readily narrated as a period in which civilians played key roles, Jorgelino Vergara's emergence from clandestine life further reinforced the idea that accomplices of all kinds were omnipresent in Chilean society. Generally speaking, throughout the country's transition to democracy, it was not the norm for perpetrators or accomplices to break long-established pacts of silence. The 1995 Univisión interview with the civilian torturer Osvaldo Romo Mena, which later became the basis for Nancy Guzmán's book *Romo: Confesiones de un torturador* (Romo: Confessions of a Torturer, 2000), or General Manuel Contreras's television interviews are perhaps marked exceptions to this rule—although neither of these men ever truly repented or offered any information that human rights organizations did not already know.[4]

For many years, Chile could not produce a confession as significant as that of former Argentine naval captain Adolfo Francisco Scilingo, who declared on Argentine television in March 1995 that detained and disappeared people had been drugged and thrown alive into the sea.[5] In Argentina, Scilingo's confession caused an enormous stir and had a major political impact: it generated renewed public interest in the "Dirty War" in a mid-1990s moment in which impunity still reigned, and it also created the conditions of possibility for Argentines to hear the voices of human rights organizations more forcefully than ever before.[6] To that end, Claudia Feld has shown for the Argentine case that even when perpetrators like Scilingo are unrepentant, the weight of their words can produce unanticipated and often positive consequences for societies in transition.[7]

Although a testimony similar to Scilingo's surfaced in Chile in July 2003 (on the eve of the thirtieth anniversary of the coup)—I am referring to the case of a retired soldier named Juan Carlos Molina, who had participated in Chile's version of the "death flights"—it did not receive the same sort of media attention, nor did it produce lasting or memorable effects for Chilean society.[8] Given this state of affairs, the case of Jorgelino Vergara becomes all the more significant because it managed—finally—to create a noteworthy and sustained presence of the accomplice figure in the public sphere. Artists, journalists, and intellectuals noticed him, not just judges and the police. Furthermore, as the country approached an important anniversary of the coup that would blow the Pandora's box of the past wide open, Chilean society now appeared ready to opine about a lowly collaborator figure like Vergara whom the country's collective memory narrative had previously excluded.

At the same time, the fortieth anniversary moment brought a noteworthy expansion of the notion of the *victim*. Chilean memory discourse for a long time defined the victim somewhat narrowly: the term was usually limited to naming those who had suffered (or who were related to those who had suffered) the direct effects of torture, exile, forced disappearance, or other acts of state terror. But suddenly, after about 2010, other actors began to appear—military conscripts forced into service, civilian underlings who did the regime's dirty work—all of whom would now also claim to be victims and even demand reparations from the state. This redefinition of victimhood begged difficult questions: To what extent should the dictatorship's foot soldiers—people like Jorgelino Vergara—also be considered victims of the regime? And to what extent could they, or should they, be held individually responsible for their participation in the machinery of state terror?

To be sure, September 2013 and the lead-up to it brought a momentary expansion in Chileans' field of vision regarding the dictatorship years. In that regard, several other happenings also merit mention. First, the National Television Network (TVN) ran a miniseries based on "forbidden images"—previously unseen—from the dictatorship years (*Chile: Las imágenes prohibidas*, Chile: Forbidden Images, 2014). The series garnered hefty ratings and was widely discussed by people from all walks of life. Second, the Supreme Court, which had never offered a mea culpa for its involvement in impeding justice during the dictatorship, confessed that it had acted erroneously by turning a deaf ear to the victims' plight for so many years. And finally, in his September 11 speech at La Moneda, then-president Sebastián Piñera shocked the country when he referred specifically to the *passive accomplices* who supported the dictatorship. This "outing" of people from his own political coalition—without naming names—caused a momentary stir and generated critiques from many politicians on the right.[9] Suffice it to say, then, that the topic of memory in September 2013 became virtually unavoidable because of the bombardment in public spaces of media coverage, films, and events related to the recent past. All of this, in aggregate, produced some lasting impact—although the full extent of that impact still remains to be assessed more carefully.

Still, we should take care not to overstate the fortieth anniversary's transcendence. As we know, memory ebbs and flows. It sometimes appears predictably (as with commemorative dates)—and sometimes unexpectedly. It can likewise fade from the public eye just as quickly as it came. Memory booms also warrant an additional caveat: while the cultural products, figures, and novel voices that flood the public scene may indeed be plentiful and sensationalistic, on closer scrutiny one realizes that many of them contribute very little to deepening our understanding of history. When ambiguous and contradictory figures like Jorgelino Vergara appear on the scene, they are not always subjected to rigorous deconstruction, that is, to a true "critique of memory."[10] We must therefore remain on our guard and proceed with caution, attuned to the nuances of the memory products that take center stage in moments of memory frenzy.

"El Mocito" Bursts onto the Scene (2010–14)

As early as 2010, in a good example of what Alexander Wilde once called an "irruption of memory," a pathetic figure known as "El Mocito" burst into the public eye and quickly agitated the fragile calm of Chile's post-dictatorial memory saga.[11] Jorgelino Vergara, one of the dictatorship's most lowly accomplices, was tasked in his adolescence with serving coffee to the head of Pinochet's secret police, General Manuel Contreras, as well as to Contreras's cronies. Furthermore, he was asked to work in several clandestine detention and torture centers, most notably in the one located at 8800 Simón Bolívar Street (in Santiago), a place of terror from which it is said only one prisoner emerged alive.[12] As part of his abhorrent work, Vergara spent his days cleaning blood off the floor, "packing" prisoners' bodies, and loading them into military planes to be thrown out to sea. He did this, he claims, because he wanted to be like the military men he admired—powerful, omnipotent. In other words, he wanted to be just the opposite of what he was: a completely marginal figure from a poor town in the South, down on his luck, and unlikely ever to become anyone important in life.

Motivated by aspirations of upward mobility, over the course of twelve years (1974–85) Vergara dutifully served the dictatorial state, first while still a minor as part of the Dirección de Inteligencia Nacional (National Intelligence Directorate, DINA) and later when he was a full-fledged adult as part of the Central Nacional de Informaciones (National Information Center, CNI), Pinochet's second secret police organization. Wrongly accused in 2007, almost thirty-five years later, of having killed the famed Communist Party leader Víctor Díaz López, Vergara emerged from his clandestine and nomadic life—or, more aptly put, he was hunted down by detectives—only to testify soon thereafter before Judge Víctor Montiglio in an attempt to clear his name and avoid judicial reprisal. A key detail: had detectives never accused him of murder, it is likely that Vergara never would have talked or come out of hiding.

Nevertheless, Vergara's appearance on the scene was more than just a mere curiosity or an untold story. His testimony triggered noteworthy and important advances in the work of truth and justice. For example, thanks to the accomplice's declarations in court, human rights organizations were able to confirm the existence of the previously unknown Simón Bolívar detention center. More important, seventy-four former DINA and CNI agents were convicted of crimes. And, perhaps most important, because of leads Vergara provided, forensic investigators were able to unearth the remains of four of the dictatorship's disappeared victims. Families who for years had searched to no avail were finally able to bury tiny shards of bone that had been dug up in Cuesta Barriga, a mountainous area outside Santiago. The recovery of some trace, *any* trace, of their loved ones afforded those families at least some semblance of "closure," twenty-six years after the three communist militants disappeared.[13]

Despite these positives, a point of clarification seems necessary for defining Vergara's role in the apparatus of state repression. Unlike military conscripts who were forced into service and sometimes coerced to participate in torture and forced disappearances, Vergara—significantly—*chose* to enter the world of DINA and was quickly seduced by the opportunities he thought it could offer him. He was never tortured or forced to serve. Quite literally, he knocked on Contreras's door because he thought there was something to be gained by doing so; once inside, even if he wanted to, it became difficult to leave.

Given these circumstances, Vergara's case illustrates how authoritarian systems prey on the weak, the powerless, and the uneducated; it also points to overarching structural inequities that feed authoritarian systems. Yet, even more than that, it offers a telling example of how seemingly anonymous bodies can become seduced by dictatorial power and redefine their ethical compasses to reflect the state of exception that a society is living. These weak subjects later benefit—however much, however little—from others' suffering.

In the expanse of four years (2010–14), this character, "El Mocito," cropped up repeatedly in a series of representational formats motivated by differing authorial intentions. First, in 2010, a documentary film called *El Mocito* (The Little Butler) debuted. Its directors, Marcela Said and Jean de Certeau, set out to draw an intimate psychological portrait of Vergara as a "survivor" (Said's word) who, thirty-five years later, still struggles to resolve his personal shame. Said's film left much to the imagination given that its goal was not necessarily to portray the "facts" of the case but rather to document Vergara's day-to-day existence and to highlight the pathetic, idiosyncratic behaviors of a kind of strange specimen that the dictatorial state managed to produce. For Said, Vergara was an unfortunate man, a victim of his circumstances, a man to be pitied, and, consequently, her portrayal of him (quite generous, as I will argue, on balance) sought to elicit sympathy in the viewer. Said's film purposefully takes distance from what Vergara did (or did not do) and instead turns him into a *character*—a character, I would add, that she dangerously divests of both agency and ideology. In the final assessment, her film is an invitation to reconciliation.

Following the premier of *El Mocito*, a book appeared on the scene, penned by a young journalist, Javier Rebolledo, who had worked with Said as an investigator during the process of filming her documentary. Unsatisfied on some level with the film's "artistic" approach to the character, Rebolledo, as any good journalist would do, strove to create a detailed accounting of the facts of Vergara's case, which was later published in the form of a best-selling book called *La danza de los cuervos* (The Dance of the Ravens, 2012).[14] The book, which to date has had multiple editions and sold more than twenty thousand copies, provides a much more balanced view of Vergara's experience than Said and de Certeau's film and resists the temptation to pass judgment on him morally. Judgment in *La danza* is left to the reader, who can assess the accomplice's narrative—and his silences—and form opinions based on hard evidence.

After the publication of Rebolledo's book, Vergara appeared yet a third time before the public (in July 2012), now as an interviewee on the journalist Tomás Mosciatti's evening television program, *La Entrevista*, which airs weekly on CNN Chile. This journalistic montage was, in a word, offensive. Not only did it treat and represent Vergara abusively, capitalizing on the spectacular nature of his marginality; it also sensationalized violence and torture in ways that were equally off-putting.

The four-year-long cycle of representations closed with two final television appearances, one national, the other international: an interview on the program *Mentiras verdaderas* (True Lies, 2013), which aired just days before the fortieth anniversary of the coup, and an ABC News Australia program called *Foreign Correspondent: Facing the Past* (2014), in which Vergara played the role of key informant.[15] Both programs cast the reformed accomplice figure as a "hero for human rights," dangerously divesting him of any responsibility for his role in DINA and CNI. In a way, the programs signaled a move from the more complex and "gray" visions of the accomplice figure that we found in Said's film and Rebolledo's book toward more simplified, media-ready versions whose intentions and representational strategies beg even more intense critique.

I am interested in this multigenre archive shaped around "El Mocito": a film, a book, and several television interviews, all quite different in their framings, uses, and even abuses of the character. I will reflect in turn on the nature and ethical consequences of each one of these representations, fully recognizing how delicate a matter it is to evaluate materials such as these, particularly because all of them have undeniably triggered positive effects in

Chilean society. Because of Vergara's testimony, as I mentioned, there are perpetrators in jail, and Chilean society has deepened its understanding of yet another aspect of the multilayered and secretive dictatorial state. There are also family members who have gained a modicum of peace by burying their dead. But, despite these positive effects, we cannot shy away from our critical responsibility to approach such representations carefully and cautiously, wary of the nature of each one and ready to condemn (as Nelly Richard suggests) the "triviality" of representations so crude and irresponsible that they run the risk of betraying the victims' memory or of evading potential justice.[16]

We should resist normalizing the accomplice and not let ourselves get carried away by the *Mocito phenomenon*. Rather, we should seize upon this unusual irruption of memory to do a critical accounting and reflect, yet again, on the ethics of representing a past whose history is far from fully written.

Humanizing the Accomplice: Marcela Said and Jean de Certeau's *El Mocito* (2010)

From the very first moments of Marcela Said and Jean de Certeau's film *El Mocito*, Jorgelino Vergara appears as a solitary, pathetic figure: a poor man, one of twelve siblings who went to work by chance and out of dire necessity in the home of General Manuel Contreras. After working for years in the heart of the Pinochet regime's apparatus of terror, Vergara finds himself living clandestinely in the south of Chile, far from urban life and the reaches of justice. Decades after he leaves the DINA/CNI, the filmmakers track him down, follow him, and film him in a somewhat hyperbolic light as he goes about his daily routine. The man's poverty and abjection are noteworthy; he appears to the viewer as something of a rare bird. In a lengthy early sequence, Vergara is shown killing a rabbit in a cold and calculated way, a necessity for his subsistence. The filmmakers focus on how Vergara skins the creature and drains its blood. In other early sequences, we see the protagonist bathing in a river, refining his skill with nunchakus, as if he were Bruce Lee, and staring into space contemplatively. These sequences pique the viewer's interest in the protagonist's idiosyncrasies and compel the viewer to wonder how Vergara honed such a methodical capacity to kill, particularly considering that he has consistently denied having killed or tortured anyone while working for Pinochet's secret police.

To be fair, Said and de Certeau recognize certain ambiguities in their main character. Throughout the film, they are interested in exploring the fine line that separates the victim from the victimizer. They are also attuned to the contradictions in Vergara's discourse and make it a point to highlight those at certain moments in the film.

Nevertheless, the film follows a clear narrative progression. If at first the camera shots distance us from Vergara, treating him as a somewhat grotesque or disturbed figure, later camera shots draw him closer to us, humanizing him. If we consider the film as a whole, then, it becomes possible to identify a narrative arc that takes us from *distance and deformity* to *humanization* and an acceptance of the accomplice as another kind of "victim" of the dictatorship. As Marcela Said explained to me in an interview: "We can say that in some sense [Vergara] was also a victim of his circumstances, of his lack of education, his poverty, his ignorance at the time, his naiveté when pretending to be a soldier because he thought it was fun. . . . He is an attractive character precisely because of his complexity."[17] Consequently, even though Vergara is an accomplice to the dictatorship and is probably hiding certain important information, Said and de Certeau maintain that he is, above all, a traumatized man who should be given an opportunity to tell his story, to understand it more deeply and, even more important, to heal. They argue that Vergara has tried valiantly to remake his life and to do what is ethically correct. In short, they contend that he has gone from being a collaborator with state repression to becoming what he is at present: in Said's words, "a collaborator with justice."[18]

Said and de Certeau's film was selected by the National Human Rights Institute (Instituto Nacional de Derechos Humanos) as one of a number of documentaries that can be used "informally" in classroom settings for educational purposes. To help teachers spark discussion about the film, Marina Loreto Donoso Rivas, in consultation with the directors, prepared a packet of pedagogical materials that contains activities, reflection questions, and suggestions for debate.[19] Somewhat predictably, these teaching materials echo the directors' focus on the ambiguity of Vergara's actions, on his "fluctuation between [the categories of] victim and victimizer." The materials sum up the film's thesis as follows: "[The Pinochet regime espoused a] politics of recruiting vulnerable people to participate directly or indirectly in the dictatorship's crimes. In this context, the film proposes that people like Jorgelino are but one more consequence of state terrorism." Discussion activities compel teachers and students to think about Vergara in relation to concepts like *memory, forgiveness, truth,* and *reparation* or to select three words that best describe Vergara from the following field of choices: *marginal, astute, strong, accomplice, assassin, traitor, charlatan, repentant man,* and *victim.* Another activity asks students to subject Vergara to a mock trial in which two students play the role of prosecutors, two play the role of defendants, and several play the role of judges. Toward the end of the packet, a final activity asks students to consider the film's over-all progression—that is, Vergara's journey from the "inferno" to "purgatory" to "redemption"—and to decide if such a characterization of the film's narrative arc is accurate or appropriate. It is worth noting, therefore, that the accompanying didactic materials, on the whole, echo the film's desire to portray Vergara as an ambiguous character, a vulnerable subject who ultimately follows a path toward redemption because of his willingness to testify in court. By asking questions and proposing activities that prime or lead students to acknowledge that Vergara might also be considered a *victim*, the directors manage to reinforce pedagogically the humanized view of the collaborator that their film espouses.

What I wish to emphasize, then, is how, on balance, *El Mocito* provides a generous portrayal of the accomplice meant to evoke sympathy or empathy on the spectator's part. This interpretive vision develops gradually, starting with the film's earliest sequences. When toward the beginning of the documentary Nelson Caucoto, a prominent human rights attorney, interviews Vergara, the accomplice argues that he was an "involuntary actor" who "practically felt like one more prisoner." Vergara's conversation with Caucoto allows viewers to perceive that the accomplice reads himself as a *victim*; it plants a seed in the viewer's mind that the accomplice can (and perhaps *should*) be read in this way. In later sequences, Vergara is no longer the only one affirming his victim-hood; other informants evoke pity for the accomplice by reading him as a victim *from the outside*. In one of these sequences, for example, Vergara appears seated at a table and remains silent while another man, his brother-in-law, speaks on his behalf. The brother-in-law notes that Vergara "was never the same" after joining DINA: "His memory is full of gaps that no one else can know; only he knows." All the while, Vergara remains there, entranced, drink-ing yerba mate. Later, others who knew Vergara also testify that he joined DINA out of economic need and that, while he worked there, the regime "brainwashed him." These other voices sprinkled throughout the film bring to mind Dori Laub's notion of the "empathic listener," whom Laub sees as vital to the survival of trauma victims.[20] By including scenes of empathic listening at several points in their documentary, the filmmakers generate a cumulative effect of empathy that has the potential to influence the viewer and compel him to understand—and perhaps even forgive—Vergara's collaboration, his silences notwithstanding.

The generous vision of the accomplice that we find in *El Mocito* culminates in the penultimate sequence, in which Vergara, having stared into a mirror at length, convinces himself that by telling the truth he is working to advance the cause of human rights. If in the beginning of the film we see a destroyed, alien-ated, and very strange Vergara going about his daily routines—skinning rabbits,

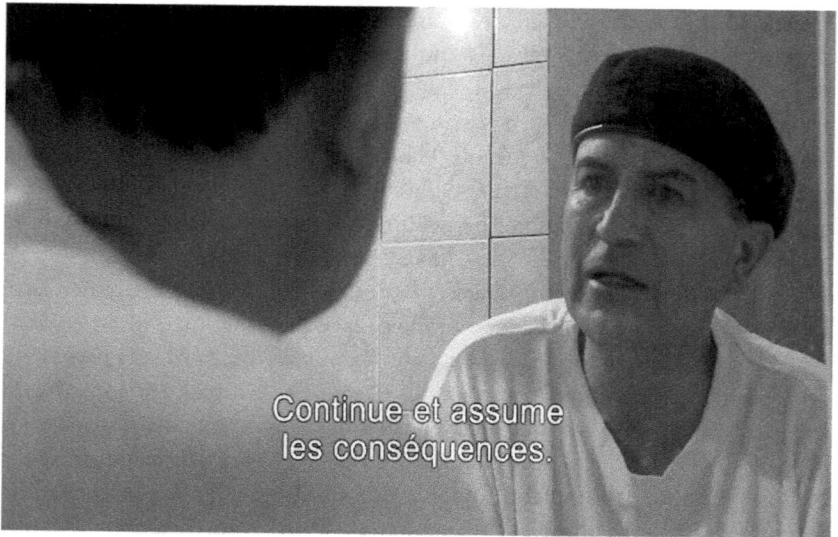

Jorgelino Vergara contemplates his image in a mirror (*El Mocito*).

playing with nunchakus, and bathing in the river—later sequences, like those in which Vergara participates in a religious parade or stares at himself in a mirror, seem to want to convince us that the accomplice is a reformed or perhaps even a redeemed man. Aesthetically speaking, the progression from a strange and hyperbolic world to another that is clean-cut and austere reinforces this notion of redemption. That the film emphasizes Vergara's deepening faith in God, which corresponds to his biographical "maturity," merely exacerbates this feeling. Standing in front of a mirror, Vergara shaves; he literally cleans up his physical appearance as an outward manifestation of the change that is occurring within him. He then mutters to himself: "You are the most important man on Earth. . . . I hope the rest of the world realizes what you are doing. You are doing something good *for human rights, for human rights, for human rights*" [emphasis mine]. Repetition serves to convince him. He is fearful, but his self-directed pep talk eventually gives him the courage to meet with the family of one of the victims.

In the final sequence, Vergara meets with the children of Daniel Palma, a communist militant who disappeared from the Simón Bolívar detention center in 1976. Two years before the encounter, Vergara recognized a photograph of Palma that he was shown in court by Judge Víctor Montiglio. When Vergara sits down with the Palma children, the scene is dramatic. The children hope to find out who, specifically, tortured and killed their father. The attitude of one

Framing the Accomplice

of the sons, Ricardo Palma, is striking. He claims to want not drama but peace, and this, he acknowledges, implies that *both* sides must make concessions. Palma is well aware that for Vergara to share what he knows, the family, too, must be willing to sacrifice some justice for truth.[21] Vergara, doing his part, upholds his end of the bargain and reveals the desired names to the Palma family, writing them on a piece of paper. The scene is truly unique because in the space of a film we witness a dynamic that not even the 1999–2000 "Mesa de Diálogo" (Dialogue Roundtable) could achieve: a genuine, honest, and significant exchange between victim and victimizer.[22] The sequence seems to suggest that some kind of reconciliation is possible in Chile if only victims and victimizers can manage to set aside their anger in the interest of transparency and truth. Quite notably, the film ends on a reconciliatory note and casts the accomplice as a reformed character who has found God, seen the light, and done what is right.

Why Said and de Certeau decide to portray Vergara in this rather generous fashion is difficult to pinpoint with certainty. Any hypothesis falls within the realm of speculation. However, it does seem relevant that Said, as she has revealed in interviews, comes from an upper-class family, several of whose members supported Pinochet.[23] I find it intriguing that the daughter of pinochetistas has dedicated almost the entirety of her documentary production to date, which also includes her documentaries *I Love Pinochet* (2001) and *Opus Dei: Una cruzada silenciosa* (Opus Dei: A Silent Crusade, 2006), to decoding the mentality of ordinary people who supported Pinochet. Given this trajectory, it seems that the main question inspiring much of her work is: Who are the pinochetistas, and what motivates their actions? Because of this, it is almost as if she is using her filmic project to explore her own biography, subjectivity, and lineage as both a Chilean citizen and a "daughter" of the generation that lived through the coup and that, in many ways, inherited its violence without being directly responsible for it. If we accept this possibility, it is perhaps less surprising that her vision of Vergara is so generous and that she portrays him, on balance, as a reformed figure whose subjectivity is, as she says, "complex."

As is often the case in the cultural production of the children of dictatorship (either direct or indirect) or of their descendants, one who has inherited a sordid and complex past often strives to take distance from it, "to defy it"; yet in so doing one also risks "mystifying" the past in ways that can be self-serving.[24] In Said's case, it seems reasonable to assume, given the critical tenor of her films, that she is on some level uncomfortable with her own inherited biography. An equestrian enthusiast, she has a direct connection, for example, to Juan Morales Salgado, the head of the Lautaro Brigade of DINA, which operated at Simón Bolívar 8800; he is now in prison and appears as an informant in *El*

Mocito. Shockingly, Morales Salgado was Said's riding teacher![25] Her personal link to this man makes it easier for her to access him and convince him to appear in her film, although it is also true that Morales is already heading to prison at the time of filming and likely has little to lose by talking. Such biographical links to the world of pinochetismo, therefore, may help to explain why Said emphasizes the ambiguities of her main character rather than condemn him outright.

Furthermore, I find it compelling that Said's aesthetic, which takes distance from Vergara as much as it brings him up close to us, encapsulates a broader trend at work among Chilean filmmakers and writers whose productions, like Said's, emerged in the 2000s.[26] These artists readily employ a number of distancing mechanisms—sometimes irony, sometimes humor, satire, or parody—to mark a position of impotence, disagreement, or shame in the face of questionable actions taken by the generations who came before them or by the Chilean state. By employing a diverse array of distancing mechanisms, they seek to disidentify with the Chile they have inherited.

I am thus left asking whether Said's humanized treatment of Vergara can be read as an attempt to grapple with her own familial and generational association with the world of pinochetismo—an association that, as an artist and person, she actively rejects but from which she also cannot entirely escape. The discourse of reconciliation, from that perspective, might very well pose a logical resolution to a complex and fraught problematic.

A Portrait in Gray: Javier Rebolledo's *La danza de los cuervos* (2012)

Like Said and de Certeau's film, Javier Rebolledo's *La danza de los cuervos* paints a portrait of Jorgelino Vergara rooted in his humble origins (his poverty, his status as an orphan) in the southern Chilean city of Curicó. Yet, unlike Said, Rebolledo does not interpret Vergara's impoverished background as an excuse for the accomplice's behavior. Instead, the journalist frames his main character as an example of what we might call "popular fascism": a vulnerable and precarious subject who internalizes the discourse of dominant power—another "nomadic body," to quote an expression made popular by the Chilean writer Diamela Eltit.[27]

Having finished only the third grade, Vergara, lacking formal education and stoked by an instinct to survive economically (although I should note that he also shows evidence of an alarming craving for upward mobility at any cost), *seeks* his education among the military. His military fantasies are striking, and Rebolledo draws this out in the text. Vergara wants to be like the military officers he sees. He considers living in General Contreras's house a "luxury" and, in a relatively short time, begins to crave "professionalization."[28] Chapter 16, titled "The Young Foundling's Baptism," is key in this sense because it describes the initiation ritual required for Vergara's indoctrination into the male-dominated military world. As part of this ritual, he learns to drink alcohol and fire a gun. He even goes through something of a sexual initiation; Rebolledo insinuates that Vergara sleeps with one of the female DINA agents at the end of a drunken bacchanal. The "orphan," consequently, finds a family among the military: the soldiers educate him, program him, and transform them into their subordinate, in body and soul.

Nevertheless, if Vergara is for Rebolledo a vulnerable subject who was undeniably abused by the dictatorial state, the journalist is not willing to admit that Vergara lacked agency. The military world generates for the accomplice a blinding attraction that Rebolledo readily acknowledges. Holding a weapon in his hand brings Vergara pleasure. At times, he fantasizes that he is Rocky Balboa or Bruce Lee. He even learns to "hate" the enemy.[29] Performing the role of a military man, in some sense, winds up convincing Vergara of the correctness of his actions. In short, the military world opens a space in which Vergara can gain a level of prestige and notoriety of which he could otherwise only dream—although we must necessarily recognize that he never ceases to be quite marginal within that world, despite his delusions of grandeur. Moreover, and perhaps even more important, being part of DINA provides Vergara a modicum of financial stability, a minimal salary on which to subsist. His body, therefore, is shot through with the insidious intermingling of power, money, and violence.

The journalist Jorge Escalante, author of the prologue to *La danza de los cuervos*, is correct to affirm that "violence forms the core of Rebolledo's narrative."[30] Indeed, readers find passages that leave them aghast in the face of the perpetrators' brutality and barbarism. The book's lexicon contains words like *corvos* (curved, double-bladed knives, used for gutting an enemy, that were prevalent during the nineteenth-century War of the Pacific and revived by the Pinochet regime) and *empaquetamientos* (the packaging or preparation of bodies that are to be thrown out of military planes into the sea), all of which become part of a vocabulary that is chillingly naturalized and normalized within a repressive context. The text, moreover, is extraordinarily graphic and direct in its descriptions of the horror that prisoners suffered. Still, Rebolledo always manages the representation of the morbid with intentionality. Far from wanting to promote a purely voyeuristic or sensationalistic look at the macabre, the journalist seems motivated to reveal what the philosopher Giorgio Agamben, following Martin Heidegger, called the "bureaucratization of horror": an extermination camp that functions like a bureaucratic machine whose goal is to produce cadavers like products on an assembly line.[31]

In any interview, power is volleyed back and forth between interviewer and interviewee. Rebolledo's book is based on more than thirty hours of interviews that he frames and manipulates skillfully. At every turn, the journalist mediates Vergara's voice, and, because of this, his own intentions take precedence. And this is precisely as it should be given that, as we know, Vergara's truth has had limits, particularly regarding the period between 1977 and 1985 when, no longer a minor, he continued to carry out functions for CNI.

Significantly, in all the episodes from Vergara's period as "El Mocito" (1974–77), Rebolledo integrates his informant's voice organically into his text by intentionally eliminating quotation marks whenever Vergara speaks directly. Rebolledo does this to signal to readers that everything Vergara claims regarding that period (1974–77) has been well documented by the courts and, for the most part, "proven." In contrast, when Vergara refers to his years in CNI, that is, the years after 1977, the journalist always deploys quotation marks as a graphic strategy for taking distance from his informant's words. Quotation marks serve to question the veracity of the accomplice's discourse. This typographical detail is significant because, in the final assessment, Rebolledo approaches the accomplice skeptically, bringing into relief the ambiguity or grayness of his status as victim or victimizer. Unwilling to overhumanize, aestheticize, or redeem his informant, Rebolledo ends his book by emphasizing that which Vergara continues to hide. In this sense, he never passes definitive judgment on the accomplice-figure. Instead, he leaves it to the reader to decide how to interpret the ethical grays and silences that glaringly *speak* through Vergara's discourse and poetically permeate the book.

Horror for Mass Consumption: The Tomás Mosciatti Interview (2012)

On the night of July 11, 2012, Chile's television audience was once again assaulted by Jorgelino Vergara's image, this time as he was interviewed by the journalist Tomás Mosciatti (Chile's version of Larry King) on his weekly interview program *La Entrevista*. This program, in general, is known for its thoughtful and hard-hitting political commentary; it reflects Mosciatti's respected trajectory as a lawyer, journalist, radio personality, and now co-owner of Radio Bío-Bío.[32] However, despite this good reputation, Mosciatti, in a scene that evoked what the Argentine critic Leonor Arfuch once called the "performative nature of an interrogation," exposed the popular accomplice and his "truth" to the consumptive eye of the television spectator.[33]

To be blunt, Mosciatti's interview added nothing new to the debate. Everything had already been said in Rebolledo's book. Mosciatti played the role of neither judge nor detective. His function, plain and simple, was to reveal: to stage what had been said in Rebolledo's book and seize upon its newsworthiness. In that sense, Mosciatti's lengthy interview with Vergara—fifty minutes in total—unfolded like a parade of sound bites taken virtually in chronological order from Rebolledo's book and, in a way, neutralized the character's complexities. Driven by the rapid-fire pace of the media message, it was clear that the goal of this journalistic mise-en-scène was, above all, to jar and shock the audience with the indecent exposure of abjection.

Leigh Payne, in *Unsettling Accounts: Neither Truth nor Reconciliation in Confessions of State Violence* (2008), points out that media versions of perpetrators' testimonies have a tendency to "obliterate" the original content of those testimonies.[34] This was certainly the case with Mosciatti's interview of the accomplice as well. The first half hour focused on sketching out—yet again—the precarious origins of a strange, pathetic, and marginalized subject: his impoverished upbringing, the physical and psychological abuse he suffered as a child, his precipitous and happenstance landing in the house of Manuel Contreras. Dressed humbly, much in keeping with the representation he *had to give* of himself, Vergara spoke slowly and sparsely, carefully measuring his words so as not to self-incriminate or overstep the boundaries of the script he had rehearsed so well. (And this makes sense! After the courts, the film, and the book, he certainly had his script down pat; he had memorized it skillfully.) To round out the scene, Mosciatti also acted for the cameras. His voice—somber, drawn, dour—masterfully intoned a gravity befitting his subject matter. Suffice it to say that for the first half hour the interview offered little novelty.

After a commercial break, however, the tenor of the interview changed brusquely. Mosciatti's goal was no longer to highlight the accomplice's humble origins but rather to focus on the Simón Bolívar torture center's mechanics of repression. The macabre, graphic details of dictatorial violence suddenly took center stage: the *gigí* (an instrument used to electrocute detainees), the "dry submarine," the "wet submarine," the "packing" of cadavers. Nothing was left out of this horrifying account whose mise-en-scène implored us to recall Nelly Richard's critiques, offered years ago, of the April 11, 1995, Univisión interview with Chile's notorious torturer Osvaldo Romo.[35] What sense was there in revisiting all the macabre details that had been well documented by the country's official truth commissions and in myriad other sources? What sense was there in this irresponsible assault on the memories of victims and their families, particularly considering that it was Vergara, the accomplice, who largely controlled the scene? What kind of ethics were at play in this sensationalistic exposé of marginality and horror that left viewers—including me—at once offended and entranced by a voyeuristic spectacle, a spectacle that made viewers want to turn off the television but at the same time compelled them to keep watching?

But perhaps what most stood out in the Mosciatti interview was the power play between Mosciatti and his interviewee—quite different from the power play I pointed out in *La danza de los cuervos*. This time Mosciatti and Vergara competed to control the spoken word, each one volleying skillfully, hoping to win the battle. It was apparent that Vergara protected himself at every turn, although at times he risked slipping up.

> MOSCIATTI: Who were the assassins in that place?
> VERGARA: Everyone. Practically.
> MOSCIATTI: Everyone killed?
> VERGARA: No, not everyone killed, but there was a complicity that
> practically made [them all / all of us] assassins. [No, no todos mataron,
> pero hay una complicidad que en el fondo prácticamente los hacía ser
> asesinos a todos.]

Practically. It is striking that Vergara excludes himself from the ranks of the perpetrators even though, paradoxically, he speaks of a complicity that included *everyone.* If, in this moment, through a minor slippage in his wording, he almost self-incriminates, immediately thereafter he shields himself from harm, affirming that he never packed bodies, that he only "helped" to pack them and move them from one place to another.

Regarding his participation in CNI operations after 1977, Vergara denies all involvement and prefers to remain silent. Mosciatti, of course, tries to catch him in a lie by evoking the final sentence of Rebolledo's book, in which Vergara insinuates—in the conditional tense, always hypothetically—that he *could have* participated in raids on shantytowns in the early 1980s that *could have* resulted in deaths: "Estas son situaciones que se podrían haber dado muchas veces" (These are situations that could have happened many times).[36] In *La danza de los cuervos*, this hypothetical and conditional answer serves a clear purpose: it opens a door so that the journalist can challenge the veracity and legitimacy of his informant's discourse because he *knows* that Vergara continues to harbor secrets. By contrast, when Mosciatti confronts Vergara with his prior conditional statement, hoping that Vergara will change that conditional to a past-tense verb—that is, hoping that he will affirm once and for all, "Yes, I *participated* in raids and killings in shantytowns"—Vergara clings for dear life to the hypothetical nature of his discourse. This, for Mosciatti, is a lost opportunity. The journalist presses his interviewee no further, allowing the accomplice to maintain strict and rigorous control of his speech act. Mosciatti thus squanders a key opportunity to force Vergara to elaborate on the role he played in the shantytown raids of the early 1980s; he misses a chance to "out" the accomplice for what he most likely was at that time: a paramilitary operative carefully groomed to kill.

Seated before CNN's cameras, a marginalized subject, an accomplice, savors his five minutes in the limelight, skillfully toying with the authority figure who, at several points, tries to catch him in a lie. When Mosciatti asks Vergara if he is worried that a judge will investigate his acts during his final years as a CNI agent, Vergara smiles and retorts, "Why? Why should I worry if I'm telling you everything right now?" Only his body language gives him away. He controls his discourse tersely, and the smile on his face reveals that he enjoys it.

In the final assessment, even though Vergara's discourse is confessional in nature, it is not really a confession in the strict sense of the term. As Leonor Arfuch notes, confessions, in their Christian version—and we should remember that Vergara claims to have discovered Christ—usually lead to an act of repentance and expiation.[37] This is clearly not the case with Vergara.

> MOSCIATTI: What are you repentant for? Are you repentant for anything?
> VERGARA: No.
> MOSCIATTI: Not for anything?
> VERGARA: Not for anything. Shall I explain why? What would I gain by
>   repenting at this stage of the game, especially because I didn't become
>   a professional within that system [the secret police] like I wanted to?

This brazen lack of repentance is jarring and calls into question the status of "victim" that other prominent commentators have ascribed to Vergara. In the end, there is no doubt that he is a vulnerable subject; nevertheless, there he sits, still harboring the fantasies of an unrepentant "wannabe" soldier, a detail that challenges the ethics of his word. The confessional subject exposes himself, yes, but not to the point of handing himself over fully and transparently to the judgment of the public or the authorities.

What perhaps would have helped to heal Chile's damaged social fabric forty years after the coup would have been to hear a repentant voice whose *full* confession truly embraced the philosophy of "Never Again." Falling far short of that goal, Mosciatti's abusive journalistic montage did nothing more than recycle a discourse we had already heard years before from General Manuel Contreras himself: that of the military man who felt abandoned—hung out to dry—by his cowardly superiors (in Contreras's case, by Pinochet).[38]

The language of the television interview brought no greater understanding of Vergara's experience; in fact, it flattened that experience. The media flash exploited an iconography of Vergara as a popular subject (dressed in a *boina*, or beret-style hat, and in clothing reflective of his humble socioeconomic status) who was sucked into the whirlwind of dictatorial violence but has now seen the light. The interview dwelled on the obscene details of torture and confronted viewers with the abject nature of the lowly aides who sometimes carried it out. At the same time, Vergara's brazen lack of repentance and his evasive, power-mongering desire for control made him nothing more than a metonymic stand-in for myriad civilian accomplices—be they weak or powerful—who still fail to recognize or fully acknowledge the role they played in aiding and abetting the Pinochet regime. Perhaps brandishing this lack of repentance in the face of the Chilean public, however vile and distasteful, was the ultimate service that Mosciatti's interview provided for Chile's collective memory. The interview made abundantly clear that for accomplices—as for the right and the military—truth, forty years later, still has firm limits.

Responsibility and Representation

In a 1964 essay titled "Personal Responsibility under Dictatorship," Hannah Arendt offers some ideas that merit consideration. First, in reference to the phenomenon of *due obedience* (the idea that one was merely following a superior's orders), Arendt observes that "there is no such thing as obedience in moral and political matters."[39] Without ignoring the immense gamut of complicities that authoritarian regimes generate, Arendt affirms with conviction that "much would be gained if we managed to eliminate from our moral and political vocabularies that pernicious word 'obedience.'"[40] According to Arendt, the question that should be posed to the person who collaborated and obeyed orders is not "why did you obey" but "why did you support."[41] In contrast to Primo Levi, who in "The Gray Zone" writes that the ultimate guilt resides in the totalitarian system itself, Arendt reminds us that guilt and innocence are not functions of a "system" but rather have meaning only when they are applied concretely to real individuals in specific cases.[42] Arendt, in other words, is wary of divesting accomplices of their agency and of attributing guilt to impersonalized systems.

With these contrasting arguments in mind, I find the comments of the esteemed Chilean human rights attorney Nelson Caucoto regarding the "Mocito" case surprising. In an interview that aired on Radio Cooperativa (December 12, 2011), Caucoto, adopting Levi's line of argumentation, stated unequivocally that Vergara was "a victim of his circumstances": "He's a very damaged person who was damaged by the Chilean state. He could perfectly well apply to the state for a pension [or some kind of reparation] on which to live [that would] help repair the damage that [the state] caused him."[43]

On some level, Caucoto's reasoning with respect to Vergara interfaces with the controversial case of Chile's former military conscripts, who over the past few years have been in the news demanding that the Chilean state pay them reparations for their forced service during the dictatorship.[44] Similarities notwithstanding, the case of Jorgelino Vergara seems different for two reasons: first, because it was Vergara's *will* to be part of the military (he clearly states this many times); and second, because he has made a number of statements (particularly in *La danza de los cuervos*) in which he appears to have supported the Pinochet regime in ideological terms. On the basis of the evidence, it also seems quite clear that had Vergara not been relieved of his duties as an agent following a 1985 parachuting accident (during paramilitary training), he likely would have continued as a loyal agent for some time thereafter. It is equally evident that if he had felt more valued by his superiors, he would have been unlikely to sell them out. And finally, if detectives had not hunted him down in 2007 to accuse him of killing Víctor Díaz, he would never have broken his long-standing pact of silence with the military.

Certain social, political, and economic structures make it possible for subjects like Jorgelino Vergara to exist. Indeed, repressive systems prey on subjects devoid of economic power, on those who lack culture and family support, or on those who hunger for power. It is undeniable that the systems that create subjects like Vergara also exploit them. But it is equally true that such subjects learn to exploit the very systems that exploit them and later fail to claim responsibility for their actions.

Moreover, when Mosciatti or Said try to create points of identification (either sympathy or empathy) between the accomplice and the spectator, they run a tremendous ethical risk. By presenting Vergara as an "everyman"—a poor guy, down on his luck, who was coopted by the dictatorial state—they risk diluting responsibilities. Naturalistic or deterministic narratives that seem to argue that people necessarily act in evil ways because their circumstances leave them no other option do not serve us well in analyzing cases like that of Jorgelino Vergara. According to this logic, which displaces guilt onto a "system," the category of the victim can become stretched beyond all recognition.

In addition, societies become susceptible to producing victims retroactively, thus losing sight of who the real victims were.

It has lately been common in Chile for actors of all political stripes to invoke the idea that during a state of exception, "we were all victims." By this logic, even the former president of Chile (the right-wing, former pinochetista Sebastián Piñera) can claim, as he has, that he and his wife were almost detained by the military soon after the coup (though they were not!) and that, consequently, on some level, they were also "victims." Such statements are not only irksome but also insensitive considering that Piñera, in the 1970s, found himself on the same side of the ideological spectrum as Pinochet and staunchly supported the violent neoliberalization of Chile.

Put differently, the postdictatorship period has had a tendency to produce a generalized notion of victimhood that can dangerously morph to encompass just about any subject position. This is a key danger that lurks behind a vision of Jorgelino Vergara that deemphasizes his personal desires and commitments to a violent counterrevolutionary state. It is my contention that we must never forget his *agency*. We must never forget that some people did the killing (or aided and abetted it), while other people were killed.

Normalizing the Accomplice: Vergara the "Human Rights Hero" (2013–14)

By the time the fortieth anniversary of the coup arrived, and even beyond it, Jorgelino Vergara lingered in the public eye—both in Chile and now also abroad. Two more representations hit the airwaves that spoke to the questionable manner in which the figure of *El Mocito the heroic human rights advocate* had become naturalized in the media. Whereas Rebolledo's book took a different approach, casting doubt on Vergara's discourse and calling attention to the limits of his truth, these new media representations— shockingly and in a deeply concerning way—normalized the accomplice figure: they portrayed him, on balance, as someone whose candor should be celebrated and who, consequently, should not be held responsible in any way for his participation, either direct or indirect, in the dictatorship's crimes.

The first of these two representations, which I will discuss briefly in turn, aired on the popular television program *Mentiras verdaderas* (September 9, 2013); it featured a ninety-minute interview with Vergara, admittedly more nuanced, well conceived, and eye opening than Mosciatti's rapid-fire tour of the highlights from Rebolledo's book. The second aired on ABC News Australia's program *Foreign Correspondent* (March 24, 2014). The Australian interview took as its main object of inquiry the case of Adriana Rivas, the personal secretary to General Manuel Contreras, another accomplice from Simón Bolívar 8800, a fugitive living in Sydney whom the Chilean justice system had accused of playing a role in interrogating and torturing prisoners.[45] Vis-à-vis his fellow accomplice, Vergara would play the part of the *professional witness* whose job would be to shed light on the deeds of the "real criminals." The implication here, is, of course, that *he* did not figure among them.

In the days leading up to the fortieth anniversary, the host of *Mentiras verdaderas* (La Red television network), Jean-Philippe Cretton, staged a cycle of interviews that drew public attention to a wide array of actors—victims, perpetrators, and accomplices—whose lives had all, in very different ways, been indelibly affected by state terror. Among those interviewed were two female survivors of the Villa Grimaldi detention center; a man who spoke graphically and jarringly about male rape, an unprecedented subject for Chilean television audiences; the cellmate of General Alberto Bachelet, father of President Michelle Bachelet (a "constitutionalist" Air Force general who died while serving time in prison for treason in 1974 after being tortured); children left orphaned following Operation Condor; the son of Manuel Contreras; and Jorgelino Vergara, "El Mocito." All the interviews garnered high ratings and instantly became trending topics on Twitter.

Reminiscent of the Mosciatti interview, Cretton's interview with Vergara included some sensationalistic elements but was, on the whole, much more measured than Mosciatti's. It ran at a slower pace, and this allowed the accomplice to reflect on and fill in valuable details regarding different chapters in his life. It was also reluctant to exploit Vergara's status as a "popular subject" (*sujeto popular*). Moreover, the longer time slot permitted viewers to scrutinize Vergara's public persona with greater care than before and to assess more judiciously how the former collaborator sees himself in the present; less pressure from the interviewer let Vergara linger in his answers, recount stories, and generate unsolicited anecdotes that tellingly revealed his thought patterns.

Yet, despite Cretton's more measured approach and well-thought-out questions, the program as a whole—interested (like most TV programs) in securing ratings—could not help but insist on Vergara's *exceptionality* as a tactic for attracting viewers. Within the first minute, Cretton surprisingly touted his guest as "the man who changed the course of human rights in our country"— a questionable statement that both implicitly silenced years of valiant efforts by family members and activists and overplayed Vergara's heroism as a hook to rope in viewers, making it sound as if Vergara had single-handedly changed the course of memory and justice efforts in post-Pinochet Chile. Even more unbelievably, Cretton's introductory remarks lent further credence to the uniqueness of Vergara's testimony by calling attention to how the accomplice had, for a long time, spoken freely and graphically about torture in ways that were—laudably, in his estimation—not "euphemistic." While it is true that perpetrators and actors of the political right have frequently resorted to euphemisms to avoid tackling the subject of torture directly, it is entirely untrue that Chilean society had never before heard graphic, *noneuphemistic* details like those that Vergara had been reciting in various forums since 2007. Several truth commission reports, the Vicaritate of Solidarity's archives, and myriad testimonial accounts by victims would alone suffice to counter Cretton's assertion. To echo the interviewer's "exceptional" framing of the accomplice turned hero, the text banners running across the bottom of the screen, full of superlatives, confirmed the exclusivity and uniqueness of the information provided by the informant that La Red had managed to lure to its studio: "EXCLUSIVE: Former DINA and CNI agent reveals secrets about one of the worst detention centers."

La Red, of course, had its motivations for framing the accomplice as it did, but Vergara, too, came ready to act the part he wanted to sell. At every turn, Vergara resisted feeding the sensationalized framework the network had established. Compared to his prior appearance on CNN, his self-performance had changed markedly: the man who before sat in front of Mosciatti—the exemplary popular subject—had now become "clean-cut": a reformed man and an authority figure on human rights issues. His wardrobe conjured the illusion that he was just like any other middle-class Chilean—despite the fact that life, admittedly, had dealt him a rough hand. Instead of a stocking cap and modest clothing, he now donned a dress shirt and tie, which gave him an added air of authority. His speech was also plainer and clearer than in the Mosciatti interview, his physicality less evasive. To consolidate his authority all the more, he subtly bolstered his stature as a professional witness by implying, in a sense, that he had *coauthored* both Rebolledo's book and Said and de Certeau's film: he refers, using a subtle grammatical nuance, to "el libro que *hice con* Javier Rebolledo" (the book I did with Javier Rebolledo) and "la película que *hice con* Marcela Said" (the film I did with Marcela Said).

Buying into Vergara's self-projected authority, Cretton goes on to invite him to talk not only about what happened at the Simón Bolívar detention center but also about topics that likely ranged far afield from the purview of a lowly lackey. The informant's answers unveil a vast breadth of knowledge: for example, he knew *at the time* that Paul Shäfer, a former Nazi coronel who headed the infamous Colonia Dignidad (Dignity Colony) in southern Chile, had harvested organs from the regime's victims to be sold abroad. He also claims to have known about Michael Townley's reprehensible experiments on prisoners using sarin gas and electric darts. These revelations of an expansive knowledge base "out" Vergara's commitments to Pinochet's secret police while, at the same time, his denials and matter-of-fact tone downplay the gravity of those commitments.

As one watches the accomplice turned professional witness on television, it becomes clear that after so much rehearsal and fine-tuning he had finally become convinced of his own story. (This, as I said before, was already starting to become clear in the Mosciatti interview.) By September 2013, though, he had successfully internalized and consolidated the public image he had worked hard to cultivate: that of *Jorgetino the human rights hero*. If at times Cretton excitedly floats "smoking gun" questions hoping that his informant will give never-before-heard responses, Vergara, unshaken, remains calm and confident in his chosen role and opts instead for a staid and relaxed approach. Put differently, the accomplice resists stoking the journalist's sensationalism because he no longer seems to think of himself as newsworthy at all. He speaks nonchalantly of the horrors that occurred, as if the things he saw and did *back then* were part of a remote past that he had now completely accepted and internalized—a normalization that may very well echo the deadening of emotion we saw occurring in Mariana Callejas in later years (see chapter 1).[46] As Vergara reminisces, images pass across the screen of street repression happening in the 1970s and of naked, tortured bodies subjected to the *pau de arara* (the Brazilian torture method referred to in English as "the perch"); a product of journalistic montage, these images appear to the viewer—strangely—as if they were *of another time*, a time that is, in fact, *not* that of Vergara's present-day candor and heroism. A careful viewer can, of course, decode and reject this temporal separation—that is, the black-and-white *then* pitted against the *now* of the professionalized witness—but the stark juxtaposition dangerously harbors a potential to disconnect (and perhaps even absolve) the accomplice of certain still-unclear involvements in state repression, as if to say that the reformed man who speaks to us on screen may have once been related to but now stands worlds apart from the disturbing images we are simultaneously being forced to consume.

The *Mentiras verdaderas* interview therefore provides yet another opportunity for Vergara to sell (and consolidate) his self-image, to contradict misconceptions, to receive buy-in from the media, and to perfect his messaging: "I was never technically a DINA agent even though you say I was"; "I only saw, heard, and witnessed torture and killing but never participated"; "I am guilty of nothing."[47] At most, he admits to being an "indirect participant" (*un partícipe indirecto*) in the dictatorship's repressive apparatus. While for a long time he claims to have felt "unjustly guilty" for being part of the dictatorial system, he clarifies that he no longer feels that way because he has realized over time that he had "no personal responsibility in detentions, torture, or killings." The only guilt he still feels stems from his having kept silent for so many years, from his having respected and fueled the military's pact of silence. Now that he has finally come clean, his conscience is clear even in that regard. He can finally sleep soundly at night.

Media buy-in to the public image of Vergara the human rights hero intensified and broadened in scope when ABC Australia's news program *Foreign Correspondent*, hosted by the reporter Sally Sara, cast Vergara as the key informant who could help to catch a fugitive accomplice (potentially a perpetrator), Adriana Rivas, a female DINA agent who left Chile to settle with her husband in Sydney in 1978. Having spent years working as a nanny, she traveled freely to her home country for decades until she was finally arrested in 2006. After three months spent in jail for her suspected role in the Lautaro Brigade, the unit responsible for Víctor Díaz López's murder, among other crimes, Rivas eventually was let out on bail. She fled to Argentina in 2007 and from there came back to Sydney, where her life in impunity continues. As part of the investigation, the journalist tracks down Rivas at her home, but the accused woman slams the door in the reporter's face, refusing to talk. Still, we come to understand something of Rivas's discourse and thought process via a series of intercalated video clips taken from Australian public television (SBS). In these clips, Rivas vehemently defends the use of torture as the only effective "way to break people." Like Vergara, she denies all specific involvement in the crimes of DINA, though, unlike Vergara, she fails to display even the slightest tinge of shame or remorse: "The best years of my youth are the ones I lived in DINA." Today she remains thankful for the economic security and "opportunities" that DINA provided. She admits that without Pinochet's secret police, she would never have been able to wear nice clothes, ride in limousines, or eat dinner in embassies: "I do not regret having worked [with DINA] because for me it was a job, a life opportunity, [and] a chance to survive [economically]."

Because Adriana Rivas is the report's main object of inquiry, Vergara's own complicity takes a back seat to hers. His role as an informant nevertheless remains pivotal. Dressed in blue jeans and a polo shirt and looking like a more casual version of the middle-class, normalized subject we saw on *Mentiras verdaderas*, he strolls with Sally Sara through Santiago's streets pointing out details of the Pinochet regime's geography and mechanics of repression, including the location of the Simón Bolívar detention center—now a condominium complex. The very first words that come from his mouth attest to his innocence and plant a seed for viewers ultimately to understand him as a human rights hero: "I'm honest and humble when I say that I'm not a bad man; I'm not a bad

Former site of the Simón Bolívar 8800 detention center in Santiago's La Reina neighborhood, now a modern condominium complex. Photograph by Michael J. Lazzara.

person." Just as in the *Mentiras verdaderas* interview, Vergara asserts that he long ago felt pangs of conscience (*cargos de conciencia*) but that he has gradually overcome them by realizing that "[he] did not act like the agents did." While it is true that the report fleetingly acknowledges that Vergara's testimony came late in the game, that is, only after he was arrested and accused of killing Víctor Díaz, Sally Sara quickly moves on from that point to emphasize Vergara's role as a hero for justice. Shockingly, the report completely silences his involvements with the Simón Bolívar detention center! Sara narrates that the witness "saw" despicable things (torture, murder) but brushes past them to focus exclusively on the present: the phase of his life in which he began to cooperate productively with authorities. She never inquires, however, about what Vergara *did*. Her report therefore paints him as a rogue actor who boldly broke longstanding pacts of silence, motivated primarily by an altruistic desire to do the right thing.

> SALLY SARA: [Military] officials trusted Vergara to keep quiet. He didn't!
>
> VERGARA: I started to cooperate fully with authorities, and then the truth began to come out.

To add pathos to the report, Estela and Luisa Ortiz, the daughters of Fernando Ortiz Letelier, a communist militant who disappeared from Simón Bolívar 8800 in 1976, appear on screen as women in pain who have spent years of their lives working tirelessly to achieve justice for their father's murder.[48] In their comments, they implore Rivas to break her silence and say what she knows about Fernando Ortiz and others, in the interest of national healing.

No grays exist in Sally Sara's story of complicity. The television-reportage format prefers a black-and-white narrative in which roles are clearly delineated. The idea of "Facing the Past," which frames the episode and also serves as its title, becomes a litmus test against which the report's main characters are judged: Who has faced the past, and who has not? If the Ortiz sisters have done so valiantly from their position as *victims* of state violence, Rivas, the *perpetrator* living in impunity, plays the role of the one who clearly *has not* faced her past. Vergara, in stark contrast to Rivas, is cast as the accomplice who "saw" (though never *did*) terrible things: he overcame fear and, in the end, acted ethically. Francisco Ugás, a human rights lawyer, validates this idea by signaling Vergara's truthfulness and the reliability of his testimony: the accomplice's declarations, he claims, align with other evidence and should therefore be considered "plausible."

A certain irony and unsettledness, of course, arises when one accomplice to state terror "outs" another and garners accolades for doing it. Even though Vergara has spoken out, his hands remains stained, and his role in the dictatorship's violence continues to be ambiguous. We still do not know the extent of his involvements with CNI or in shantytown raids in the 1980s. For that reason, the two recent media representations I have just examined strike me as dangerous. Not only do they normalize the accomplice figure and implicitly pardon him; they also fail to probe the real depth of his commitments. Moreover, they go to an extreme by casting him as a national hero, implicitly or explicitly.

The interviewers ultimately responsible for constructing these reports appear seduced by both the accomplice's truth and his newsworthiness. By framing their reports through simplified or schematic lenses (e.g., heroism, reconciliation, the reformed accomplice, the man who collaborated with justice), they shy away from Levi's admonition to see the grays that state terror generates and instead risk lapsing back into binary constructions of positionalities that do nothing to further our understanding of how state terror really worked.

۱۶

The Mocito phenomenon calls to mind one final danger: that which emerges when the archive and its contents migrate toward the realm of the spectacle. As

I hope to have shown in this chapter, a "character" like Jorgelino Vergara lends himself to many framings and readings. If Marcela Said's film de-ideologizes the accomplice, takes distance from him, and seeks to evoke a sympathetic view of him, Javier Rebolledo's book (more responsibly, I think) re-ideologizes him, focusing on the facts as well as the omissions that pepper the accomplice's truth. Rebolledo paints a more nuanced view of the accomplice figure that allows readers to question the ethics of his comportment. Tomás Mosciatti's interview, in contrast to both of these other versions, engages in overt sensationalism of the character, urging a pedagogy of memory (as horror) that leads citizens to consume the past voyeuristically rather than debate it vigorously or reflect on it productively. Subsequent media representations on Chilean and Australian television have normalized the accomplice figure, holding Vergara up in the limelight as a human rights hero and professional witness while gradually (and dangerously) divesting him of any responsibility for his role in DINA and CNI.

The case of Jorgelino Vergara invites reflection on the kinds of complicities on which the Pinochet regime was built and on the complicities that shaped the subsequent transition to democracy. In a country in which there has been almost no judicial movement toward convicting or trying accomplices of any kind, this debate is more urgent than ever. If the judicial realm is unlikely to be the one in which complicity is tried and made publically visible, cultural production and the court of public opinion become all the more important. It seems to me that the fortieth anniversary of the 1973 coup opened a space in which this debate could begin to take place. However, I fear that we may ultimately find this to be a squandered opportunity insofar as the normalization of the accomplice figure, which emerges in the last two media representations of Vergara that I analyzed, may be signaling a tendency in Chilean society to shy away from future judicial prosecutions of accomplices who took orders from superiors and who can argue "due obedience." It may simply be easier for a country whose quest for justice has been long and difficult to stick to pursuing the cases in which responsibility is most clearly defined and to avoid gray zones altogether.

Has Chile, then, through the gradual normalization of Vergara in the public sphere, allowed us to glimpse its ultimate position on prosecuting certain kinds of civilian accomplices in court?[49] The question therefore remains regarding how willing Chilean society will ultimately be to engage in an honest reckoning with the accomplice within.

5

Complacent Subjects

(Max Marambio, Eugenio Tironi, Marco Enríquez-Ominami)

Why, [we] thought, should we not become modern, especially if Pinochet introduced us to postmodernity? How
could [we] not leave behind [our] illusory, tired [revolu-
tionary] identities, [our] Guevara-era [ideas of] "fatherland or death" or "advancement without negotiation"?
Why not assume the historical truism that what once
existed no longer does? Because it's much better to be
something that we never dreamed of being: it's better to
be a millionaire than a revolutionary.

Gabriel Salazar

n his book *Pensar entre épocas: Memoria, sujetos y crítica intelectual* (Thinking between Eras: Memory, Subjects, and
Intellectual Critique, 2004), the Argentine essayist Nicolás Casullo tackles the
question of whether it is possible to capture an era—that of 1960s and 1970s
revolutions and armed struggles in Latin America—from the vantage point of
our neoliberal, globalized present. Like Beatriz Sarlo, John Beverley, and other
intellectuals who have recently written on this topic, Casullo wonders if we, as
inhabitants of today's neoliberalized world, possess the affective and intellectual tools necessary to understand in a deep and situated way the spirit and
politics that years ago fueled desires for revolutionary change—what we might
call the true political and social face of the revolutionary era. This challenge
becomes all the more daunting when assumed from a present whose journalistic
and media production frequently does little more than cite the revolutionary

era as bygone (that is, of another time that is not *ours*) or reference it in carica-turesque fashion.

Particularly critical of revolutionary comrades who have now become stalwart capitalists and who operate constricted by the *politics of the possible*, Casullo perceives a tendency among some former proponents of armed struggle to silence their pasts or renege on certain aspects of their revolutionary subjec-tivities. To that end, in a 2007 essay titled "History and Memory," he argues: "The political history of 'the seventies' that has effectively been imposed on us is [plagued by] anecdote, anomaly, esperpentism, accusation, extremism, partial testimony, errors, curiosities, ignorance of what really happened, vilification, forgetting . . . and commonplaces."[1] To add to this list, one could also mention a number of other key factors that indelibly marked the revolutionary actors of the 1970s and that undeniably color present-bound narratives about revolu-tions, armed struggle, and the left, among them trauma, defeat, torture, disap-pearances, exile, and the struggles that the left has faced globally both during and after the Cold War. The potency of these factors must be taken into ac-count if we are even to begin to reflect on how memories of revolution and armed struggle become dehistoricized, mythologized, or simply passed over in the present.

In parallel to Casullo's post–Cold War reflection, theoretical interventions on memory by scholars such as Nelly Richard, Leonor Arfuch, and Fernando Blanco have made abundantly clear that our memory-obsessed era teems with a vast range of first-person accounts, of differing tenor, about the recent past.[2] Indeed, this has been a central idea running through all the chapters of this book. Arfuch teaches us, for example, that the consumption of intimacy through confessions, biographies, social media, and reality genres bespeaks the exis-tence of a "biographical space" in contemporary culture that has clear links to the individualistic, privatized ethos of neoliberalism.[3] Pushing this one step further, Nelly Richard cites the emergence in the postdictatorship period of a *mercado de lo confesional* (confession market) composed of biographies, auto-biographies, testimonies, and documentaries by people of all walks of life and political stripes—both right and left—who share their thoughts and craft their public personae through acts of self-representation. They offer up their textual lives to readers and spectators who are willing to consume them.[4]

As I have argued in previous chapters, it is clear that when intimate, personal experience becomes public, what we read on the page or see on screen is not the real life of the person being represented but rather an "exemplary life" that the autobiographical subject wishes to show us.[5] First-person genres, generally speaking, reveal a mask, a fictionalization of a self. Displaced in time, people struggle to find ways to explain the sometimes contradictory twists and turns their lives have taken. As they write themselves into history, they rationalize their life paths into reasonably coherent, harmonious narratives that, despite all best efforts, inevitably remain riddled with gaps, silences, and unanswered questions.

In the specific case of some (*not all*) former revolutionaries who once advocated for armed struggle, which is the concrete scenario that interests me here, we are faced with subjects adrift on history's tides, subjects who have chosen to reimagine and reinvent themselves in a new era—the neoliberal era—whose current values and beliefs do not cohere with those they held in their militant youth. Sometimes, though not always, such subjects continue to identify with the left; all those I analyze here, coincidentally, do. But even when they do, it is also clear that they are today much less ideologically radicalized than in their youth and have long since abandoned the militant imperative to "advance without negotiation" (*avanzar sin transar*), a mantra that guided their revolutionary zeal to bring about socialism at any cost and by means very different from the peaceful, unarmed "Chilean Road to Socialism" that Allende espoused. Estranged from their militant selves, today they cast their memories through fantasy, selectivity, or metamorphosis. Fernando Blanco captures this dynamic eloquently when he affirms that, in a sense, "the [neoliberal] model also produced its own subjects, subjects whose collective identities . . . were pulverized by the recombinatory rules of globalization and the flexibility of markets," as well as, I would add, by the violence of dictatorship and the pain of exile.[6]

When one era disappears, it takes with it something of the lives that fueled it.[7] This state of affairs triggers a need in former revolutionaries to reinvent themselves so as to survive (and thrive) in a scenario in which the rules of the game have clearly changed. As I hope to show, often the result of such processes of self-reinvention is the production of normalized subjectivities that adhere within the dictates of neoliberal socialization. As subjectivities normalize, the revolutionary self, viewed retrospectively from the present, tends to become fetishized, merely cited, rejected, critiqued, muted, or outright denied through figurations like resignation or repentance.

While I could point to many figures on the current Chilean political scene to prove my point, I will focus selectively (and symbolically) on a few public personalities from among the country's transition and posttransition elite class whose autobiographical accounts call up tensions between past and present, or, in Casullo's language, "between eras." In telling ways, these figures highlight the crisis that the Chilean left has experienced during the transition as well as the neoliberalization of some of its key protagonists. A common thread runs through their accounts: a self-justifying vision that speaks at once to the difficulty of thinking between eras, to the dangers of complacency, and to a disavowal of radical political action as a viable alternative in the present.

Complacent Subjects

Taken together, the texts I have selected show different tendencies and narrative dynamics at play in the self-fashionings of revolutionaries turned neoliberals. These range from the transformation of subjectivity, to the parsing of the self, to unmitigated fantasy—dynamics similar, at least in a mechanical sense, to those I found at work in accomplice and bystander narratives. Like other kinds of complicit subjects I have studied, "converts" (*conversos*) to capitalism, to recall Mónica Echeverría Yáñez's provocative term, sell versions of themselves hoping that readers will buy into their self-fictions and validate their belief that revolutionary change has ceased to be viable or even desirable in today's world.[8]

As proponents of—or, in an interesting inversion of terminology, as "revolutionaries" for—neoliberalism, these subjects would, on the one hand, prefer us to believe that the revolutionary era has inevitably (and for the better) given way to the neoliberal "end of history." On the other hand, their unquestioning adherence to the neoliberal model causes them to become what I choose to call *complacent subjects*: that is, subjects who fervently adhere to and uphold the neoliberal status quo, generally satisfied with themselves, their actions, their politics, and the current state of affairs in which Chile (and the world) finds itself. Although complacent subjects may indeed push for change and seek ways to mitigate poverty, inequality, and other social ills, they do so "progressively," always already bounded within the strictures of an inherited neoliberal model that they efficiently and implacably administer, content with change that is incremental in nature rather than far-reaching. As the self-proclaimed "heroes" of the transition—because they managed to help Chile leave Pinochet in the past and, at the same time, brought many Chileans out of extreme poverty—complacent subjects fail to question the fundamental philosophical underpinnings of a status quo that they are reluctant to upset and from which they also clearly benefit.

In this chapter, I want to situate complacent subjects—subtly—within the matrix of complicity that this book has laid out, fully acknowledging that their complicity is of an entirely different nature from that of criminals who participated directly in the dictatorship's violence (like Callejas), who aided and abetted the dictatorial state (like Jorgelino Vergara), who stood by and said nothing (like Hugo Zambelli), or who served during the 1970s and 1980s as the regime's founding ideologues or economic advisors (like Pablo Longueira or Sergio de Castro). To be fair, at the height of dictatorial violence, many of those who today qualify as complacent subjects found themselves fighting vigorously against the dictatorship from exile. Later, they worked tirelessly to bring down Pinochet in the 1988 plebiscite. Their identities as people of the left therefore remained largely intact when the goals were clear and immediate and when the dictator served as a figure against whom to rally political energies.

Yet, even at that time (in the 1980s), their identities were already undergoing important modifications. As the transition unfolded, prior experiences of defeat and exile caused them to reevaluate their political tactics and turned them into what Chileans now frequently refer to as "renovated" leftists: people who chose to shed their revolutionary zeal in exchange for a more pragmatic approach to politics. Motivated for deeply existential reasons by a desire to avoid the political upheaval that had characterized their earlier lives, they came to accept neoliberalism as doctrine while still seeking ways to be "of the left" within the bounds of present-day geopolitical conditions. Many of these same figures, especially those who played a founding role in establishing the Concertación and in designing the transition, soon thereafter rose to positions of extreme political, economic, or intellectual power. Their vantage point from the top served only to consolidate their belief in the overall efficacy of the neoliberal model.

Given these circumstances, should we understand the complacency of revolutionaries turned neoliberals as a form of complicity? Do these figures mark a kind of ethical limit at which vehemently upholding the dictatorship's economic legacy out of self-interest or fear implicitly becomes a form of validating the regime's work by failing to respond adequately to the needs of the popular classes? These are, of course, complicated questions with no clear-cut answers.

As I mentioned in my introduction to this book, it was not an easy decision to include a chapter on complacent narratives within a broader reflection on complicity. I found it difficult precisely because many of the actions that led the complacent subjects I study here to become rich or influential or both are not overtly criminal in nature. Nevertheless, as I write this book, cases are appearing in the news every day in which complacent subjects—the very founders and designers of and intellectual spokespeople for the transition—are being investigated for their connections to corruption scandals such as the 2015 Soquimich and Penta-gate cases.[9] Figures of both the right and the left appear linked to one another by deeply seated forms of economic and political collusion that seek to protect the country's elites. Such cases are now making visible the complicities between the economic and political classes that have long been known to characterize Chile's transition to democracy. Moreover, these cases are drawing increased public attention to the collateral forms of violence that neoliberalism generates—forms of violence that, as Mónica Echeverría Yáñez accuses, derive from a "centrifugal [neoliberal] machine that marginalizes everything and everyone that it does not find useful or beneficial, or that does not generate wealth or money."[10]

After much reflection, then, I am convinced that complacency should be understood as a form of complicity that, while not necessarily legally prosecutable, is at the very least ethically condemnable. To my mind, complacency forms part of a broad and variegated spectrum of moral and ethical responsibility that the dictatorship and transition generated. A full accounting for complicity in postdictatorial Chile must therefore take into account the complacency of certain actors whose self-serving actions or inactions (and memories) serve as barriers to stemming social and economic injustices. My desire, as in previous chapters, is to attend critically and responsibly to their textual self-fictions so as to unveil the dynamics behind the stories they tell.

To carry out this exercise of showing how complacency manifests *as text*, I have constructed a canon of three books and a film that were all created by figures whose lives and public actions have evinced mixed reactions in Chile: Max Marambio's *Las armas de ayer* (The Arms of Yesterday, 2008), written by a former member of the Movimiento de Izquierda Revolucionaria (Left Revolutionary Movement, MIR), Chile's most radicalized 1970s revolutionary group, who later became a businessman and one of the richest men in Chile; Eugenio Tironi's *Crónica de viaje: Chile y la ruta a la felicidad* (Chronicle of a Journey: Chile and the Road to Happiness, 2006), a book by a sociologist and lobbyist who owns an important public relations firm called Tironi Asociados (Tironi and Associates) and who played a major role in the design of the country's transition to democracy; and Marco Enríquez-Ominami's documentary film *Chile, los héroes están fatigados* (Chile, the Heroes Are Worn Out, 2002), written by a young politician, twice a presidential candidate and also the biological son of the founder of MIR, Miguel Enríquez. In the case of Marco Enríquez-Ominami, I consider, too, a book he coauthored with his adoptive father, the Socialist senator Carlos Ominami, titled *Animales políticos: Diálogos filiales* (Political Animals: Conversations between a Father and a Son, 2004). This last book stages a spirited, intergenerational dialogue that pits the values of the revolutionary era against those of the neoliberal present. All these examples draw attention to the logics and self-fictions according to which former revolutionary subjects have deradicalized since the 1980s. They also suggest how younger politicians of the renovated left, such as Marco Enríquez Ominami, have inherited and channeled similar tendencies and narratives.

Complacency

The two figures of the revolutionary generation whose works I analyze closely in the next two sections of this chapter, Max Marambio and Eugenio Tironi, have their roots in MIR and the Movimiento de Acción Popular Unitaria (Popular Unitary Action Movement, MAPU), respectively.

Both groups were highly influential during the Popular Unity period and belonged to the Chilean New Left movements that emerged starting around the mid-1960s. While MIR advocated openly for armed struggle and, for that reason, sustained constant tension with Allende regarding the most effective means for bringing about socialism in Chile, MAPU, a splinter group of the Christian Democratic Party "composed of elements of the most important political and elite networks in the country," including the Catholic University Law School, progressively radicalized during the Popular Unity years, so much so that a faction of it known as MAPU-Garretón, by 1973, began to advocate for armed struggle and an acceleration of the revolutionary process.[11] Deeply influenced by the Cuban Revolution, the Vietnam War, anticolonial movements, and Liberation Theology (in the case of the Catholic MAPU), as well as by Marxist and Leninist thought, both groups channeled the widespread desire for radical change that permeated the Chilean left at the time.

Following the September 11, 1973, coup, MIR and MAPU suffered very different fates. While MIR faced implacable repression at the hands of DINA, which culminated in the swift deaths of many of its members, MAPU was targeted with violence, though less vigorously. As a result, MAPU militants enjoyed a higher survival rate and, in some cases, more readily found paths to exile.[12] Nonetheless fragmented, beaten down, tortured, and victimized, MAPU members would, from there, initiate a decade-long process of renovation—shot through with intense debates between those who stayed in Chile and those who left—whose end result would be the abandonment of the group's belief in armed struggle and the embrace of a more measured, "progressive" path toward the future. Cristina Moyano Barahona, the scholar who has most closely mapped MAPU's evolution, identifies several stages within this renovation process: (1) an immediate stage of profound self-critique in which MAPU accepts its defeat and rallies around the idea of a "crisis of the left" as a basis for its renovation (1973); (2) a gradual transition away from the dogmatic language and conceptual apparatus of Marxism and Leninism (1974–77); and (3) an eventual acceptance of the idea that not only had the military defeated the left but also that the left, in its own regard, had failed to come up with a broad-based, inclusive project that could hold real potential for societal transformation (1977–80). Its renovation process would lead MAPU, by 1980, to propose what came to be known as the Socialist Convergence, a coalition-based project that was ideologically grounded in a belief in democracy, personal liberty, modernization, and free markets, tempered by progressive social reforms. Eugenio Tironi, who during those years came to embrace the merits of European-style social democracy and who, along with many of his colleagues, grew skeptical of "real socialisms," became one of the main intellectual authors and promoters of the Socialist Convergence.

In short, between the 1960s and the 1990s, MAPU gradually left behind a messianic and ideological vision of the left in exchange for a reformed vision premised on skepticism and pragmatism.[13] If its once-chosen revolutionary path to change had failed, the group would now opt for the "politics of the possible," a mantra that would guide its perspective as founders and architects of Chile's transition to democracy. By the end of the dictatorship, MAPU would dissolve, and its membership would be absorbed primarily by two main parties of the newly minted Concertación coalition, the Socialist Party (Partido Socialista, PS) and the Party for Democracy (Partido por la Democracia, PPD). Many former MAPU members remain active today in the Nueva Mayoría (New Majority) coalition that replaced the Concertación in 2013.

As architects of the transition, ex-MAPU concertacionistas would choose a future-oriented political vision based on modernization, symbolic amounts of truth and justice, and a pragmatic acceptance that a "pacted" transition was the necessary formula for pacifying strained relations with a still-volatile military and political right. Tacitly or actively validating the right's modernizing project as "the new ideology for a future Chile,"[14] figures such as José Miguel Insulza, Óscar Guillermo Garretón, Eugenio Tironi, Enrique Correa, and José Joaquín Brunner would accrue considerable power and influence by serving as ministers, deputies, senators, ambassadors, lobbyists, or key communications specialists during the administrations of Patricio Aylwin (1990–94), Eduardo Frei Ruíz-Tagle (1994–2000), and Ricardo Lagos (2000–2006). As they consolidated their power and advocated for neoliberalism "with a human face," to recall Aylwin's famous phrase, they would religiously embrace modernization without adequately interrogating its pitfalls or underlying tenets. In that vein, Katherine Hite remarks: "What appears to be absent from the[se] [political] entrepreneurs' adoption of modernization into contemporary political discourse is any questioning or critique of modernization itself. . . . There is something self-assured and safe [for them] about the images that modernity conveys— access to material desires, market freedoms, educational excellence, freedom from the state, and so forth. . . . [But] underneath the entrepreneurs' use of a consensus-based language of modernization has been an exaggerated fear of political conflict, stemming from a political legacy that continues to haunt protagonists of the Chilean left."[15]

Haunted subjects (like many of the others I have studied in this book), these former revolutionaries found it easier to forget their radical political subjectivities of the past and to cling instead to their new identities as neoliberals. Divested of utopias and mired in a shrinking horizon of political possibilities, they adopted a process of political unlearning and relearning that resulted in the abandonment of *homo politicus* and of any ability to dream that "another world [was] possible."[16] Reborn as *homo oeconomicus* and having bought into the neoliberal rationality that the dictatorship imposed by force, on some level these subjects "surrender[ed] to a felt and lived condition of human impotence, unknowingness, failure, and irresponsibility."[17] Bounded, they clung to a salvific narrative different from that of the military, yet salvific all the same: if the military had "saved" the country from Marxist tyranny, the Concertación would take pleasure in having "saved" it from lapsing back into the kind of political polarization that drove it to a breaking point in 1973. To rationalize their worth, Cristina Moyano explains, Chile's once "rebellious sons" now recast themselves as the "prodigal children" of democracy.[18]

My description to this point of the neoliberal recasting of some former revolutionaries' political identities might lead one to think that this process unfolded without self-critique. This was not at all the case. In fact, at many moments in time, concertacionistas, responding to public discontent with persistent socioeconomic inequality, questioned the directions their policies had taken. As evidence of this, we can cite specifically a debate that materialized in 1998 following the widespread nullification of ballots in the December 1997 parliamentary elections. Concerned about voter apathy and waning support, Concertación political elites drifted into two camps that came to be known colloquially as *autocomplacientes* (complacents) and *autoflagelantes* (self-flagellators). Tironi was one of the major spokespeople for the complacents. Patricio Navia lays out the difference between these camps: "While the complacents emphasized the noteworthy achievements of the Concertación governments, the self-flagellators underlined the errors and shortcomings of a social and economic model that did not leave them fully satisfied. If the complacents celebrated the important advances [the Concertación had made] by fighting poverty, bettering health, education, and housing, and consolidating democracy, the self-flagellators lamented the obstinate inequality that existed as well as the difficulties [that the coalition had experienced] in consolidating democracy."[19] Navia goes on to explain that the debate between the complacents and the self-flagellators ultimately proved backward-looking insofar as it forced political actors to adopt positions that dwelled either on their historical pasts or on their present-day successes and failures. Consequently, it failed to take into account the real, future-oriented concerns and demands of those who did not feel represented or interpreted by the infighting of either self-deprecating or self-congratulatory political elites.

I want to clarify at this point that complacency is more than just a simple moniker I am inflicting on certain figures from my critical vantage point. Rather, drawing on the preceding discussion, I see it as a notion born out of former revolutionaries' own self-evaluative language. In an etymological sense, complacency has the idea of "pleasure" bound up within it. The *Cambridge*

Dictionary defines it as "a feeling of calm satisfaction with [one's] own abilities or situation that prevents [one] from trying harder." Such a definition begs asking what it is exactly that brings these subjects pleasure or, put another way, what it is that makes them complacent in the first place. While the simplest and most accusatory explanation might hold that their pleasure simply derives from the wealth and status they have accrued since the 1980s, another possibility is that their pleasure stems instead from a belief in a political job well done, that is, from a conviction that they made the most of an impossible situation and brought the country, despite persistent problems, to a point of relative stability. In still another sense, complacency also has to do with mitigating risk. The dire consequences that stemmed from these subjects' former political choices have today made them tend toward moderate stances that reduce risk to themselves and the country.[20] Avoiding undue conflict or polarization, perpetuating their own power, and doing as much "good" as they can while maintaining that power all become key ingredients that shape their complacent worldview. Understood in this way, complacency is much more than a critical accusation levied against certain historical figures. Instead, it functions as a kind of capacious memory framework: a vantage point from which these figures, wittingly or unwittingly, interpret past, present, and future. However, by suggesting that complacency acts as a frame for memory, I by no means wish to imply that complacent subjects readily admit to their complacency or actively elect to frame their memories through a complacent lens. It is highly unlikely that anyone would say the words "I am complacent." More accurately, complacency should be understood as an attitude toward politics, a way of being in the world that shapes how one understands oneself, one's relation to the other, and the very purpose of the political.

Complacency is thus a complex phenomenon. Steve J. Stern holds that it is overly simplistic to think that "the middle classes and the wealthy, as beneficiaries of the economic prosperity created by the military regime, developed the habit of denial or looking the other way on matters of state violence" simply because they enjoyed material wealth—in other words, that they entered into a kind of "Faustian bargain" in which moral complacency and forgetting became the price for economic comfort.[21] While forgetting a violent past might be one possible way in which complacency manifests, in most cases complacency as a memory frame is far more layered, colored not only by a sense of who one is in the present but also by a sense of who one was in the past (and perhaps no longer wants to be), as well as by the intervening violence and the destruction of dreams and life-worlds that the dictatorship wrought on radical political subjectivities. To introduce this kind of nuance into the discussion is not to forgive the complacent subject's turning a blind eye to the plight of others but rather to acknowledge the entangled strata of experience on which present political attitudes and visions of the self are built.

Needless to say, Chilean commentators' views of complacent subjects have been mixed. For example, from his perspective as a historian of political elites, Alfredo Jocelyn-Holt Letelier acerbically critiques the design of the transition to democracy in his book *El Chile perplejo: Del avanzar sin transar al transar sin parar* (Perplexed Chile: From Advancement without Negotiation to the Never-Ending Transition, 1998). In this book, written around the time of the autocomplacientes-autoflagelantes debate, he takes the Concertación to task for its lack of courage in upsetting the constitutional order it inherited from both the dictatorship and Jaime Guzmán; he accuses Chilean political elites of accepting and fomenting a "normality" now defined as the politics of the possible and boldly "outs" former MAPU members such José Antonio Viera-Gallo who have publicly supported such logic.[22] Much more recently, Mónica Echeverría Yáñez, the ninety-five-year-old mother of *mirista* Carmen Castillo and widow of Jaime Castillo Velasco, a Christian Democrat and former rector of the Catholic University who led the historic 1968 "reform" of Chile's most conservative institution of higher education, published a book-length diatribe, *¡Háganme callar!* (Just Try to Shut Me Up, 2016), which takes direct aim at the *conversos* of the Concertación ("converts" from socialism to capitalism). In her book, Echeverría Yáñez declares her "hatred" for a series of figures, including Marambio and Tironi, who betrayed their revolutionary ideals and sold out to the almighty dollar.[23] Holding nothing back, she writes that these figures make her want to "vomit" when she thinks about the paths their lives have taken. In contrast to their questionable political choices, as a woman who unwaveringly chose to side with the *pueblo* despite the twists and turns of recent history, she holds up her own political choices as more laudable and ethically consistent: "The utopia of thinking that another world is possible, of a more human, dignified, and solidarity-based society is the one to which I subscribe and that years ago motivated my 'converts' [*mis conversos*]. How can these people who are so intelligent and cultured not realize that they have taken up a dangerous and perverse cause? They call themselves *realists*, but their faith in a reality driven by globalized markets is pure fantasy. Their past ideals no longer make sense to them, so they have to hide them or file them away in the dustbin of [history]."[24]

From more attenuated perspectives, we also find critiques of the transition in books by sociologists and political scientists such as Tomás Moulian and Patricio Navia. Moulian's famed *Chile actual: Anatomía de un mito* (Chile Today: Anatomy of a Myth, 1997), published around the same time as Jocelyn-Holt's essay, became an instant best seller that offered a biting critique of the "pacted" transition and of the unequal "consumer paradise" that Chile had become.[25] Moulian, like Echeverría Yánez, holds little back in his overall assessment of Chilean reality, but as a former member of MAPU he is curiously reluctant to "name names" or to take his former comrades to task individually; his book is therefore bold and groundbreaking as an analysis of Chilean political processes since the 1970s but admittedly silences certain realities that might prove inconvenient for Moulian's own biographical persona. As a final example, Patricio Navia, in *Las grandes alamedas: El Chile post-Pinochet* (The Wide Avenues: Chile after Pinochet, 2004), levies his own critiques of the transition and attunes us, in great detail, to debates such as the one that took place in the late 1990s between the complacents and the self-flagellators. Importantly, however, Navia points out the Concertación's shortcomings not to seek an alternative model for doing politics but rather to show us where the Concertación went wrong so that it might, with luck, reform its ways and figure out how to govern more effectively. His book, though critical, is therefore ultimately penned from a pro-Concertación and highly pragmatic perspective.[26] Taken together, then, we find that Chilean commentators of the right, center, and left have variously portrayed revolutionaries turned capitalists as "victims," "heroes," "traitors," or a strange admixture of all of these.

If we shift our perspective to the figures themselves, we find that their narratives show varying degrees of self-analysis or willingness to admit to the contradictions of their lives. While figures like Marambio clearly shy away from such contradictions, people like Tironi, who seek to seduce and convince readers with their rhetoric and perspectives, engage in more complex processes of rationalization peppered with stronger doses of metadiscourse. Illustrative of this point, Tironi confesses in the prologue to his recent book *Sin miedo, sin odio, sin violencia: Una historia personal del NO* (Without Fear, without Hatred, without Violence: A Personal History of the NO, 2013) that the "intimate" dimension of the dictatorship is, admittedly, the most difficult to face: by this he means "the guilt, fears, and most private fantasies that [we former revolutionaries] don't dare confess to ourselves—not then and not now."[27] As a sociologist, he tells us that he has read classic texts such as Erving Goffman's *The Presentation of Self in Everyday Life* (1959) and is keenly aware that people write their life stories by putting on masks.[28] This is perhaps why, significantly, he chooses to title the first chapter of his book "Masks." Furthermore, citing the psychologist and behavioral economist Daniel Kahneman's *Thinking, Fast and Slow* (2011), he asserts that self-narratives can be seen as a kind of machinery whose goal is to make sense of a life: human beings' "useful fictions" [Kahneman's term] allow them see the world as "more tidy, simple, predictable, and coherent than it really is."[29] This is why memories are so often at odds with lived experience. Tironi takes comfort in these ideas and finds in them a liberating impulse. He confesses that writing about his own life ceased to be difficult only when he finally embraced the idea that telling one's life story is not really about telling it "how it was" but about "how [one] s[ees] it."[30]

Given Tironi's metadiscursive analysis of his own writing, Cristina Moyano Barahona could not be more correct when she concludes that former *mapucistas* who took the helm of the socialist renovation speak to us today as "uprooted subjects, bifurcated subjects, subjects who have had to adapt."[31] In that sense, she continues, "the socialist renovation can be read as an imperative ontological discourse whose goal is to avoid the dismemberment of identity, to avoid the dilution [of former mapucistas] as political actors."[32] To remain relevant, play the political game, and conserve power, former revolutionaries had to get with the times. They had to fabricate useful fictions. Doing so was indeed vital to their survival.

Max Marambio: The Past as Citation

The very title of Max Marambio's *Las armas de ayer*, a book that bears the imprint of a center-right publishing house linked to *La Tercera* newspaper, relegates armed struggle to the dustbin of history. Figured in preterite time (i.e., *ayer*, or yesterday), the 1970s revolutionary moment becomes a mere citation, an anecdote to be shared, a curiosity wholly disconnected from the here and now.

The narrative voice, that of former *mirista* Max Marambio, educated and trained in Cuba with the expressed goal of importing armed struggle to Chile, is that of a severed subjectivity whose militant youth gives way to his current, neoliberalized self, the contours of which we only vaguely begin to intuit by the end of the book. Purposefully, I think, Marambio's jet-set life as a businessman receives no specific mention in the text; no effort is made to reconcile his "reformed" self with the revolutionary he once was.[33] We learn nothing of his life as a business magnate who, not without controversy, became rich in Cuba in the 1980s and 1990s. By virtue of its absence from the text, this later phase of his life, for those who know something of Marambio's life, appears entirely disconnected from his youthful *guerrillero* escapades and his bold 1970s revolutionary ideals.

Because the textual time of the book is entirely situated in the past, the subject of enunciation is thus able to speak of his militancy in a self-aggrandizing, romanticized tone whose goal is to iconicize (and temporally compartmentalize) his youthful adventures. Marambio, the son of a former Socialist congressman and diplomat, Joel Marambio, sketches a pantheon of heroes—such as Che Guevara and Fidel Castro—who stoked his youthful revolutionary desires. These references, however, are always communicated in a preterite (utopian) key and are never linked to the present: "In my idealized, youthful vision, Che was invincible, and the possibility of being with him sustained my revolutionary dreams."[34] To justify the moral rectitude of his militant choices of yesteryear, Marambio is eager for the reader to carve out a place for him within the pantheon of leftist heroes he describes.

Written in an affable style and aided by the editorial savvy of the noted Chilean writer Germán Marín, Marambio's autobiography adheres strictly to the paradigm of the epic hero—the call to adventure, the crossing of thresholds, subjective transformation, and the return home—that Joseph Campbell outlined in his classic text *The Hero with a Thousand Faces* (1949).[35] Marambio leaves Chile, goes to Cuba with his father at age seventeen, works hard to become a guerrilla, trains in the mountains, and even considers himself an adopted son of Fidel. When he returns to Chile, he sets out to train other MIR militants in the use of arms because he thinks it to be his duty. Rooted in altruistic idealism, his narrative thus paints the early 1970s as an era of dreams, illusions, adventures, and utopian aspirations.

Arriving for the first time in Cuba, the narrator-protagonist appears as an impressionable, impetuous, and wide-eyed young man whose narrative gaze parallels that of the early Spanish chroniclers of the Americas. The Cuban landscape exudes for him an exotic air of the "marvelous real": "When the airplane door opened, I felt enveloped by a mouthful of dense air, as if that air had been expelled by a savage animal; I succumbed to the rare heat, to the intense colors [that surrounded me]."[36] After that, it does not take long for him to discover his fledgling militant devotion: "In Cuba, I found my model society"; "I was moved by epic passion"; "socialism was still a very real possibility, and it [had not yet] occurred to anyone to announce the end of history"; "my goal was to pursue my father's beliefs, but with an armed component."[37]

As the text progresses, we see Marambio trying the role of the guerrilla on for size by participating in militarized exercises; in fact, he becomes so quickly vested in his emerging persona that he thinks that if he does not hurry he will miss his chance to reach his own metaphorical "mountaintop," that is, to live out a personal moment of glory that, he feels, assuredly lies on the horizon.[38] Pushed along by a rapid-fire narrative inertia that envelops the reader, too, in the swift pace of events, Marambio, just like Campbell's epic hero, therefore winds up profoundly transformed: he is now a *guerrillero* to his very core. And this transformation manifests quite literally and in a performative way:

Marambio sets aside his "civilian clothes" and opts instead for an "olive green uniform."[39] A third of the way through the book, he declares his transformation complete: "I was no longer the person I once was."[40]

When he returns to Chile in 1968, Marambio becomes part of the hierarchy of MIR, cultivates a close friendship with Miguel Enríquez (the group's top leader), and participates—not without remorse when he evaluates his actions from the present—in the "expropriation" (i.e., the robbing) of banks. He even assumes a role as one of Allende's personal bodyguards in the president's legendary Grupo de Amigos Personales (Group of Personal Friends, GAP). Proximity to Allende on a daily basis thus allows Marambio to foster an intimate relationship with yet another monumental figure of the Latin American left. Allende joins Fidel and Che in his pantheon of heroes.

But nothing lasts forever. If, until this point, the book has explained the commitments of a Chilean "faithful to" (*consecuente con*) his militant beliefs— that is, those of a man who rejects his bourgeois roots and becomes a radicalized guerrilla—what remains of *Las armas de ayer* does little more than chart how that same narrator takes distance from his militant past via an exercise in historical revisionism and a reframing of his subjectivity under the aegis of *defeat*. The epic hero, trained in Cuba, gradually embraces a new identity as the antihero of a lost epic battle.

Halfway through the book, a chapter titled "Contradictions of MIR" inaugurates Marambio's telling of how he took distance from Miguel Enríquez and MIR's leadership; this fulcrum chapter sets in motion the denouement of his entire autobiographical act. Highly critical of how, with the passage of time, the organizational structure and politics of MIR began to resemble more and more the structure and politics of the parties MIR wished to critique, Marambio takes distance not only from the party to which he not long ago pledged allegiance but also from Allende—always rhetorically careful, however, not to renounce his identity as a leftist: "And so, I took distance from any kind of militancy."[41] Allende's death, on September 11, 1973, seals Marambio's identity as a defeated man and marks the end of his grandiloquent, utopian horizons: "Now I was only motivated to combat the little abuses that were right before my eyes and to salvage whatever dignity I could, which is the only privilege life permits the defeated."[42] Here, then, we see an overt concretization in the text of the "politics of the possible."

The final chapters of *Las armas de ayer* chronicle Marambio's ten-month clandestine stay in the Cuban Embassy in Santiago; from there he secures safe passage to exile in Sweden. Ironically, the Swedish extract him from the embassy in "one of the few Mercedes Benz [automobiles] to circulate [in Chile] at the time."[43] The last three pages of his account concentrate, briefly, on the waning revolutionary's life in Sweden and on his return to Cuba, where he temporarily joins Castro's Special Forces but then defects. Regarding his life after 1974, he says not a word.

By the end of Marambio's book, the narrator's desire to "normalize" his life stands out. Although he does not yet consider himself a neoliberal, little by little he begins to seal a pact with neoliberalism. When offered an opportunity to participate in a clandestine, 1978 MIR mission to infiltrate Chile and overthrow Pinochet militarily (Operación Retorno, or Operation Return), Marambio refuses.[44] He explains his refusal by claiming that "[he] ha[d] completed a cycle in Chile"; perhaps this refers to the historical "cycle" of his militancy.[45] He also takes distance from his comrades in exile and lacks any motivation to participate in their political debates. Alternatively, he prefers a "normal" life: "I tried to take distance from the alienating life of my exiled [comrades] and firmly resolved to live a life, in the company of Anna, that was as normal as possible."[46]

References abound to the banal, everyday life Marambio so desperately craves. Plagued by defeat and feeling the pain of friends who are then suffering at the hands of a brutal regime, he has written a text that eventually becomes depoliticized in tandem with his own subjectivity. A slew of inconsequential details speaks to his status as a defeated and normalizing subject. While still holed up in the Cuban embassy, he becomes obsessed with the Mexican soap opera *Simplemente María* (Simply María) and writes letters to La Payita (Miria Contreras Bell, Allende's personal secretary and mistress who was then living in exile) to tell her how the television series ends. Later, in Sweden, Marambio learns to cook and concentrates his energy on mastering certain Swedish dishes. These details stand out not because of the activities in which Marambio engages but rather because he chooses to focus the final pages of his autobiography on banalities rather than engage in deep historical analysis or even offer a personal summation of his life as a revolutionary.

Nothing remains of the young guerrilla we saw in earlier chapters—only, as Marambio says toward the beginning of his book, "an ethical commitment that has accompanied [him] for the rest of [his] life."[47] He never expounds on the nature of that ethical commitment, nor does he tell us if that commitment bears any relation to the "arms of yesterday."

Marambio leaves much out of his account. He says nothing, for example, about the role that the "bases" (or nonelite supporters) played in sustaining MIR, choosing to focus exclusively on the group's elite leadership. Neither does he divulge his real reasons for taking distance from MIR: at a certain point, the party abandons its armed strategy and opts instead for an approach based on mass politics (*política de masas*), a move with which Marambio disagreed.[48] And finally, he fails to mention the complex relationship that existed at the time between Cuba and Chile or the real tensions that existed between MIR and Allende. His laudatory portrayal of Allende seems anachronistic if we consider that, despite the admiration Allende felt for MIR, the Socialist president never embraced the group's armed tactics.

Reluctant to reassert his bygone belief in armed struggle or to admit to contradictions that would disturb his nostalgic remembrance of a figure like Allende, Marambio avoids deep historical analysis, which lies beyond the scope of what he wishes to accomplish. Instead, he seems content to give us an idealized, self-centered, and somewhat megalomaniacal account of a past time that casts his militancy in a noble, ethical, and even heroic light. Embedded in the text we find the idea that times have changed; consequently, even if he wanted to, it would no longer be possible for Marambio to be the person he once was. In the end, it is much easier for him to accept the "end of history," which he names as such early in the book, than to problematize what it might mean to think between eras. To do this would require him to account for several things: for how his past life as a guerrilla dialogues with his later life as an investor and businessman; for his break with the Castro family; for the financial scandals that assail him; and for his 2011 conviction for bribery, fraud, and falsification of bank records. The real Marambio therefore remains hidden from view. To maintain a coherent image, his autobiographical self resorts to fantasy, to a reading of the past that leaves no room for the present.

It is no minor detail that the last sentence of Marambio's book returns us to the motif of the *chapa* (false name), that is, to the diverse identities that the speaking subject assumed at different points in his story: "When I went back to Cuba, I changed my name again; no longer would I be called Ariel Fontana"— his false name while in MIR.[49] Having proclaimed the metaphorical death of Ariel, Marambio remains unwilling to reconcile any of his future identities with his false name of the past. And this stands to reason. To do so would mean disrupting the narrative harmony that he, as an autobiographical subject, so fervently desires to preserve; it would also mean inhabiting an unstable zone of experience that would logically feel entirely intolerable to him. In short, bridging past and present would imply risking a comfortable present-day subject position that—at the moment of writing—had become fully normalized and accommodated to the neoliberal framework.

Eugenio Tironi: The Repentant Militant

In his book *Latinamericanism after 9/11* (2011), John Beverley provides an interpretive key to understanding the narrative texture of certain autobiographical and testimonial accounts that recall the era of militancy and armed struggle. According to Beverley, a *paradigm of disillusion* permeates many present-bound narratives written by former militants. Their texts read like "coming of age" stories in which the subject's "romantic adolescence" (generous and courageous but also prone to excess, error, and irresponsibility) gives way to "biographical maturity."[50] This period of maturity corresponds to the normalization of the subject (as a professional, as a parent) in the neoliberal era.

Drawing on this logic, Beverley describes a tendency in former revolutionaries' autobiographies to emphasize militancy's negative aspects: what "we" did wrong, our misguidedness. Often, he says, former militants reject their past militancy outright, fail to engage in a critical accounting for their past selves, are reluctant to consider the merits of bygone revolutionary imaginings, or resist examining or admitting to the historical continuities that assuredly exist between 1960s and 1970s forms of militancy and Latin American social movements today. In other words, a wide temporal abyss generates not only a biographical compartmentalization of subjectivity but also a deep cleavage in history. Autobiographers feel a kind of "residual guilt" that causes them to repent the folly of youth, and, as a result, "then" and "now" become mutually exclusive or only distantly related. Such a dynamic obfuscates any true sense of history but also blurs any true sense of a "life."

Beverley's paradigm of disillusion pithily encapsulates the case of the sociologist, lobbyist, advertising executive, and former MAPU militant Eugenio Tironi. From the very start of his book *Crónica de viaje: Chile y la ruta a la felicidad*, Tironi knows perfectly well—and demonstrates repeatedly—that his text is not just the story of Chile's historical, social, political, and economic trajectory since the 1970s but also the intimate narrative of a historical subject complicit with that trajectory. He says so point blank: "This essay is, then, a reflection on Chilean identity; but wrapped up in it, I have no doubt, is a reflection on my personal identity."[51] Nevertheless, Tironi's book does not read like a typical autobiography because it does not dwell obsessively on the first-person singular. In many moments, the authorial "I" hides conveniently behind a third-person discourse more characteristic of traditional sociological writing. The occasional surfacing of the "I," however, permits readers to engage with the fictions of a self that wants to appear as an integral, harmonious, noncontradictory subject when assessed from a present-day vantage point.

We know that Tironi belonged to MAPU starting in the late 1960s. Moved by Marxism, the newly formed MAPU rejected any alliance with bourgeois politics.[52] Eduardo Aquevedo, a former militant of the group, characterizes Tironi as "an unorthodox Marxist, but a Marxist in the end like all of us," a characterization that seems reasonable if we recall that Tironi belonged not only to MAPU but also to MAPU-Garretón, the movement's most radicalized faction, named for its leader, Óscar Guillermo Garretón.[53] To further drive home Tironi's youthful rebelliousness, a 2001 article published in *Qué Pasa* magazine alerts readers to the fact that he was the one who in 1973 coined the famous slogan *avanzar sin transar* (advance without negotiation), which was adopted by those who disagreed with Allende's "reformist" tactics.[54] Although Tironi continued to critique openly the Chicago Boys and the neoliberal model throughout the 1980s, during that same decade, now in exile in Paris, he would initiate a rupture with his Marxist past. According to a study by Héctor Hermosilla, "Tironi, in his trips around Europe, began to embrace an alliance-based politics that no longer privileged armed insurrection but rather dialogue and consensus-building."[55] Furthermore, as I mentioned earlier, in the early 1980s a crisis erupted in the heart of MAPU that would call into question the movement's future. Tironi would go on to lead the sector that proposed dissolving the movement and embracing the so-called Socialist Convergence, whose efforts, after many years of groundwork and accrual of political capital, would culminate in Ricardo Lagos's presidency (2000–2006).[56]

Curiously, Tironi's revolutionary past is almost entirely silenced in *Crónica de viaje*. The references we do find to the early 1970s focus mainly on Allende, whom Tironi represents as a man vacillating between revolution and reform and whose epic death, ironically and paradoxically, may have effectively helped to consolidate Pinochet's neoliberal crusade. Rather than offer a critical and balanced assessment of the Popular Unity years, the disillusioned and repentant autobiographer does little more than zero in on the profound and irreversible nature of Allende's defeat: "We shouldn't be ashamed; those of us who are old enough to have been Allende's contemporaries know full well that his project was destined to fail; we hoped for something else; perhaps we secretly wanted him to die."[57]

For Tironi, as for Marambio, there is no going back. One era gives way to another, and defeat becomes the tessitura that resounds in his book. Tironi's writing thus allows us to bear witness to the process of founding "another society" (*otra sociedad*), a phrase that serves as the title for one of the book's chapters.[58] Throughout *Crónica de viaje*, the author incessantly announces the death of ideology and of politics. In fact, he signals that one of the Pinochet regime's main goals was to "put an end to politics as such," to privilege the free market as the primary source of happiness and individual reward.[59] Accepting this state of affairs, he argues that the (ideological) Cold War of his generation has today metamorphosed into a new cold war between a European brand of neoliberalism (social-democratic in nature) and a US brand (with a smaller social safety net). He feels that by opting for the US version of neoliberalism,

Chile has strayed from its historical path of social concern and from any sense of imagined community that may have been present in earlier historical periods: therein resides his main and *only* critique of the neoliberal model. Time spent living in Paris again in 2006 teaches Tironi that European capitalism has a more "human" face than US capitalism; consequently, he feels that Chile would be well served to reprise its pre-1973 historical trajectory, which he understands to be inspired, at bottom, by European social democracy.

It does not take much of a mental leap, however, to see that Tironi's book is ultimately an apology for the Concertación and its twenty years of work, precisely because the center-left governing coalition mitigated the nefarious effects of pure, unbridled US-style neoliberalism by introducing necessary and beneficial social-democratic reforms. In Tironi's estimation, the Concertación caused Chile to veer toward the "East Coast"—a United States–inspired metaphor that connotes a more democratic and less republican existence—and did a relatively good job of constructing a "mass democracy" characterized by better access to education and health care for less advantaged sectors of society.[60] He unflinchingly admits that socioeconomic inequality is "Chile's greatest shame," but instead of questioning the neoliberal model outright, he finds an adequate solution in Europeanizing Chile, in line with a long-standing tradition of Latin American thinkers who at different times and for different reasons have fetishized Europe.[61]

Quite obviously, Tironi's ideas and assertions are highly questionable and his metaphors reductive. Yet this is not what interests me primarily. What concerns me instead is how he creates his textual persona. In that vein, a key to understanding his book lies in a chapter titled "Sin relato" (Without a Story). In this chapter, citing Richard Rorty, the autobiographer admits: "There is no way to recount the history of a country that is not at once mythological and ideological"; perhaps the same could be said regarding individual life stories.[62] For Tironi, the problem with the Concertación governments' "modernizing revolution" is that it left the Concertación without epic roots in the popular imagination: "[The Concertación could never manage] to anchor itself in the collective imaginary"—an argument that echoes Navia's argument that I cited earlier.[63] Why? According to Tironi, the answer is that "the Concertación never managed to assume its work as truly its own: [it never managed to embrace and celebrate how it] redirected Chilean modernization toward a more democratic and inclusive path without breaking the unquestionably US model forged under dictatorship. The Concertación [instead] feels guilty about its historical work. It sees what it did as 'what was possible given the circumstances.' It is never proud of its work; it [never] says, 'look at what we wanted and managed to do to transform the face of Chile.'"[64] Tironi argues that the Concertación should abandon its historical traumas and narrative of self-blame and instead stalwartly defend its twenty years of accomplishments. Only then will it forge a "moral identity" that justifies its existence.[65]

Like the now-defunct (or transformed) Concertación coalition that he discusses, Eugenio Tironi, in a way, appears as a subject "without a story" (*sin relato*), a kind of shipwrecked sailor adrift on history's tides who, like the two rowers in a canoe who adorn his book's cover, seeks a compass to orient his existence. *Crónica de viaje* is his attempt to affix on paper a "moral identity" — a justification of his good works as a "capitalist reformer" — because he perhaps suffers from the same residual guilt that he attributes to his colleagues from the Concertación elite.[66]

In an interview titled "Soy un capitalista reformador" (I Am a Capitalist Reformer), published in *La Tercera* on August 11, 2012, Tironi affirms: "I supported the [neoliberal] economic model quite early on, at the end of the 1970s."[67] By making this claim, he conveniently pushes the birth of his current capitalist ideology farther back in time to make it appear less abrupt and therefore less dissonant with his present self. (Recall Acevedo's testimony, cited earlier, that Tironi maintained his Marxist ideas until the mid-1980s.) Additionally, in a 2006 interview published around the same time as his book, Tironi goes one step further and explicitly reneges on his past; he claims "not to feel like part of the MAPU generation" because, on the one hand, he is younger than many of his former MAPU colleagues and because, on the other hand, he did not pursue a political career in the Concertación as many of them did.[68] Consequently, the autobiographer responds for his past (*da la cara*) because he is convinced it is the right thing to do; however, in the process he flounders (*esconde la cara*) due to the discomfort his chameleonic life instills. Tironi is ultimately, then, a subject consumed by silences and self-fictions. And he admits it: "I am part of a generation of survivors. And people who survive often do so by maintaining silences, by swallowing secrets about things that happened. I will not break that norm—not now, not ever."[69]

Marco Enríquez-Ominami: The Unsettling Inheritance of Revolution

> At bottom, I am the son of the yin and yang of the left, of social democracy and revolution, of two aesthetics that acknowledge and despise one another in today's world: the revolutionary and the reformist.
>
> Marco Enríquez-Ominami

If the previous two cases exemplify complacent subjects from the revolutionary generation who invent epic self-fictions to justify their present-day neoliberal subjectivities, I would now like to recast the issue of thinking between eras from an intergenerational perspective.

Marco Enríquez-Ominami, often referred to as ME-O, is a phenomenon of recent Chilean politics whose biography also—in another way—brings the crisis of thinking between eras into sharp relief. The son of two fathers—his biological father is none other than Miguel Enríquez, legendary leader of MIR, and his adoptive father is the former MIR militant and Socialist senator Carlos Ominami—ME-O embodies the unresolved tension between the radical legacy of armed struggle and the politics of consensus that characterized Chile's transition to democracy. Trapped between a utopian ideal of radical change and the progressive neoliberalism of the "renovated" left, ME-O, first as a congressman (2006–10) and twice as a presidential candidate (in 2009 and 2013), constantly mediates and negotiates between the legacies of his two emblematic fathers (one a radical, the other a radical turned reformer).

Although it is clear that ME-O descends from a long line of Chilean political elites, his political project and strategy have been to disrupt the establishment from within. Aware that by 2009 the Concertación had reached its twilight after twenty years in power, ME-O in his first presidential campaign responded to Chileans' generalized discontent with traditional political parties and with a political class that they felt was not responding adequately to their needs. In his book *El díscolo* (The Disobedient One, 2009), Patricio Navia speculates that if President Michelle Bachelet (and her bottom-up leadership style) created the conditions of possibility for ME-O's entrance onto the Chilean political scene, the son of Miguel Enríquez ultimately went much further than Bachelet in his "disobedient" (*díscolo*) zeal to shake things up; like his adoptive father, ME-O cut ties with both the Socialist Party and the Concertación. His independent candidacy therefore made him attractive to many voters and jump-started his career early on. These characteristics help to explain how ME-O managed to garner 20.14 percent of the vote in the first round of the 2009 presidential election. Nevertheless, his identity as an "independent" did not necessarily mean that his stances were radical. Commenting on ME-O's congressional voting record for the 2006–10 period, Navia concludes: "His positions are not staunchly statist in nature. In fact, ME-O has doubts about the role of the state because he believes profoundly in individual liberties and fears that the state can be coopted by private interests. He instead believes in a state capable of fomenting, permitting, facilitating, and guaranteeing competition. ME-O is a capitalist; in line with the Concertación, he believes in a pro-market and pro-competition state, more so than in a state that is pro-corporations and pro-business."[70]

ME-O's reputation as a "progressive" neoliberal makes one wonder, then, about his relationship to the legacy of his biological father, Miguel Enríquez.

To answer this question requires going back in time to the period before ME-O became a congressman. In 2002, prior to his formal entrance into politics, ME-O worked as an independent filmmaker for Rivas and Rivas Productions. That same year he directed a documentary called *Chile, los héroes están fatigados* that clearly positions him as an intermediary in the battle between eras. The film sets out to ask a bold question: What had become of some of Miguel's former comrades in arms?

Echoing logic that we have already observed in the cases of Marambio and Tironi, the film's opening sequence states the given information: Chile has irreversibly passed from one era to another, and there is no going back. Interestingly, seven years later that same sentiment would serve as the slogan for ME-O's first presidential bid: "Chile cambió" (Chile has changed; note the use of preterite time to mark a definitive temporal rupture). As the film begins, ME-O's narrative voice remarks: "[Miguel's] followers still sing to him fervently in local gymnasiums, but no one cares about them. Chile has changed. It moved from poverty to growth." This quip interfaces directly with the film's context: the 2000 election of the socialist president Ricardo Lagos, which for ME-O marks not only the culmination of three decades of socialist struggle to take La Moneda but also the pinnacle of Chilean socialism's "renovation" (i.e., its neoliberalization). Because Lagos will not grant ME-O an interview, likely out of fear of what Enríquez's son might ask him, ME-O finds contentment in acerbically critiquing—not without much irony—the destinies of several of Miguel's former comrades who have accommodated their lives to the neoliberal status quo.

Among ME-O's prime targets we find Óscar Guillermo Garretón, Enrique Correa, José Miguel Insulza, José Joaquín Brunner, and Eugenio Tironi: in brief, a group of former mapucistas who all participated in designing and negotiating the country's "pacted" transition with the military. Interviews with these figures show constant oscillation between "then" and "now," as well as a strong generational desire to relegate the past to the past. In true concertacionista style, all of ME-O's informants look toward the future. An intercalated film clip of Garretón shows him preaching to a massive crowd about "popular force" (*fuerza popular*) during the Allende years; to this image ME-O juxtaposes more current footage of Garretón the businessman seated in his corporate office. Garretón explains that even when armed struggle leads to victory, it ultimately "creates societies that [he] doesn't like." Having spent fourteen years in exile, Garretón was later accused of sedition, imprisoned for revolutionary statements he made in his youth, and subsequently exonerated by the Supreme Court. When that happened, ME-O tells us, "Garretón publicly recanted and asked forgiveness for his 'revolutionary confusions' [*confusiones revolucionarias*]." He thus represents another case of a repentant revolutionary.

In the same vein, several interviewees refer to how subjectivity and politics become normalized under neoliberal rule. Correa claims, for example, that passion and affect, in pure Machiavellian style, have no role to play in political life; politics instead should be "terrain for the purest and strictest operation of reason." For his part, Tironi acts with a market-driven mentality that comes across as almost fundamentalist in nature—at least in ME-O's portrayal of the character—and as lacking in all scruples: "I do business, and when one does business there is no mention of life. When I do business, I do it with people who have different stories. I'm not interested in those stories. Some of them aren't even Chilean, and I have no idea where they come from." Brunner, in contrast to the other two, is less extreme in his pronouncements; he seeks autobiographical legitimacy on the basis not of his present self but rather of a claim to a more generalized "leftist historical identity" that he believes he still possesses: "If for some reason a person were to ask me if I am still a leftist, I would legitimately say that I am because I can reference an element of my historical identity." His rhetorical strategy reads as yet another way of compartmentalizing the fragments of a subjectivity torn apart by defeat.

Toward the end of *Chile, los héroes están fatigados*, the journalist and academic Faride Zerán, in counterpoint to the other testimonial voices already heard in the film, reads all these subject positions (Garretón, Tironi, Brunner) from the *outside*. She claims that this group collectively represents a "left that at a certain moment ceased to be leftist because it was seduced by the politics of the possible, particularly during the early phase of the transition." For Zerán, to be of the "left" means not compromising or capitulating to the norm; rather, it implies "a state of mind, a way of being in the world" that is geared in every way toward contesting the neoliberal model.

Throughout the film, ME-O plays the role of devil's advocate. He tries to maintain the feigned distance of a documentarian, but his subjectivity is undeniably complicit with his subject matter. This is most evident in a shocking sequence in which Enríquez-Ominami pays a visit to his father's tomb in Santiago's General Cemetery. Standing before the humble niche in which the fallen revolutionary is buried, the son laments the exhaustion of the left, the twilight of the Concertación, and the "transformism" (*transformismo*) that has changed many of Miguel's *compañeros* into capitalists.[71] "All of these heroes you once knew," ME-O tells his father, "became slaves to efficiency with no concern for cost. . . . I fear you died for nothing." The comment, in and of itself, is jarring, but ME-O's speculation regarding the uselessness of his father's death also seems entirely misguided if we take into account the temporal lag that gives rise to his comment. ME-O fails to historicize his father's death, to ask what it meant to be a revolutionary in another era, to give one's life for one's beliefs, or to be killed by a brutal dictatorship. His comment sounds instead like a knee-jerk reaction born in response to present-bound discontent, political disenchantment, or cynicism. Furthermore, it fails to account adequately for the legacy of armed struggle or even to ask what it meant—perhaps because the son, firmly situated in the neoliberal moment, is also reluctant to take that mental leap.

The film makes clear that, for ME-O, Miguel Enríquez—the father he never really knew—is largely a symbol, a source of moral and ethical inspiration—sort of like Allende for Marambio. Yet, in the final assessment, Miguel is little more than a "myth" with which Enríquez-Ominami is forced to live. To be a neoliberal and the son of a revolutionary martyr generates tremendous cognitive dissonance in Enríquez Ominami as a speaking subject; that dissonance leads to a sustained effort on his part to reconcile the legend of Miguel ("a certain idea of the left," as he says at the film's outset) with the renovated left that surrounds him and bothers him but of which, like it or not—independent or not—he is also a part.

It is clear, then, that ME-O salvages from his dead father's memory a certain ethical compass that guides his steps and fuels his rebelliousness against the political establishment; it is also clear that ME-O's biological father, of whom he claims to have no direct memories, represents for him *an imagined, imaginary, or inherited legacy* with which he would probably rather not contend—another haunting, so to speak—but with which he has no choice but to reckon. For ME-O, Miguel Enríquez is a problematic figure, a void in his life, a memory he has to invent. Consequently, he makes selective use of the legacy of armed struggle to fuel the political image he wants to create for/of himself but also to vindicate the coherent (*consecuente*) political actions of his adoptive father, Carlos Ominami, who emerges in the film as the real hero of the present: "Like [Miguel], Carlos embraces action, fearless of risk. He continues in the service of constructing a coherent [that is, based on ideals] political left." The imagined legacy of a mythical father therefore ultimately gives way to the redemption of the living, adoptive father. In the final assessment, both ME-O and Ominami shine in the film. And how could it be otherwise? Disappointingly, the film's flavor turns out to be quite propagandistic.

Two years after ME-O's film debuted, in 2004, the tension between eras manifested again in his book *Animales políticos: Diálogos filiales*, a lengthy intergenerational dialogue between ME-O and his adoptive father, former senator Carlos Ominami. In the book, ME-O—ever the *díscolo*—again plays the role of devil's advocate and instigator. He seems less interested in sharing his own thoughts than in facilitating the testimony of the stepfather he loves and admires. At times, though always with respect, he takes an accusatory tone toward Ominami and the revolutionary generation, chiding that generation for its sins of commission and omission. Ominami's self-critique is noteworthy. He repeatedly observes that his generation was severely traumatized and left with no epic narrative (which we have already heard from Tironi and Navia): "What's clear . . . is that Chile normalized after thirty years of much political intensity, and in so doing, lost its [chance at an] epic [story]."[72] In the former senator's estimation, Chile, at the time of the book's publication, was living a moment of low political intensity, characterized by pragmatism, efficiency, and the administration of power. Ominami goes one step further: "Perhaps because of historical circumstances and our own traumas, we have exacerbated the administration of power and left the cultivation of our deepest convictions untended."[73] But what are these "deepest convictions" to which he refers? They are never made explicit in the text. Are they the convictions of an era too painful to recall? The question of the left's future, of Chile's future (and its connections to the past), thus goes unanswered.

Starting from the premise that "MIR no longer exists" and that "it would be difficult to vindicate its legacy," both Ominami and ME-O seem to validate certain ideas as given: first, the world has taken a turn to the right, and second, globalization and market economies are here to stay.[74] *Homo politicus* has given way to *homo oeconomicus.* The only question that remains, then, is "how to be radical in those circumstances."[75] But that question, by its nature, forestalls the conversation *between eras* that it seeks to open precisely because it fails to ask or acknowledge what it meant to be radical in the 1970s and what motivated actors at that time to make the choices they did.

Final Reflection

Katherine Hite, in *When the Romance Ended: Leaders of the Chilean Left, 1968–1998* (2000), develops a taxonomy of the cognitive positions that have oriented the Chilean left since Pinochet. Among them, we find categories such as "party loyalists" (to one party or another); "personal loyalists" (e.g., to iconic figures such as Allende and Enríquez); "political thinkers" (who are capable of changing ideology); and "political entrepreneurs."[76] Although figures like those I have studied in this chapter cross over into more than one of these categories, all of them, without doubt, fit squarely within Hite's definition of the *political entrepreneur*: a fundamentally pragmatic being who is willing to change orientation (even ideologically) in accordance with his perception of the horizon of what is possible and who is also moved by a desire to maintain peace and consensus at all costs.

Political entrepreneurs are interested in forming coalitions that facilitate effective governance; they are practitioners of consensus-based politics and favor incremental change. It should come as no surprise, then, that political entrepreneurs were the ones who designed, "pacted" with the military, and consolidated Chile's neoliberal transition to democracy. And, although confrontation and conflict have been acceptable to them within certain limits, they have, on the whole, protected the neoliberal model as a sacrosanct and unquestionable bastion of modernization. In the process, they have become complacent subjects who have benefited from that system and who have proved willing to accept shameful amounts of inequality and forms of soft violence as the price of peace. While their present-day attitudes and perspectives cannot be dissociated from and are shaped by the immense traumas their generation suffered, it is clear they have traded in their political subjectivities of yesteryear and their ability to dream of a more equitable future for a techno-cratic existence tempered by "progressive" change.

Like other types of complicit subjects I have studied in this book, com-placent autobiographers (revolutionaries turned neoliberals) rationalize their lives in complex ways. While some romanticize and compartmentalize their revolutionary pasts (Marambio), others figure their pasts through repentance, end-of-history rationalizations, or "salvific" narrative lines (Tironi). Their narra-tives of disavowal of revolutionary change then filter down to a new generation of "progressive" politicians (Enríquez-Ominami) who find themselves caught in an unresolvable tension between the revolutionary era and the neoliberal one, with no easy way to reconcile the two.

First-person accounts like those of Marambio, Tironi, and ME-O/Carlos Ominami fill Chile's bookstores and can even be found in pirated versions in the street. These books reach the citizenry and dangerously strive to leave a mark on collective memory as if they were *the* definitive stories of our times. For this reason, it is incumbent upon readers to recognize these texts for what they really are: illustrations of subjective and cognitive blockages within their narrators, all of whom are products of traumas (personal and historical), tempo-ral inertia, generational change, and epochal shift. Because of these blockages, and also because of the complacency of protagonists who benefit from the system to which their subjective self-imaginings have adapted and that frames those imaginings in turn, these texts risk obscuring or cancelling out deeper understandings of what Latin America's revolutionary moment really meant or how it dialogues (or could dialogue) with the present and the future.

I choose to close with a reflection by Pilar Calveiro, an Argentine political scientist as well as a victim and survivor of her country's "Dirty War" (1976–83). She tells us that to understand Latin America's revolutionary moment requires a "double movement": on the one hand, it requires restoring the historicity of memory with an eye toward the attitudes, passions, and debates that moved that era; on the other hand, it requires revisiting the past *from the present* to question the potential that the past holds for informing current social and political movements.[77] Instead of treating seemingly opposed temporalities and the subjectivities to which they give rise as disconnected, distant, compartmentalized, or fragmented, an alternative proposal (which we are already hearing in the voices of Latin American activists and academics) might ask how we can reconcile honestly and ethically the distance separating *that time* from *our time*. Only in this way can we learn to think *between* eras and not *against* them.

Epilogue

A Call to Account

As I was writing this book, a film debuted that drove home for me in very vivid ways the fictions of mastery that complicit subjects create to protect their tormented psyches and shield themselves from reprisal. Joshua Oppenheimer's *The Act of Killing* (2013) provides a chilling look back at the Indonesian genocide of 1965–66, another chapter taken from the annals of the Cold War.[1] For those familiar with Chile's history, the overarching dynamics of what happened under General Suharto's rule (1967–98) should sound eerily familiar. Fueled by long-standing racial and class prejudices, Indonesian political elites, aided and abetted by the US Central Intelligence Agency, would oversee the massacre of more than a half-million communists, leftists, and ethnic Chinese whose mere existence was perceived by the regime as a threat to the country's future stability. They would carry out those killings not only to eliminate the "other" within the country's borders but also to consolidate their power and wealth and to pave the way for Indonesia's eventual entrance into the global economic order.

Like General Pinochet, Suharto died in impunity, convicted only of financial corruption but not of mass killing. Yet, unlike in Chile, where decades of memory work in the long run proved fruitful (though arduous, partial, or perhaps insufficient in the opinions of some), efforts in Indonesia to come to terms with a violent past have been surprisingly recent. Because Suharto and his heirs maintained a firm grip on power for decades after the genocide, they also controlled official memory. Only in 2012, nearly a half century after the genocide, did a truth commission investigate what had happened. Curiously, it was Oppenheimer's film, which appeared on the heels of the truth commission, that played a major role in opening a space for the country's process of reckoning to take root. That reckoning, however, remains fledgling and will undoubtedly prove difficult in a country where powerful forces still prefer to bury the truth.[2]

When *The Act of Killing* premiered, Oppenheimer was chided for having made a film that focused on the perpetrators rather than the victims, particularly considering that it took so long before the victims could tell their stories publicly. Detractors argued that allowing perpetrators to rehearse their tales of "heroic" conquest on film was tantamount to empowering and legitimating their voices—an argument that, though pertinent and well taken, must also be balanced against the film's many merits. Viewers are, of course, right to feel maddened and even sickened by listening to perpetrators brag about the suffering they inflicted on so many of their fellow human beings. But the film also invites consideration of the director's carefully chosen metaphors and framings, which permit viewers to deconstruct and really perceive the nuances undergirding "the fantasies and fictions by which [perpetrators and accomplices] know [themselves]" (Oppenheimer's words)—a deconstruction similar, in many ways, to that which I have tried to carry out in this book.[3]

To make his film, Oppenheimer tracked down more than forty of Suharto's cronies (some high-ranking, some not), observed them in their daily lives, and intentionally placed them in situations that would incite them to talk about or even reenact their genocidal crimes. At certain points, he dresses them in full costume and makeup, a filmic device meant to highlight the theatricality of their speech acts. In most cases, he asks them to perform their well-rehearsed roles as victimizers, but sometimes, too, he reverses the roles, asking those who were killers—or those who helped the killers—to occupy the place of their victims. The result of all this role playing is shocking: the murderers and their support staff, in almost every instance, boast about the efficiency and precision with which they carried out their deeds, taking tremendous pleasure and pride in their own omnipotence.

Most of the voices we hear in *The Act of Killing* show no signs of remorse. Much like the complicit Chilean voices I have studied, they deploy an arsenal of techniques to avoid taking responsibility for what they did: parsing subjectivity, depoliticizing the self, holding themselves up as heroes, employing escapism, claiming due obedience, silencing key details, telling skewed histories, normalizing their lives, building up walls to make themselves seem invulnerable, and so on. One voice, however, breaks the mold: that of Anwar, a perpetrator who in the film's last two sequences eventually heeds the call to account and *begins* to admit that what he did was wrong.

Somewhat predictably, Anwar's process of coming into self-awareness starts with self-deception. Seated in his living room, he invites his two young grandsons to sit on his lap and watch a film in which he and his buddies reenact a horrifying scene of torture and interrogation. On screen, Anwar plays the role of victim. Contemplating the image of himself on TV, he encourages his young grandsons to validate his performance and to praise him for his "good acting" rather than seize the opportunity, as one might hope, to teach the next generation a valuable moral lesson about how others should be treated. At first, Anwar's performance seems like a mere game—a good-natured playing along with Oppenheimer's unusual cinematic experiment. Soon, though, the perpetrator's demeanor changes: he claims that by watching himself play the role of the victim on television he is now able to sense the same sort of terror that his victims once felt. Challenging such a facile claim to empathy, Oppenheimer reminds Anwar that the terror he purports to be experiencing has been triggered merely by watching a film; Anwar's victims, in contrast, felt *real* terror because they knew all too well that they were about to lose their lives. Still, Anwar insists: "But I can feel it, Josh. Really, I feel it. Or have I sinned? [*He breaks down.*] I did this to so many people, Josh. Is it all coming back to me? [*Crying*] I really hope it won't. I don't want it to, Josh." Anwar's reference to sin (posed as a question) might be interpreted as a first sign of the blush of shame.

Despite the distance that initially separates Anwar—a fully bounded being—from a genuinely empathic position, giving himself over to the place of the victim (or at least *trying to*) eventually *does* something to him. It washes over him, works on him. It erodes his intellect's self-defensive mechanisms through affect; it creates a specular condition in which the "other"—personified here as a bifurcation of the self—calls out to him and interrogates him silently. Intelligently, Oppenheimer seizes upon this process and invites Anwar, in the film's final sequence, to return to a physical site, today a ladies' handbag store, where years ago he tortured and killed some of his victims. The scene sets the stage for a greater deepening of the perpetrator's self-awareness. Pacing around a patio that appears to have remained almost untouched since the dark days of the genocide, Anwar appears visibly disturbed, his words scant: "This is where we tortured and killed the people we captured. I know it was wrong, *but I had to do it*" (emphasis mine). Even in this naked moment of facing himself, he still clings desperately to a self-deceptive fiction—"I had to do it." The self wants desperately to flee from itself, but we perceive that Anwar's self-awareness runs deeper than his words reveal. His body begins to retch uncontrollably: he is literally sickened by who he is, by what he has done, by what he has become. In this moment, as Butler might put it, a face interrogates him that is not literally a face but rather the very cry of human suffering for which he *knows* he is, in part, responsible.[4] Anwar can do nothing more than vomit in shame, naked before himself, in a moment that is completely disarming to both him and the viewer.

Anwar's process of coming into self-awareness dramatizes what can happen when one who has done wrong renders himself vulnerable and heeds the call to account. It provides a moment—an instant—that can begin to chip away at the "moral vacuum" that perpetrators and their accomplices create when they propagate fictions of mastery whose effect is to shut out the other's pain.[5] As Oppenheimer once put it, it is a process that can erode "the scripts, the fantasies, the half-remembered, second-hand, third-rate stories that make [accomplices] who [they] are and [that determine how] they want to be seen."[6]

To be sure, certain zones of Anwar's experience will always remain opaque to him, as in the cases of all the complicit narrators I have studied. But that opacity will arguably become less so as he begins to sense (or even understand something about) the "norms" and conditions that have "[brought] him into being" as a subject, even if he can never fully explain them.[7] Thinking with Butler, an opportunity presents here for Anwar to become "undone" in relation to the other (and to himself). And this facilitates an opportunity (still unfulfilled) for both personal and social transformation—a starting point for strengthening a profoundly scarred community.[8] Unclear, however, is whether Anwar will ultimately stand up and "own" the consequences of his momentary vulnerability. Will he assume the full costs associated with his still-inchoate act of reckoning, no matter how grave those costs may turn out to be in the end?

❧

Regrettably, cases like Anwar's are not the norm. Rarely do accomplices heed the call to account, even though they do indeed speak, sometimes ad nauseam. For that reason, it falls to societies in transition to pursue them and compel them to acknowledge their complicity, using mechanisms such as trials, truth commissions, public acts of shaming like the Argentine *escraches* or Chilean *funas*, or cultural production (e.g., journalism, literature, television, theater, performance, academic work).

If we look beyond Chile, we find cases in which accomplices have been held legally accountable to differing degrees. After the Holocaust, for example, the Nuremberg International Military Tribunal (1945–46) clearly established that lesser accomplices—not just the upper echelons of the Nazi machinery— could, in fact, be convicted for their participation in the genocide. Judges, low-ranking foot soldiers, and even businessmen who contributed to the Nazi infrastructure all figured among the defendants at Nuremberg.[9] Much more recently, other important legal precedents for prosecuting accomplices have been set. The 2011 sentencing of John Demjanjuk, a guard who served at the Sobibór concentration camp and was later convicted as an "accessory to the

Holocaust," even though it could never be proved that he actually killed anyone, stands as a case in point.[10] Additionally, the case of Oskar Gröning (2015), a man known as the "bookkeeper of Auschwitz," who was responsible for stripping prisoners of their money and possessions, and that of Hubert Zafke (2016), an Auschwitz medic whose proximity to the gas chambers made him a potential accomplice to the murders of 3,681 people, provide further examples of Nazis who have been taken to court for their participation in Hitler's machinery of horror.[11]

Such legal precedents have resonated, too, in other parts of the world, including Latin America. Recently in Argentina, for example, businessmen who aided and abetted the military junta in its 1976–83 "Dirty War" have been forced to stand trial—a phenomenon that, beyond noteworthy convictions, has also produced unforeseen, very positive effects in the country. One such effect came in December 2014 when the country's Central Bank created a human rights unit that was tasked with "systematizing all the documentation produced and kept by the bank during the last dictatorship."[12] Another such effect came in 2015, when Argentina's lower house of congress overwhelmingly voted to create a special investigative commission whose job would be to identify economic accomplices with the dictatorship in hopes that trials could eventually be pursued. In the Argentine case, societal pressure to "out" economic accomplices with the Dirty War thus incited two important institutions, the Central Bank and Congress, to respond in kind by acknowledging and taking responsibility for complicity and agreeing to contribute in an important way to deepening truth and memory.

As we think about contrasting cases such as Chile in which accomplices have, broadly speaking, not paid a judicial price for their roles in aiding the dictatorial state, it is useful to keep in mind that since the mid-twentieth century, international human rights law has equipped us with tools for enabling potential prosecutions of those complicit with crimes against humanity.[13] Concretely, two classes of crimes currently exist in international criminal law: *aiding and abetting the crime of genocide* and *complicity in genocide*. Both crimes are specifically named in the 1948 Genocide Convention,[14] and they have also been ratified by important international bodies such as the International Criminal Tribunal for the former Yugoslavia and the International Criminal Tribunal for Rwanda. Though related, the two crimes differ in a key aspect. While "aiding and abetting the crime of genocide" carries a heavier burden of proof insofar as it requires proof that an accomplice *willfully* and *knowingly* intended to facilitate widespread acts of killing (*mens rea*), "complicity in genocide" carries a much lighter burden of proof in that it simply requires that an accomplice could have foreseen the end result of his or her actions, even if he or she had no specific motive to kill.[15] A businessman, for example, who sells arms or provides equipment to a dictator and does so merely to make a profit might indeed lack a specific motive to kill a given person or group of people; nevertheless, under international law, this same businessman (who wanted only to make money) might still be convicted of the crime of "complicity in genocide" if he could have reasonably assumed that, given the political climate, those weapons might be used to kill the regime's opponents.[16] Despite the existence of such legal vehicles, however, the messiness of deciding what kinds of accomplices to prosecute and where to draw the line has often meant that courts invoke the figure of "complicity in genocide" sporadically and infrequently. If adopted more readily, though, this well-established international legal precedent could pave the way toward prosecuting a wider array of accomplices in different contexts and could also have tangible effects on how laws for meting out transitional justice are both made and implemented.

In cases where legal prosecutions of accomplices have not been possible, truth commissions have also done important work to account for the role that such figures play in state-sponsored violence. The South African Truth and Reconciliation Commission (TRC), probably the most important example in this regard, became emblematic worldwide for its decision to sacrifice justice in the interest of establishing the most complete record possible of the truth. Trading justice for truth meant rewarding witnesses with amnesty if the commissioners deemed the witnesses' testimony sufficiently honest and forthcoming; doing this, the commissioners thought, would attract a larger and more diverse group of witnesses unafraid of having to face punishment for their deeds. To establish a broad-based truth, the TRC "held special hearings for businessmen, for churchmen, for the legal profession, [and] for the media, [and sought] to ascertain their degree of complicity in the apartheid system."[17]

Later truth commissions, like those in Sierra Leone, Liberia, and Kenya, have followed suit in incorporating the role of complicity. Their reports reference wide swaths of actors and decidedly include long-view historical explanations of the "root causes" that led to state-sponsored violence.[18] In the specific case of Sierra Leone, the commission's final report acknowledges that the mining industry and the transnational diamond trade played a part in crimes against humanity committed during that country's civil war; it stops short, however, of suggesting that nonstate actors be legally prosecuted. In the same vein, the commission opts to contextualize the war broadly, focusing on the legacies of colonialism and the corruption of several postcolonial governments.

The case of Sierra Leone confirms Naomi Roht-Arriaza's assertion that, at present, we seem to be witnessing a "changing panorama" of transitional justice in which counties appear willing to go further than ever before to establish that state violence does not occur in a vacuum but rather is symptomatic of deep-seated, often long-standing practices of colonialism, racism, ethnic hatred, economic disparity, or corruption.[19] It also signals that postconflict societies are starting to acknowledge more routinely (even when prosecutions are not possible or even desired) that, to be effective, state-sponsored violence requires a vast spectrum of accomplices: both state and nonstate actors, military and civilians.

❧

Mechanisms such as trials and truth commissions confirm that international precedents exist for calling accomplices to account or, minimally, for naming their responsibilities in crimes against humanity. Yet, as I have mentioned in different moments of this book, prosecuting or even naming accomplices can be an immensely delicate matter for transitioning countries in which complicit actors still hold significant political or economic clout and where courts tend to focus only on the most egregious and readily identifiable perpetrators. Delving deeply into complicity is often the place where countries in transition draw a firm line in the sand. In those cases—and I would argue that Chile figures among them—*morally condemning* complicity therefore becomes all the more important for deepening memory work and for strengthening the quality of democracy.

No one can dispute that since 1990 Chile has made remarkable strides in establishing certain basic truths about its past. The 1991 Rettig Report chastised the Pinochet regime's crimes and stood as an iconic example to the rest of Latin America and the world of how important it is for a society to acknowledge state-sponsored crimes in the interest of strengthening democracy and building a culture of human rights. It is likewise difficult to dispute that Chile, despite certain limitations, has taken important steps toward prosecuting the most noteworthy perpetrators, particularly when we consider the "justice cascade" that General Pinochet's 1998 detention in London triggered within the country.[20] At the same time, it seems equally important to acknowledge that even if Chile's processes of memory and justice-seeking stand out as emblematic and even pioneering when viewed in global terms, the country, from within, has faced important limitations and blockages to dealing with its past by actors uninterested in probing the dictatorship's crimes or in really owning up to how the dictatorship's legacy continues to shape the present. On that point, Steve J. Stern notes, "In the 1990s, on themes of memory and human rights, and social equity and economic redistribution, Chileans had to remember not to ask for too much, or too much too soon, lest they jeopardize the stability and success of the transition."[21] He adds that, despite the admirable achievements of Chile's early transition, for many years a "pent-up demand" lingered in Chile to acknowledge the economic injustices that the dictatorship had wrought on the population and that the transition governments, in many ways, preserved.[22]

Memory, though, does not remain static. It sometimes takes unexpected twists and turns. It adapts and responds to the needs and conditions of the moment. And new generations less shackled by the fears and constraints of the past begin to make their voices heard and to *use* memory as a tool to voice *their* political demands. If by the end of the 1990s (and even as late as the 2003–4 National Commission on Political Imprisonment and Torture, or Valech Commission) Chile continued to define the "memory question" somewhat narrowly as the "violent trampling of human rights and bodily dignity under military rule," the massive student protests of 2006 and, even more so, those of 2011 on have set in motion an expansion of the memory question such that it now frequently includes the dictatorship's social and economic legacies.[23] Today, young people (and older people who stand in solidarity with them) regularly flood the streets to fight for the right to education, a livable retirement pension, better health care, and a new constitution. They demand that Chile's political elites respond to their cries to mitigate poverty and bury the dictatorship's lingering legacies of widespread, inequality-generating privatization. In that sense, the past decade or so has brought new deployments of memory that focus less on human rights violations such as torture, disappearance, and exile—although these issues have certainly not gone away—and more on the false promises and extreme inequality of the "new" Chile and "its private culture of self-actualizing individuals."[24] (It bears remembering, of course, that Chile is one of the most unequal countries in the world.) Moreover, recent corruption scandals like the Penta and Soquimich cases (2015–present; see chapter 5) have only sharpened the public's focus on the tentacled ways in which the dictatorship's family tree remains firmly embedded and alive in the democratic present.

The journalist María Olivia Mönckeberg's new book, *La máquina para defraudar: Los casos Penta y Soquimich* (The Defrauding Machine: The Penta and Soquimich Cases, 2016), shows that the corruption scandals currently plaguing Chile have left Chileans reeling and more disenchanted than ever with political and economic elites. While Mönckeberg claims that it is perhaps not surprising that economic powerhouses like the Penta Group, an investment bank, spent years illegally funneling money into an ultra-right-wing political party like UDI, whose loyalties to the Pinochet regime, as I have shown, run deep, she expresses consternation and dismay that figures of the left ("those who fought against the dictatorship, or their descendants, [and] those who created the political parties that defended democracy") have also found themselves embroiled in controversy and facing legal prosecution for corruption.[25] As a woman of the left, Mönckeberg confesses that she was, perhaps, "naïve" to think for so long that *only* the political right had been deeply complicit in propagating Pinochet's neoliberal model.[26] Her brilliant research devastatingly reveals an intricate web of sordid relationships and cross-pollinations among political and economic elites—from across the wide political spectrum—that lays this myth to rest. Among those she mentions are two figures whose public discourse I have studied in this book, one of the extreme right, the other of the progressive left: Pablo Longueira and Marco Enríquez-Ominami. Both men currently face charges for having accepted bribes (*boletas ideológicamente falsas*) and illegal campaign financing. Ironically, though tellingly, the funding they allegedly received originated with a businessman named Julio Ponce Lerou (Soquimich), none other than Pinochet's former son-in-law: a billionaire, a former mogul of the forestry industry, and the man most directly responsible for privatizing Chile's nonmetallic mining industry. Longueira and Enríquez-Ominami, of course, deny any wrongdoing. They resist avowal and prefer to guard their words—and their worlds.

Mönckeberg details a vast web of complicit actors who played roles large and small in the Penta and Soquimich corruption cases.[27] In describing this web, she perceives a performative dimension within complicit actors' memories quite similar to the dynamics I have observed throughout this book: "In this realist drama," she writes, "we take note of actors who reproduce similar scripts: the manager or employee who has the big boss's back, protected by silence; the one who ritualistically spouts off a previously-agreed-upon series of ready-made statements; or the one who prefers to half confess or—perhaps—[sometimes] tell the truth. And we see the secretaries, the errand boys, the functionaries, and relatives who facilitated bribes rather unwittingly because they had little to lose or to gain in this game of power and money. Some of them have simply preferred to speak frankly, and their testimonies have been, in many cases, of great value to the investigation."[28] But even though some people—those with much less to lose—speak candidly, the vast majority deny what they have done. For that reason, Mönckeberg tells us that Chile, in the final assessment, has become a "mortgaged democracy," owned by political and economic elites that, to protect their interests, have "invested in politics to dominate the scene and the will of the citizenry."[29] Her statement is powerful, with resonance not only for Chile but also far beyond it.

Yet, even if we accept Mönckeberg's acerbic criticism of Chile's current reality, I would not want to give the impression that complicit voices are winning the battle over memory. Indeed, concerned citizens' voices loom large, and their massive protests—valiantly, repeatedly, consistently—peel back the layers of the transition's dark underbelly. But their battle is uphill, to say the least. And only time will tell its outcome.

◈

The line that runs from complicity to complacency is not always straight or easy to map. This book has nevertheless worked to affirm that it exists. The dictatorship's legacy pervades Chilean democracy, marking it indelibly and establishing its contours. If the dictatorship spawned a host of complicit bodies (such as Mariana Callejas, Jaime Guzmán, Pablo Longueira, Sergio de Castro, Hugo Zambelli, Jorgelino Vergara, and countless others who today dilute, deny, or instrumentally manipulate the idea of human rights), the neoliberal machinery of the transition has, in its way, birthed another gamut of complicit bodies and moral gray zones, removed from but also linked to those of the 1973–90 period. New figures appear who were not part of the dictatorship's neoliberalization project (e.g., Max Marambio and Eugenio Tironi) but who now covertly propagate Pinochet's legacy through their fervent embracing of the neoliberal order. As normalized, neoliberal subjects, they craft self-fictions that speak to a realist vision of politics (and of the political) in which ends justify means and in which horizons for utopian thinking have shrunk to such a degree that they have become almost invisible. At the same time, they disavow or downplay the original violence that gave birth to "our" present and sometimes choose to turn a knowing blind eye to the other, multiple forms of violence that constitute the here-and-now.

Chile's story, as we know, is not just Chile's story. It is a global story linked to the Cold War in which the United States played a shamefully complicit role—as it did and continues to do in so many other places around the world. By now the specific role that the United States played in Chile is well known thanks to multiple rounds of declassified documents that detail "more than twenty years of overt and covert US efforts to shape, manipulate, orchestrate, and influence Chile's future."[30] Within this saga, Richard Nixon and Henry Kissinger played major roles, having attempted repeatedly and in multiple ways to thwart Allende's rise to power as well as his "peaceful road to socialism." Many years later, when the Clinton administration released an important round of papers further confirming the breadth and depth of US involvement in Chile, State Department officials encouraged the administration to offer a long-overdue, official apology that would, at long last, avow for the United States' role in fomenting the coup and in actively supporting the persecution of those who opposed the Pinochet regime. Faced with this challenge, however, Clinton stopped short. His administration proved reluctant to take such a bold step, preferring instead to let the documents speak for themselves. Peter Kornbluh explains that on the occasion of the documents' release:

> The Office of Policy and Planning wrote up a simple statement to be released on presidential stationery: "The United States bears responsibility and expresses regrets for events contributing to the coup and the resulting human rights violations." . . . Senior White House officials preferred to avoid an official acknowledgment of responsibility for Chile's tragedy. Instead of an apology, the White House released a brief, unsigned paragraph focusing on the documentation and judgments that could be derived from reading it: "One goal of the project is to put original documents before the public so that it may judge for itself the extent to which US actions undercut the cause of democracy and human rights in Chile. Actions approved by the US government aggravated political polarization and affected Chile's long tradition of democratic elections and respect for constitutional order and the rule of law." As the final, symbolic document in the Clinton administration's Chile Declassification Project, this contorted press statement fell far short of acknowledging the contribution that US foreign policy had made to the national and human horror experienced in Chile—an acknowledgment needed for United States citizens and Chileans to gain closure on a painful history.[31]

Nations, like individuals, resist making themselves vulnerable. They refuse to "own" the foundational acts of violence that underlie the "peace" and that support "our" way of life. Well aware of this, I want to end by remarking that I have not written this book naïvely. I have written it in the United States, protected by guarantees of gender, race, and class and by my status as a professor in a respected US university. Yet I have also written it as someone who has spent the better part of twenty years living in Chile for lengthy periods of time; studying Chile and Latin America; forging deep, personal relationships with Chilean friends and colleagues; and thinking and acting in solidarity with those who were adversely affected by the dictatorship's violence and who continue to suffer the consequences of its policies. (Here, I pause to wonder if these words I am writing might very well be part of my own fiction of mastery . . .).

On another level, I have written this book to challenge complacency. Diana Taylor once used the term *percepticide* to refer to the ways in which all of us tend to turn away from shameful, painful, or horrifying realities for fear that if we admit to them, the contradictions of our own lives might prove suffocating.[32] It is easy to think that "we" bear no responsibility for the violence that ensues around us. We find it more comfortable, more tolerable, to avert our gaze from the "the pain of others."[33] To protect ourselves and our material comfort, we shore up our borders and ourselves. We become bounded beings. But Taylor warns of the "dangers of disconnecting violent incidents from the economic and ideological factors that [give] rise to them." Without going to the extreme of lapsing into an ill-defined scenario of collective guilt that ignores the agential roles that individuals play in fomenting violence, we must also not shy away from understanding our place within local and global matrices of complicity. Taylor notes:

> Spectacles work internationally. People cross borders, capital moves invisibly from one location to another. Fantasies, too, are exported and imported; staging techniques travel; speech acts echo each other. The neo-Nazis in the United States today who advocate white supremacy belong to the same world as the neo-Nazis in Argentina with their black shirts, and both groups mimic Hitler's performance. The totalitarian spectacle of [Argentina's] Dirty War [and Chile's] was one more "damnable iteration." It was a repetition with no single original. Through what act of negation, of self-blinding, can we maintain that what happens in another country has nothing to do with us? . . . Without letting the culprits off the hook, [then], it is [therefore] vital to recognize that we, [too], participate in creating . . . environment[s] in which certain acts become thinkable, even admissible.[34]

I have not written *Civil Obedience* to incite cynical voyeurism on the reader's part. Instead, I have wanted to offer a serious invitation to understand and challenge the fictions of mastery that shape our lives, our families, our communities, our societies, our nations, and our world. In so doing, I have worked to suggest that we will not bring about long-lasting, deep change merely by reforming institutions, writing new constitutions, or imposing political measures of various kinds—though these things are undeniably vital to transitioning societies. Rather, we will do so by modifying our political cultures, striving to change firmly entrenched and seemingly immovable attitudes, rendering ourselves vulnerable to one another, repudiating violence and discrimination in all its forms, and educating citizens, especially younger generations, in the interest of strengthening broken communities. I have likewise wanted to suggest that even when certain forms of complicity do not prove prosecutable—because of a lack of political will or of viable conditions in which to carry out such prosecutions—they must nevertheless remain subject to moral repudiation and a demand for accountability. Moral reasoning, a sense of right and wrong, must have a place in politics if democracy is to be more than just a pragmatic game of ends and means.

Last, I hope that this book has been more than just a simplistic airing of First World shame. I see it as an expression of solidarity with those whom the neoliberal order crushes most. At the same time, it expresses my conviction that another, less violent, more community-oriented world is possible if only we can somehow manage to challenge blind belief in the vital, self-serving fictions of mastery that shape our daily lives.

Notes

Prologue

1. FUNA-Chile was founded by members of HIJOS-Chile, an organization composed of sons and daughters whose parents were murdered or disappeared during the Pinochet years. The goal of FUNA, which began in 1999, is to publicly shame human rights violators by "outing" them. The group's tactics are similar to those of the Argentine escraches. The FUNA group stages public events near where torturers, collaborators, or accomplices live or work to signal the degree of impunity that still reigns in Chile. The term FUNA derives from the indigenous language Mapudungun and, loosely translated, means to "spoil" the party for someone.

2. See Julio Oliva G., *Informe Gitter: Los criminales tienen nombre* (Santiago: Editorial Siglo XXI, 2003).

3. As this book goes to press, the hotly contested 2017 Chilean presidential elections are witnessing the demise of the New Majority. The coalition that was once the Concertación de Partidos por la Democracia has fractioned yet again, this time into two groups: La Fuerza de la Mayoría (Majority Force), anchored by the Socialist Party and the Communist Party, and Convergencia Democrática (Democratic Convergence), anchored by the Christian Democratic Party.

4. Diego Portales was a nineteenth-century Chilean lawmaker and statesman who served during several regimes as Minister of the Interior and Foreign Affairs. He also played a major role in shaping the presidentialist and "authoritarian" constitution of 1833. General Francisco Franco, following the Spanish Civil War, ruled Spain from 1939 until his death in 1975. Both leaders believed in governance by decree and in doing whatever was necessary to quell opposition. It comes as no surprise that General Pinochet would laud both of these men as heroic figures. In fact, historians have observed that Pinochet looked to the Portalian state as a model for his own government. On this point, see in particular Alfredo Jocelyn-Holt Letelier, *El peso de la noche: Nuestra frágil fortaleza histórica* (Santiago: Planeta/Ariel, 1997).

5. To access this document, one can consult a more recent edition published after the dictatorship. See *"El ladrillo": Bases de la política económica del gobierno*

militar chileno, prologue by Sergio de Castro (Santiago: Centro de Estudios Públicos, 1992).

6. See Comisión Nacional de Verdad y Reconciliación, *Informe de la Comisión Nacional de Verdad y Reconciliación*, 2 vols. in 3 books (Santiago: Ministerio Secretaría General de Gobierno, 1991). The quote referenced here comes from the translated *Report of the Chilean National Commission on Truth and Reconciliation*, foreword by William Lewers, C.S.C., introduction to the English edition by José Zalaquett, 2 vols. (Notre Dame, IN: University of Notre Dame Press, 1993). The complete document can be accessed on the website of the United States Institute for Peace, http://www.usip.org /sites/default/files/resources/collections/truth_commissions/Chile90-Report/Chile 90-Report.pdf. In the web document, see 85–86. Subsequent references will be to this same document. I have modified the translation in places where I feel that my translations more accurately capture the original Spanish text.

7. Ibid., 86.

8. Ibid., 86–87, emphasis mine at the end of this passage.

9. It is worth noting that one of the coauthors of the Rettig Report was the conservative historian Gonzalo Vial, notorious for his pro-Pinochet perspective. Vial's views thus factored into the final report, which delicately played contextualization of the 1973 crisis against an affirmation that no degree of crisis justifies human rights violations. Steve J. Stern speaks to Vial's influence: "[The Commission] entrusted the conservative historian Gonzalo Vial to draft the narrative of the 1973 crisis. Two key points framed the account. First, at the level of historical probabilities, the crisis that culminated in 1973 was relevant, and responsibility for it did not fall on one small sector alone. The Commission would sidestep a deep analysis of socioeconomic and long-term causes of the crisis, considered a task for historical interpretation and debate. It would focus the historical analysis more narrowly, on political and ideological dynamics that created an atmosphere conducive to overthrowing democracy and to characterizing the political adversary as an 'enemy' unfit for rights. . . . At this level of analysis, the Commission provided a brief account of sharpening polarization and demonization. It inserted Chile's drama in a double frame, as an aspect of international Cold War and as a bitter internal conflict. . . . The Commission saw responsibilities on both left and right during the Allende years—among those who preached the necessity of armed struggle, and those who equated opposition with making society ungovernable. . . . A second key point, however, drew a sharp line between historical probability and historical justification. Probability was not inevitability; some rights were inalienable. A crisis of institutionality and bitter social division did not grant a right to organize a campaign of extermination. . . . Fundamental rights of life and physical integrity could not be renounced or excused by historical circumstance." Steve J. Stern, *Reckoning with Pinochet: The Memory Question in Democratic Chile, 1989–2006* (Durham, NC: Duke University Press, 2010), 82–83.

10. Interestingly, Steve J. Stern points out that "the most strategic sections of the [truth commission's] narrative were drafted by conservatives. The report's stinging descriptions of law and the judiciary's failure . . . came from the likes of Ricardo Martin, a former Supreme Court justice, and José Luis Cea, a constitutional scholar. In some

ways, the conservatives were more scandalized and shocked than human rights veterans such as [Jaime] Castillo and [José] Zalaquett, who had for years read many cases and experienced steady denial of habeas corpus petitions in matters of life and death." Ibid., 81–82.

11. I will return to the international and judicial dimensions of complicity in the epilogue to this book. Leigh A. Payne and Gabriel Pereira have noted that transitional justice (TJ) mechanisms have increasingly come to include nonstate actors complicit with human rights violations: "Truth commissions and trials have focused on state forces and their allies in death squads or paramilitary groups, as in Peru and El Salvador. They have also held accountable rebel or revolutionary forces fighting against the state, as in Guatemala and South Africa. The domestic prosecution of a priest in Argentina and a doctor in Uruguay for their involvement in torture provide two additional examples of the incorporation of nonstate and civil society actors within TJ's scope. The South African Truth and Reconciliation Commission (TRC) investigated religious organizations as well as businesses for their complicity in the apartheid era." Leigh A. Payne and Gabriel Pereira, "Accountability for Corporate Complicity in Human Rights Violations: Argentina's Transitional Justice Innovation?," in *The Economic Accomplices to the Argentine Dictatorship: Outstanding Debts*, ed. Horacio Verbitsky and Juan Pablo Bohoslavsky, trans. Laura Pérez Carrara (Oxford: Oxford University Press, 2016), 30. In their introduction to this same book, the editors observe for the Argentine case that as more and more military perpetrators have been brought to justice for their crimes, it has gradually become possible to "expand the scope and analyze the context in which those crimes were committed, focusing on civilian, economic, and Church accomplices, whose contributions *enabled, facilitated, or improved the efficiency in the commission of such crimes.*' Verbitsky and Bohoslavsky, *The Economic Accomplices to the Argentine Dictatorship*, 4.

12. See Javier Rebolledo, *A la sombra de los cuervos: Los cómplices económicos de la dictadura* (Santiago: Ceibo Ediciones, 2015).

13. Juan Francisco Luzoro Montenegro, former president of the Paine Transportation Workers Union, was sentenced in November 2017 to twenty years in prison for his role in the murders of four farmers from the town of Paine, Chile, in late September 1973. Paine, located about twenty-five miles from Santiago, is a rural area that served as one of the most important sites for agrarian reform under Salvador Allende. Luzoro and other civilians acted alongside Paine police (Carabineros) to kill Carlos Chávez, Raúl Lazo, Orlando Pereira, and Pedro Ramírez, all of whom had supported agrarian reform efforts in Paine To date, fifty-one civilians have been processed by Chilean courts for their links to different dictatorship-era crimes. Whether these civilians ultimately face convictions will have much to say about the possibilities for an expansion of the scope of transitional justice in the Chilean case.

Introduction

1. See Naomi Klein, *The Shock Doctrine: The Rise of Disaster Capitalism* (New York: Picador, 2007).

2. See Rafael Otano, *Crónica de la transición* (Santiago: Planeta, 1995); Víctor Osorio and Iván Cabezas, *Los hijos de Pinochet* (Santiago: Planeta, 1995); Carlos Huneeus, *The Pinochet Regime*, trans. Lake Sagaris (Boulder, CO: Lynne Rienner, 2007); and *Chicago Boys*, directed by Carola Fuentes and Rafael Valdeavellano (Santiago: La Ventana Cine, 2015), DVD.

3. Primo Levi, *The Drowned and the Saved* (New York: Vintage International, 1989), 37. An early book that eloquently captures the winner-loser dynamic is Pamela Constable and Arturo Valenzuela, *A Nation of Enemies: Chile under Pinochet* (New York: W. W. Norton, 1991).

4. Some bibliography on complicity exists for cases of political violence in different countries and time periods. In this sense, the topic is not new, though the existing bibliographies do strike me as rather focused and limited. Examples of key works that touch on the subject include, for the Argentine case, Marguerite Feitlowitz's *A Lexicon of Terror: Argentina and the Legacies of Torture* (New York: Oxford University Press, 1998), David M. K. Sheinin's *Consent of the Damned: Ordinary Argentines in the Dirty War* (Gainesville: University Press of Florida, 2012), and Horacio Verbitsky and Juan Pablo Bohoslavsky's *Cuentas pendientes: Los cómplices económicos de la dictadura* (Buenos Aires: Siglo XXI Editores, 2013); for the case of Peru, Kimberly Theidon's *Intimate Enemies: Violence and Reconciliation in Peru* (Philadelphia: University of Pennsylvania Press, 2014); for African cases, Mark Sanders's *Complicities: The Intellectual and Apartheid* (Durham, NC: Duke University Press, 2002) and Carol Rittner's *Genocide in Rwanda: Complicity of the Churches* (St. Paul, MN: Paragon House, 2004); for the Holocaust, works by Primo Levi and Hannah Arendt, as well as studies such as Victoria J. Barnett's *Bystanders: Conscience and Complicity during the Holocaust* (Westport, CT: Praeger, 1999) and Debarati Sanyal's *Memory and Complicity: Migrations of Holocaust Remembrance* (New York: Fordham University Press, 2015). While these books all introduce aspects of the "gray zones" of complicity, several of them focus on complicity only as a secondary subject matter. Other books single out specific forms of complicity (e.g., intellectual, economic); focus on complicity by certain institutions (churches, indigenous peasants during civil conflict); or delve into the moral ramifications of being a bystander. Most of them survey fiction or media or take an ethnographic approach to the subject. Treatment of this subject in the Chilean case has been quite limited. I have also not found precedent for a thorough study of complicit memories in nonfictional genres, as this study proposes.

5. Younger Chilean writers who have treated civilian complicity in a fictional mode include Alejandro Zambra, Nona Fernández, Marcelo Leonart, and Álvaro Bisama.

6. See Judith Butler, *Giving an Account of Oneself* (New York: Fordham University Press, 2005).

7. The idea of memory as a battlefield upon which different actors vie for visibility and public clout runs through Elizabeth Jelin's groundbreaking work. See Elizabeth Jelin, *State Repression and the Labors of Memory*, trans. Judy Rein and Marcial Godoy-Anativia (Minneapolis: University of Minnesota Press, 2003). Jelin's book originally

appeared in Spanish as *Los trabajos de la memoria* (Madrid: Siglo XXI Editores, 2001). Yet even prior to Jelin's book we find influential expressions of the idea of memory as battle or struggle in works such as Steve J. Stern, "De la memoria suelta a la memoria emblemática: Hacia el recordar y el olvidar como proceso histórico (Chile, 1973–1998)," in *Memoria para un nuevo siglo: Chile, miradas a la segunda mitad del siglo XX*, ed. Mario Garcés, Pedro Milos, et al. (Santiago: LOM, 2000), 11–33. We also find further deployment of this metaphor in María Angélica Illanes, *La batalla de la memoria: Ensayos históricos de nuestro siglo (Chile, 1900–2000)* (Santiago: Planeta/Ariel, 2002). Illanes, Stern, and others were already thinking of memory as battle during a 1998 conference held in Santiago that led to the aforementioned edited volume by Garcés et al.

8. Wendy Brown's book *Undoing the Demos: Neoliberalism's Stealth Revolution* (New York: Zone Books, 2015) has been highly influential in my thinking on this matter. Brown asserts: "The claim that neoliberalism is profoundly destructive to the fiber and future of democracy in any form is premised on an understanding of neoliberalism as something other than a set of economic policies, an ideology, or a resetting of the relation between state and economy. Rather, as a normative order of reason developed over three decades into a widely and deeply disseminated governing rationality, neoliberalism transmogrifies every human domain and endeavor, along with humans themselves, according to a specific image of the economic. All conduct is economic conduct; all spheres of existence are framed and measured by economic terms and metrics, even when those spheres are not directly monetized. In neoliberal reason and in domains governed by it we are only and everywhere *homo oeconomicus*." Brown, *Undoing the Demos*, 9–10.

9. See Leonor Arfuch, *El espacio biográfico: Dilemas de la subjetividad contemporánea* (Buenos Aires: Fondo de Cultura Económica, 2002).

10. See Philippe Lejeune, *On Autobiography*, ed. Paul John Eakin, trans. Katherine Leary (Minneapolis: University of Minnesota Press, 1989), 119–37. By the "autobiographical pact," Lejeune meant that the reader would enter into a kind of implied agreement with the "I" of autobiography. The reader would accept that the "I" really was who he or she claimed to be and that the "I" would agree to speak the truth of the writer's experience.

11. These metaphors can be found in Wendy Brown, *Undoing the Demos*, 33.

12. Chiara Lepora and Robert E. Goodin, *On Complicity and Compromise* (Oxford: Oxford University Press, 2013), 1–16.

13. Ibid., 31.

14. Ibid., 36.

15. General Carlos Prats was a "constitutionalist" military officer, loyal to Allende and opposed to the September 11, 1973, coup.

16. Lepora and Goodin, *On Complicity and Compromise*, 31.

17. Ibid., 44.

18. Anthony Appiah, "Racism and Moral Pollution," in *Collective Responsibility*, ed. Larry May and Stacey Hoffman (Lanham, MD: Rowman and Littlefield, 1991), 219–38.

19. Gregory Mellema, *Complicity and Moral Accountability* (Notre Dame, IN: University of Notre Dame Press, 2016), 154.

20. Ibid., 155.

21. For the complete text of the 1998 Rome Statute of the International Criminal Court, see http://legal.un.org/icc/statute/99_corr/cstatute.htm.

22. Mellema, *Complicity and Moral Accountability*, 154.

23. Ibid., 10, emphasis mine.

24. I borrow this insight from Mark Sanders, *Complicities*, 3.

25. See Christopher Kutz, *Complicity: Ethics and Law for a Collective Age* (Cambridge: Cambridge University Press, 2000), quoted in Mellema, *Complicity and Moral Accountability*, 32, emphasis mine.

26. Karl Jaspers, *The Question of German Guilt*, trans. E. B. Ashton, with a new introduction by Joseph W. Koterski, S.J. (New York: Fordham University Press, 2001), 61.

27. Ibid.

28. Ibid., 34.

29. Among the texts that I have found most influential for my own thinking are Paul de Man, "Autobiography as De-facement," *Modern Language Notes* 94 (1979): 919–30; Philippe Lejeune, *On Autobiography*; Sylvia Molloy, *At Face Value: Autobiographical Writing in Spanish America* (Cambridge: Cambridge University Press, 1991); Leonor Arfuch, *Memoria y autobiografía: Exploraciones en los límites* (Buenos Aires: Fondo de Cultura Económica, 2013); Angel G. Loureiro, *The Ethics of Autobiography: Replacing the Subject in Modern Spain* (Nashville: Vanderbilt University Press, 2000); and Judith Butler, *Giving an Account of Oneself.* These books range from "classic" reflections on autobiographical writing to specifically Spanish or Latin American reflections to more contemporary philosophical and political approaches such as Butler's.

30. Arfuch, *Memoria y autobiografía*, 47.

31. Sidonie Smith and Julia Watson, eds., *Reading Autobiography: A Guide for Interpreting Life Narratives*, 2nd ed. (Minneapolis: University of Minnesota Press, 2010), 61.

32. See Loureiro, *The Ethics of Autobiography*, 13.

33. I borrow the idea of "diversionary schemas" from the psychologist Daniel Goleman. See Daniel Goleman, *Vital Lies, Simple Truths: The Psychology of Self-Deception* (New York: Simon and Schuster Paperbacks, 2005), 107. I return to this idea in greater depth in chapter 1.

34. Loureiro, *The Ethics of Autobiography*, 14.

35. Smith and Watson, *Reading Autobiography*, 15.

36. Butler, *Giving an Account of Oneself*, 8.

37. Ibid., 16.

38. Ibid., 18.

39. Arfuch, *El espacio biográfico*, 79.

40. In the specific case of *El Mercurio*, several noteworthy exposé pieces already exist, including Paulette Dougnac, Elizabeth Harries, Claudio Salinas, et al., *El diario de Agustín: Cinco estudios de casos sobre El Mercurio y los derechos humanos (1973–1990)*

(Santiago: LOM, 2009); Víctor Herrero A., *Agustín Edwards Eastman: Una biografía desclasificada del dueño de El Mercurio* (Santiago: Debate/ Penguin Random House Grupo Editorial S.A., 2014); Nancy Guzmán J., *Los Agustines: El clan Edwards y la conspiración permanente* (Santiago: Ceibo Ediciones, 2015); and Ignacio Agüero's documentary film *El Diario de Agustín* (2008). See also much excellent work by the journalist María Olivia Mönckeberg, such as *Los magnates de la prensa: Concentración de los medios de comunicación en Chile* (Santiago: Debate/ Random House Mondadori S.A., 2009).

41. Some other texts that could be studied using the arguments developed in this book include Federico Willoughby-MacDonald, *La guerra: Historia íntima del poder en los últimos 55 años de política chilena, 1957/2012* (Santiago: Editorial Mare Nostrum, 2012), by an early civilian collaborator and mouthpiece for the regime who later became an opponent of military rule; Patricia Arancibia Clavel, Claudia Arancibia Floody, and Isabel de la Maza Cave, eds., *Jarpa: Confesiones políticas* (Santiago: *La Tercera*/Mondadori, 2002), featuring a book-length interview with Sergio Onofre Jarpa, who served in Pinochet's cabinet; Hermógenes Pérez de Arce, *Autobiografía desautorizada* (Santiago: Colección *Qué Pasa*, 2003), a book by a notoriously pinochetista journalist; and Raúl Hasbún, *Testimonios* (Santiago: Editorial Don Bosco, 1995), a book by an Opus Dei priest who served as an apologist for the dictatorship and opposed the more liberal wing of the Catholic Church, which fought tirelessly for the victims and defended them through the Vicariate of Solidarity.

Chapter 1. Fictions of Mastery

1. My initial evocation of the "face" brings to mind the Levinasian "face," which calls out and functions as an invitation to act ethically. I will return to this idea later. At the same time, the "face" appears as an operative notion in autobiographical theory, particularly in poststructuralist iterations such as Paul de Man's notion of *de-facement*. Linda Anderson summarizes de Man's claim well: "[Paul de Man] identifies autobiography with a linguistic dilemma which is liable to be repeated every time an author makes himself the subject of his own understanding. The author reads himself in the text, but what he is seeing in this self-reflexive or specular moment is a figure or a face called into being by the substitutive trope of prosopopoeia, literally, the giving of a face, or personification. The interest of autobiography, according to [d]e Man, is that it reveals something which is in fact much more generally the case: that all knowledge, including self-knowledge depends on figurative language or tropes. . . . What the author of an autobiography does is to try to endow his inscription within the text with all the attributes of a face in order to mask or conceal his own fictionalization or displacement by writing. Paradoxically, therefore, the giving of a face, prosopopoeia, also names the disfigurement or defacement of the autobiographical subject through tropes. In the end there is only writing." Linda Anderson, *Autobiography* (New York: Routledge, 2001), 12.

2. Caught up in this semantic web that equates "face" with "truth" we also find the legal concept of the *careo*. The term describes a scenario in which two opposing

sides "face off" in court and in which each opponent is expected to testify truthfully to what he or she knows.

3. The psychologist Ulric Neisser refers to how the human mind naturally tends to divert one's attention from anxiety-causing experiences. The mind creates filters, "diversionary schemas," or ways of understanding the world, that protect the mind from hurtful pasts. Such schemas provide frameworks that promote the subject's mental equilibrium and impede troubling pasts from creeping unwantedly back into conscious awareness. See Ulric Neisser, "John Dean's Memory: A Case Study," *Cognition* 9 (1981): 1–22.

4. Leigh A. Payne, *Unsettling Accounts: Neither Truth nor Reconciliation in Confessions of State Violence* (Durham, NC: Duke University Press, 2008), 20.

5. On this point, my choice of vocabulary differs from Payne's (2008), though the dynamics at play in the narratives that she calls "confessions" and that I refer to as "fictions of mastery" may indeed be similar.

6. Steve J. Stern develops the idea of "salvationist" memory, largely espoused by the military and the political right, in *Remembering Pinochet's Chile: On the Eve of London 1998* (Durham, NC: Duke University Press, 2004), 7–38.

7. Ibid., xxvii.

8. See Roberto Bolaño, *Nocturno de Chile* (Barcelona: Anagrama, 2000) (English translation, *By Night in Chile*, trans. Chris Andrews [New York: New Directions Books, 2003]); Pedro Lemebel, "Las orquídeas negras de Mariana Callejas (o 'el Centro Cultural de la DINA')," in *De perlas y cicatrices: Crónicas radiales* (Santiago: LOM, 1998), 14–15; Roberto Brodsky, "Amores que matan (autobiografía de Michael Townley y Mariana Callejas)," in *Con pasión*, ed. Marco Antonio de la Parra et al. (Santiago: Planeta, 2000), 143–60; Carlos Iturra, "Caída en desgracia," in *Crimen y perdón: Cuentos* (Santiago: Catalonia, 2008), 183–219; and Nona Fernández, *El taller*, in *Bestiario: Freakshow, temporada 1973/1990*, ed. Marcelo Leonart, Ximena Carrera, and Nona Fernández (Santiago: Ceibo Ediciones, 2013), 135–203.

9. Prats, a "constitutionalist" general loyal to Allende, was killed with his wife, Sofía Cuthbert, in a car bombing that Townley and Callejas executed in Buenos Aires on September 30, 1974. This crime, along with the 1976 assassination of Orlando Letelier (one of Allende's ministers), in Washington, DC, and the 1975 assassination of Bernardo Leighton (a prominent Christian Democrat), in Rome, was carried out as part of Operation Condor, a consortium of terror that coordinated the efforts of several South American dictatorships to eliminate enemies and "subversives." It included Chile, Argentina, Uruguay, Paraguay, Bolivia, and Brazil. Townley and Callejas were also responsible for carrying out the Letelier and Leighton crimes. On Operation Condor, see John Dinges, *The Condor Years: How Pinochet and His Allies Brought Terrorism to Three Continents* (New York: The New Press, 2004).

10. There are many sources available on the role the United States played in aiding the Chilean coup. Peter Kornbluh's *The Pinochet File: A Declassified Dossier on Atrocity and Accountability* (New York: The New Press, 2003) continues to be one of the best.

11. Many of the facts relayed here can be found in John Dinges and Saul Landau, *Assassination on Embassy Row* (New York: Pantheon Books, 1980), and in Juan Cristóbal Peña's 2010 journalistic investigations: "Mariana Callejas, cómplice del crimen de Carlos Prats y su esposa (I): Vida literaria en el corazón de la DINA"; "Mariana Callejas (II): Las dos vidas de su casa-cuartel en Lo Curro"; and "Mariana Callejas: 'Es tan triste escribir y que no te publique nadie,'" all of which can be found online at www.ciper chile.cl.

12. Dinges and Landau note: "When Espinoza recruited Townley in mid-1974, DINA had about 600 full-time paid military agents and civilian contract employees. About 20 percent of the staff were civilians, mostly recruited in slum areas from among thugs and petty criminals. Townley joined a more elite group handpicked from Patria y Libertad and other opposition groups, most of whom entered DINA in March and April 1974." Dinges and Landau, *Assassination on Embassy Row*, 132.

13. Ibid., 130.

14. Callejas for years held out hope that DINA would justly reward her and Michael for their service by gifting the couple the deed to the house. This never happened, and, consequently, she continued to harbor bitterness against Pinochet and Contreras. Townley's personal secretary during his years in DINA, Alejandra Damiani, alias "Roxana," once described her boss in court as a "very poorly paid mercenary." (See Peña, "Mariana Callejas [II]: Las dos vidas de su casa-cuartel en Lo Curro.") Although Callejas claimed that she and her husband were never motivated primarily by money, she could not help feeling that they were undervalued in financial terms.

15. This story is anthologized in Callejas's book *La larga noche* (Santiago: Editorial Lo Curro, 1981), 89–95. It is ironic that *El Mercurio*, a newspaper that supported the Pinochet regime, gave Callejas this special recognition for her literary talents.

16. Operation Colombo refers to a false media campaign waged by DINA to convince Chileans that 119 leftist militants had killed one another—in the newspaper's words, they had been "exterminated like rats"—in Curitiba, Brazil, and Buenos Aires, Argentina, in 1975. This psychological warfare and extermination campaign should be understood as part of Operation Condor. In this instance, the Chilean media cover-up was supported by Brazil and Argentina. For more information on Operation Colombo, see Lucía Sepúlveda Ruiz, *119 de nosotros* (Santiago: LOM, 2009). Carmelo Soria (1921–76) was a Spanish diplomat whom DINA murdered as part of Operation Condor.

17. When Callejas wrote *Siembra vientos*, she had already suffered through Townley's 1976 trial in the United States, though she had yet to see legal action against herself or Michael for the roles they played in the Leighton and Prats cases. She therefore remained, to some extent, untouched by the law and perhaps felt that she was untouchable. Curiously, Delle Chiaie would testify against Townley in Italy in the very same year that Callejas published her memoir, opening a new judicial phase. Later, in 2003, Callejas would be tried for her role in the Prats murders.

18. Ironically, *Siembra vientos* was published by Editorial ChileAmérica Cesoc, a house founded by a group of anti-Pinochet Chilean exiles, among them Bernardo Leighton, a man targeted in one of Operation Condor's best-known crimes, in which

Callejas played a role. The literary critic Patricio Pron cites this unusual and surprising detail, calling it "one of many contradictions within recent Chilean history." Patricio Pron, "Mariana Callejas: La literatura nazi en América," *Letras libres*, March 2014, http://www.letraslibres.com/revista/letrillas/mariana-callejas-la-literatura-nazi-en-america.

19. Emmanuel Levinas, *On Escape (De l'évasion)*, trans. Bettina Bergo (Stanford, CA: Stanford University Press, 2003), 64.

20. I have opted to use feminine pronouns in this chapter to avoid cumbersome repetitions of "he or she." In other chapters in which I study male accomplices, I will prefer the masculine pronoun. The reader can assume here that when I speak of the dynamics of shame in general, I am also speaking about the case of Callejas specifically.

21. Claudia Welz, "Shame and the Hiding Self," *Passions in Context: International Journal for the History and Theory of Emotions* 2 (2011): 82.

22. Ruth Leys signals that a shift from guilt to shame in contemporary culture can become a strategy for evading moral or even legal responsibility. We should therefore be on guard when subjects claim to be ashamed but not guilty: "What is crucially at stake in the current tendency to replace guilt with shame is an impulse to displace questions about our moral responsibility for what we *do* in favor of more ethically neutral or different questions about our personal attributes. Normally we cannot be held responsible for who we are in the same way we can be responsible for what we do." Ruth Leys, *From Guilt to Shame: Auschwitz and After* (Princeton, NJ: Princeton University Press, 2007), 131. For this line of argumentation, see also Emanuela Tegla, *J. M. Coetzee and the Ethics of Power: Unsettling Complicity, Complacency, and Confession* (Boston: Brill/Rodopi, 2015), 95–108.

23. Agnes Heller, *The Power of Shame: A Rational Perspective* (London: Routledge & Kegan Paul, 1985), 4.

24. Welz, "Shame and the Hiding Self," 80.

25. Levinas, *On Escape*, 64.

26. Ibid., 65.

27. See Daniel Goleman, *Vital Lies, Simple Truths: The Psychology of Self-Deception* (New York: Simon & Schuster Paperbacks, 1985), 105. Goleman also notes that Freud uses the term *repression* to explain how the subject shields itself from psychological pain. "The pain can be of many varieties: trauma, 'intolerable ideas,' unbearable feelings, anxiety, guilt, shame, and so on. Repression is the quintessential lacuna; it lessens mental pain by attenuating awareness, as does its cousin, denial. The concept of repression underwent many permutations in Freud's writing and has been further refined by successive generations of his followers. This conceptual evolution culminates in the 'mechanisms of self-defense,' the most detailed map to date of the ways in which attention and anxiety interplay in mental life" (112–13).

28. Ibid., 115.

29. In the late 1970s, Callejas shared these diaries with the journalist John Dinges prior to the 1980 publication of *Assassination on Embassy Row*. I am grateful to John

Dinges for sharing these rare manuscripts with me. The quote reproduced here comes from these unpaginated documents.

30. Mariana Callejas, personal diary, April 12, 1978, n.p., emphasis mine.

31. By integrity, I mean "to be integral," to think of oneself as a whole person with a rational life story.

32. Heller, *The Power of Shame*, 21. Heller's use of the phrase "social justice" has to do with evening the playing field after one member of a society has committed a wrong against another. It has nothing to do with questions of socioeconomic injustice.

33. Judith Butler, *Giving an Account of Oneself* (New York: Fordham University Press, 2005), 33.

34. Butler summarizes the complexity of Levinas's concept of the "face" in *Precarious Life: The Power of Mourning and Violence* (New York: Verso Books, 2004), 144. She writes: "[In the Levinasian view], there is a 'face' which no face can fully exhaust, the face understood as human suffering, as the cry of human suffering, which can take no direct representation. Here the 'face' is always a figure for something that is not literally a face. Other human expressions, however, seem to be figurable as a 'face' even though they are not faces, but sounds or emissions of another order. The cry that is represented through the figure of the face is one that confounds the senses and produces a clearly improper comparison: that cannot be right, for the face is not a sound. And yet, the face can stand for the sound precisely because it is *not* the sound. In this sense, the figure underscores the incommensurability of the face with whatever it represents." The face interrogates us and calls us to act ethically, to acknowledge the other's humanity as equal to our own.

35. Butler, *Giving an Account of Oneself*, 136, emphasis mine.

36. Ibid., 130.

37. Mariana Callejas, *Siembra vientos: Memorias* (Santiago: Ediciones ChileAmérica CESOC, 1995), 21.

38. Ibid., 141.

39. Ibid., 144.

40. Shoshana Felman, "After the Apocalypse: Paul de Man and the Fall to Silence," in *Testimony: Crises of Witnessing in Literature, Psychoanalysis, and History*, ed. Shoshana Felman and Dori Laub, MD (New York: Routledge, 1992), 149.

41. Callejas, *Siembra vientos*, 144.

42. Ibid., 29.

43. Ibid., 127.

44. Ibid., 144.

45. Ibid., 127.

46. Dinges and Landau, *Assassination on Embassy Row*, 95.

47. The quote comes from Callejas's personal diaries, n.p.

48. Callejas, *Siembra vientos*, 33.

49. Nelly Richard, "El mercado de las confesiones: Lo público y lo privado en los testimonios de Mónica Madariaga, Gladys Marín y Clara Szczaranski," in *El salto de*

Minerva: Intelectuales, género y Estado en América Latina, ed. Mabel Moraña and María Rosa Olivera-Williams (Frankfurt: Iberoamericana/Vervuert, 2005), 309. Richard adds that in certain cases "the feminine testimonial utterance serves as a pretext for drawing the public's attention toward intimate confessions while the real secrets of state remain unconfessed" (311).

50. Callejas, *Siembra vientos*, 159.

51. The Chicago Boys were economists, mostly from the Pontifical Catholic University of Chile, who were sent to the University of Chicago to study neoliberal economic policy with Milton Friedman. They, in turn, became the designers of Pinochet's economic reforms.

52. I will return at greater length to the ideas of parsing subjectivity and to the ways in which "human rights" have been instrumentalized by Pinochet's supporters when I analyze Pablo Longueira Montes's *Mi testimonio de fe: El servicio público, el sentido del dolor* (see chapter 2).

53. See Philippe Lejeune, *Le pacte autobiographique* (Paris: Seuil, 1975).

54. Leonor Arfuch, *Memoria y autobiografía: Exploraciones en los límites* (Buenos Aires: Fondo de Cultura Económica, 2013), 47, 51.

55. Here I am adapting some of Erving Goffman's classic ideas on performativity to the autobiographical act. See Erving Goffman, *The Presentation of Self in Everyday Life* (New York: Doubleday, 1959), 44. His fourth chapter, "Discrepant Roles," is also relevant to this discussion.

56. Butler, *Giving an Account of Oneself*, 40.

57. Callejas, *Siembra vientos*, 23.

58. Raúl Hasbún Zaror (b. 1933), an Opus Dei priest and professor of theology, was director of Chile's Catholic University television network from 1972 to 1974. His ideological opposition to the Allende government was blatantly clear in the network's programming. After the coup, he wrote regularly in support of the military regime in the pages of *El Mercurio* and other Chilean newspapers. He also appeared frequently on television speaking out against "Marxist subversives." He was accused of complicity in the asphyxiation of worker Jorge Tomás Henríquez G., but the case was thrown out in 1974 by the military tribunal charged with hearing it.

59. Callejas, *Siembra vientos*, 89.

60. See Peña, "Mariana Callejas: 'Es tan triste escribir y que no te publique nadie.'"

61. Callejas, *La larga noche*, 111.

62. Ibid., 113.

63. Ibid., 114.

64. Ibid., 76.

65. Ibid., 78.

66. See Robert Jay Lifton, *The Nazi Doctors: Medical Killing and the Psychology of Genocide* (New York: Basic Books, 1986), and Ervin Staub, "Moral Exclusion, Personal Goal Theory, and Extreme Destructiveness," *Journal of Social Issues* 46, no. 1 (1990):

47–64. See also Ervin Staub, *The Roots of Evil: The Origins of Genocide and Other Group Violence* (New York: Cambridge University Press, 1990).

67. Victoria J. Barnett calls attention to both Lifton's and Staub's theories in *Bystanders: Conscience and Complicity during the Holocaust* (Westport, CT: Praeger, 1999), 27–30.

68. Callejas, *La larga noche*, 117.

69. Ibid., 72.

70. Ibid.

71. Jorge Escalante, Nancy Guzmán, Javier Rebolledo, and Pedro Vega, *Los crímenes que estremecieron a Chile: Las memorias de* La Nación *para no olvidar* (Santiago de Chile: Ceibo Ediciones, 2013), 182.

72. Ibid., 137.

73. Ibid.

74. Although I cannot think of any cases in which Chilean accomplices to the Pinochet regime have committed suicide as a means to escape shame, guilt, public persecution, or legal prosecution, a number of military men have chosen this route. Germán Barriga Muñoz (2005), Odlanier Rafael Mena Salinas (2013), and Hernán Ramírez Rurange (2015) are cases in point. Odlanier Mena, a former director of the Central Nacional de Informaciones (National Information Center, CNI), left the military in 1975 but continued to serve the regime as a civilian collaborator. In this sense, his figure evokes both military and civilian complicity.

75. Callejas, *La larga noche*, 26.

76. Ibid., 124.

77. Because of the capaciousness of the idea of *culpa* in Spanish, I am choosing to interpret the concept as "shame" for the purpose of my argument. This is because the biographical Callejas refused to admit to legal guilt. I recognize that her own vocabulary in some of the passages I cite throughout this chapter is imprecise, so I am introducing a degree of precision in my own translations to make clear that Callejas felt shame, not guilt. *Culpa*, here, carries a connotation of *vergüenza*.

78. Jacques Derrida, *Sovereignties in Question: The Poetics of Paul Celan*, ed. Thomas Dutoit and Outi Pasanen (New York: Fordham University Press, 2005), 96.

79. Ibid.

80. See Mariana Callejas, *Nuevos cuentos* (Santiago de Chile: Editorial Puerto de Palos, 2007).

81. Ibid., 21.

82. Ibid., 20.

83. Ibid., 21. Fittingly, the quote Callejas took from Pablo Neruda comes from his apolitical love poetry and not from his politically committed work. See Neruda's famous "Poema 20," printed bilingually in Spanish and English in Pablo Neruda, *The Essential Neruda: Selected Poems*, ed. Mark Eisner (San Francisco: City Lights Books/ Fundación Pablo Neruda, 2004), 9–11.

84. Callejas, *Nuevos cuentos*, 21.

85. Several critics have offered interesting readings of this novel, though Susana Draper's is perhaps most relevant to my analysis of Callejas. "In *Nocturno de Chile*," she wrote, "Bolaño recounts what could perhaps be the official right-wing mea culpa and accuses the neoliberal left (the 'Concertación' coalition) of lacking courage. . . . The entire novel focuses on what the author describes as the great national silence: the right-wing conscience (home) pursued and haunted by the ghosts of its hunting. . . . *Nocturno* is a text about protected democracy (immunity and impunity) figured as an architecture that attempts to prevent (protect) the return of an event (its discovery, its irruption); the uncanny stems from the impossible attempt to control and immunize the entire future of politics." Susana Draper, *Afterlives of Confinement: Spatial Transitions in Postdictatorship Latin America* (Pittsburgh: University of Pittsburgh Press, 2012), 127, 150–51. Draper's comments on haunting inspire my writing here and will becomes even more relevant in chapter 2, which deals with how subjects of the right who do not experience shame attempt to control and narrate ghosts from the past. In particular, I will focus on the specter of Jaime Guzmán, neoliberal Chile's main ideologue. Bolaño's accusations of complicity against the neoliberalized left, which Draper also notes, foreshadow my treatment in chapter 5 of the "complacent subject."

86. A general consensus exists among literary critics that Urrutia Lacroix is a fictional double for José Miguel Ibáñez Langlois (1936–), an Opus Dei priest and literary critic whose "official" reviews of literary works filled the pages of the ultraconservative newspaper *El Mercurio* during the dictatorship years. Better known by his pseudonym, Ignacio Valente, as of this writing Ibáñez Langlois continues to publish occasionally in *El Mercurio*.

87. Bolaño, *By Night in Chile*, 125.

Chapter 2. Specters of Jaime Guzmán

1. See Tomás Moulian, *Conversación interrumpida con Allende* (Santiago: LOM-Arcis, 1998).

2. Jacques Derrida, *Specters of Marx: The State of the Debt, the Work of Mourning, and the New International*, trans. Peggy Kamuf, introduction by Bernd Magnus and Stephen Cullenberg (New York: Routledge, 1994), 37.

3. Ibid.

4. Belén Moncada Durruti, *Jaime Guzmán: Una democracia contrarrevolucionaria; El político, de 1964 a 1980* (Santiago: RIL, 2006), 16.

5. Ibid., 20.

6. Renato Cristi, *El pensamiento político de Jaime Guzmán: Una biografía intelectual*, 2nd ed. (Santiago: LOM, 2011), 19.

7. Ibid., 21–22.

8. Cristián Gazmuri, *¿Quién era Jaime Guzmán?* (Santiago: RIL, 2013).

9. Ibid., 55.

10. Ibid., 15–16.

11. Derrida, *Specters of Marx*, 58.

12. Ibid.

13. Pablo Longueira Montes, *Mi testimonio de fe: El servicio público, el sentido del dolor* (Santiago: Grijalbo, 2003).

14. *El tío*, directed by Mateo Iribarren (Santiago, Chile: Santa Cruz Producciones, 2013), DVD.

15. Ignacio Santa Cruz, in broad terms, identifies publicly with the left. As I later show, however, he supports neoliberalism in his discourse. Ideologically, he is therefore difficult to place because of his biological connection to the extreme right and also because he does not often make public statements that permit us to categorize him ideologically. One might therefore consider Santa Cruz, objectively viewed, to be of the center left or center right: his positions are morally liberal but fiscally conservative. For my purposes, I accept his assertion that he is a man of the "left," but I also urge readers not to forget that this man of the left bears intimate ties to the right that also shape his subjectivity and from which he finds it difficult to break free. In that regard, I read Santa Cruz as a subject in tension.

16. Mario Garcés, "Chilean Social Movements in Confrontation with Neoliberalism," in *Neoliberalism's Fractured Showcase: Another Chile Is Possible*, ed. Ximena de la Barra (Chicago: Haymarket Books, 2012), 232.

17. Carlos Huneeus, *The Pinochet Regime*, trans. Lake Sagaris (Boulder, CO: Lynne Rienner, 2007), 228. Much of the biographical information that I include here is derived from Huneeus's excellent work. For a complete profile of Guzmán, see Huneeus, *The Pinochet Regime*, chap. 7.

18. Huneeus, *The Pinochet Regime*, 229–30.

19. Steve J. Stern, *Battling for Hearts and Minds: Memory Struggles in Pinochet's Chile, 1973–1988* (Durham, NC: Duke University Press, 2006), 57.

20. Ibid.

21. Steve J. Stern adds an important caveat: "Guzmán was from the start important in the emerging [memory] framework of war and salvation. It goes too far, [however], to convert him into the deus ex machina behind each and every act of building political legitimacy and official memory, or to free military leaders of responsibility for their own words and deeds, including decisions to accept or reject advice by civilians. It is also true, however, that Guzmán and *gremialismo* provided crucial intellectual backing, advice, and language that blended well with Pinochet's own instincts and that drew on strands of conservative thought and critiques of democracy influential before 1973. The gremialista emphasis on antipolitics fit well with the idea that recent history proved the need for a drastic tearing down of Chile's political culture. It also fit well with Pinochet's need for ongoing 'war' to consolidate his power." Stern, *Battling for Hearts and Minds*, 58.

22. In his brilliant, unpublished paper "Piñera and the Pyramids: The Problem of Historical Memory Relating to the Tension between Human Rights and Free Markets in Chilean Neoliberalism," Hassan Akram shows how Guzmán drew on Friedrich Hayek's notion of the "liberal dictator" as a tool for "defend[ing] [both] freedom and dictatorship at the same time." Cristi, in *El pensamiento político de Jaime Guzmán*, also points to the influence of Hayek on Guzmán. For deeper insight into Hayek's rationale,

see especially Friedrich Hayek, *Constitution of Liberty* (Chicago: University of Chicago Press, 1960).

23. For a detailed analysis of Pinochet as hero and "savior" of the nation, see Steve J. Stern, *Remembering Pinochet's Chile: On the Eve of London 1998* (Durham, NC: Duke University Press, 2004), 7–34.

24. Jaime Guzmán Errázuriz, *Escritos personales*, 3rd ed. (Santiago: Zig-zag, 1993), 133. Critics of memory and transitional politics such as Nelly Richard among others have regularly observed that the right and the Concertación have frequently treated human rights as a "theme" to be dealt with so as to make it go away rather than as a guiding principle to defend. In that regard, it is worth noting that Guzmán deployed the same phrase (*el tema de los derechos humanos*) that later became commonplace in official political discourse during the early transition.

25. Ibid., 136.

26. Ibid., 137. Unlike other supporters of the Pinochet regime who claim to have suddenly become aware of human rights violations only after the 1976 assassination by DINA of Orlando Letelier in Washington, DC—which many scholars recognize as a turning point in the regime's human rights saga—Guzmán purported to have cared deeply about human rights "long before 1973" and to have always acted "in accordance [*en consecuencia*] with his beliefs."

27. Ibid.

28. Ibid., 139.

29. Ibid., 141.

30. Ibid., 155.

31. Huneeus, *The Pinochet Regime*, 241.

32. Gazmuri, *¿Quién era Jaime Guzmán?*, 64–65.

33. Ibid., 68.

34. Guzmán, *Escritos personales*, 137, emphasis mine.

35. For Giorgio Agamben's analysis of Eichmann's defense, see *Remnants of Auschwitz: The Witness and the Archive*, trans. Daniel Heller-Roazen (New York: Zone Books, 1999), 23–24.

36. For a detailed accounting of this whole episode, see Steve J. Stern, *Battling for Hearts and Minds*, 118–21. I follow Stern's lead in my summarized narrative of these events.

37. For a more complete version of Guzmán's words, see Steve J. Stern, *Battling for Hearts and Minds*, 119.

38. Regarding Guzmán's role as a strategist, Sofía Correa Sutil adds that "Jaime Guzmán revised his early doctrinal positions linked to corporatist Catholicism and adapted them to the historical necessities he was living. To be sure, Guzmán was lucid enough to foresee the long-term interests of the right and [consider] its capacity to politically guarantee its survival through an institutional order that would become consolidated independently of military tutelage, which he knew was, by definition, precarious." Sofía Correa Sutil, *Con las riendas del poder: La derecha chilena en el siglo XX* (Santiago: Editorial Sudamericana, 2004), 278.

39. Cristi, *El pensamiento político de Jaime Guzmán*, 25.

40. I have elsewhere written extensively about the Chilean right's tendency to "parse" the dictator, particularly around the time of his death in 2006. See Michael J. Lazzara, "Pinochet's Cadaver as Ruin and Palimpsest," in *Telling Ruins in Latin America*, ed. Michael J. Lazzara and Vicky Unruh (New York: Palgrave Macmillan, 2009), 121–34.

41. Akram points to this dynamic in "Piñera and the Pyramids": "According to U.S. embassy cables (released by WikiLeaks), Piñera has privately defended the neoliberal economic model by attempting to detach it from the violent circumstances through which it came into being. 'One would not destroy the pyramids because people died in their construction,'" Piñera claimed while on the campaign trail in 2010. Akram adds: "In an interview with *La Tercera* newspaper on the eve of the commemoration events for the fortieth anniversary of the 1973 coup, Piñera gave a public interview in which he repeated a version of the 'pyramid thesis.' In doing so, Piñera echoed the language of Socialist Party president Ricardo Lagos's book on Chile's bicentenary that described the country's history as a juxtaposition of light and shadow. Similarly, Piñera argued the dictatorship had both 'the darkest shadows such as the repeated, permanent, and systematic violation of human rights by agents of the State' and 'certain lights like moderni[z]ation . . . and the creation of a social market economy.'" For the Lagos reference, see Ricardo Lagos Escobar, *Cien años de luces y sombras*, vol. 1 (Santiago: Taurus, 2012). In the same vein, Rosario Guzmán Errázuriz frames her brother's legacy in terms of "light" and "shadows" in her book *Mi hermano Jaime*, 4th ed. (Santiago: Editorial Ver, 1992), 91–107. Chapter 4 of Rosario Guzmán's book is aptly titled "Sus ángeles y demonios" (His Angels and Demons).

42. See Akram, "Piñera and the Pyramids."

43. Michel Foucault, *Wrong-Doing, Truth-Telling: The Function of Avowal in Justice*, ed. Fabienne Brion and Bernard E. Harcourt, trans. Stephen W. Sawyer (Chicago: University of Chicago Press, 2014), 17.

44. Ibid., 15, emphasis mine.

45. Ibid., 28.

46. For information on the Spiniak case, see Pablo Vergara E. and Ana María Sanhueza, *Spiniak y los demonios de la Plaza de Armas* (Santiago: Editorial La Copa Rota/ Universidad Diego Portales, 2008), and Gustavo González Rodríguez, *Caso Spiniak: Poder, ética y operaciones mediáticas* (Santiago: LOM/ Universidad de Chile, Instituto de Comunicación e Imagen, 2008).

47. Longueira, *Mi testimonio de fe*, 38.

48. Ibid., 60.

49. Ibid., 77.

50. See Rigoberta Menchú, *I, Rigoberta Menchú: An Indian Woman in Guatemala*, ed. Elisabeth Burgos-Debray, trans. Ann Wright (New York: Verso, 1984).

51. See Javier Rebolledo, *A la sombra de los cuervos: Los cómplices civiles de la dictadura* (Santiago: Ceibo Ediciones, 2015).

52. Longueira, *Mi testimonio de fe*, 59.

53. Ibid., 60.

54. To understand the full implications of this statement, see Wendy Brown, *Undoing the Demos: Neoliberalism's Stealth Revolution* (New York: Zone Books, 2015), 9–10. Brown writes: "As a normative order of reason developed over three decades into a widely and deeply disseminated governing rationality, neoliberalism transmogrifies every human domain and endeavor, along with humans themselves, according to a specific image of the economic."

55. Longueira, *Mi testimonio de fe*, 25. The complete "La Paz Ahora" proposal can be found on UDI's website, http://www.udi.cl/sitio/wp-content/uploads/2009/03/la_paz_ahora_propuesta_ddhh_udi_2003.pdf.

56. Juan Carlos Gómez Leyton, *Política, democracia y ciudadanía en una sociedad neoliberal (Chile: 1990–2010)* (Santiago: ARCIS/CLACSO, 2010), 295.

57. Ibid., 296.

58. Ibid., 297.

59. Longueira, *Mi testimonio de fe*, 125.

60. One of the memory frameworks that Steve J. Stern identifies is that of "persecution and awakening." Those whose memories fit into this framework understand the dictatorship as a "long winter of repression and self-discovery" followed by a period of "awakening" to dark realities that they perhaps did not know were such at the time. Reminiscent of this logic, Longueira situates his awakening to human rights violations in 1989—conveniently, at the *end* of the dictatorship—when he was elected as a congressman (*diputado*) for Paine, a rural area on the outskirts of Santiago where seventy men, mostly farmworkers who favored agrarian reform, had been rounded up by the military and disappeared in October 1973. Longueira writes: "While I was a deputy for that district, the doors to my congressional office in Paine, located right in front of the Municipal Building, were always open to families who lived the theme of political violence [*el tema de la violencia política*]. Year after year, many mothers asked me to help have their sons excused from military service. Every time I was asked, I quietly complied." He continues by telling the story of one victim's mother who confessed to him that, despite all that had happened, she still supported Pinochet because "he made it so that other wives wouldn't lose their husbands like [she] did." Longueira's "awakening" while a deputy for Paine in the late 1980s and early 1990s therefore set the stage for his magnanimous gesture of reaching out to the families of Pisagua in 2003. Note that this did not occur for more than a decade. Prior to 1989, he claims to have known nothing of human rights violations. See Longueira, *Mi testimonio de fe*, 127. On the framework of persecution and awakening, see Steve J. Stern, *Remembering Pinochet's Chile*, 109–10.

61. Longueira, *Mi testimonio de fe*, 25–26, emphasis mine.

62. To understand Luz Arce's use of the phrase *dar el paso*, see Michael J. Lazzara, *Luz Arce and Pinochet's Chile: Testimony in the Aftermath of State Violence*, trans. Michael J. Lazzara and Carl Fischer, foreword by Jean Franco (New York: Palgrave Macmillan, 2011), 124.

63. Longueira, *Mi testimonio de fe*, 129.

64. The "Peace Now" document reads: "Having listened to the requests of the families that approached UDI as well as public declarations by groups of Families of the Disappeared, we propose—with the goal of facilitating knowledge of the whereabouts of their family members—that a law be established according to which a time period be set in which judges assigned to [human rights] cases would receive, by any means and without formality, information that would productively contribute to that goal. . . . The law would establish a reduction in sentencing or, alternatively, an attenuation of consequences [*una atenuante calificada*] for whomever would offer such information, whether that person were the author of or an accomplice to the crime; if the person were an accessory to the crime, he or she would be exempt from responsibility."

65. In his contribution to Longueira's book, UDI senator Juan Antonio Coloma Correa frames his life similarly to Longueira. Coloma's narrative therefore functions as a mirror of and support for Longueira's. See Longueira, *Mi testimonio de fe*, 73.

66. Patricio Fernández, "Editorial: El bajón de Longueira," *The Clinic Online*, July 17, 2013, http://www.theclinic.cl/2013/07/17/editorial-el-bajon-de-longueira/.

67. "El último día de Longueira en la UDI," *The Clinic Online*, March 9, 2016, http://www.theclinic.cl/2016/03/09/el-ultimo-dia-de-longueira-en-la-udi/.

68. Longueira, *Mi testimonio de fe*, 23.

69. Several works refer extensively to de Castro's role in the Pinochet regime and serve as my main source material here. I draw especially on Juan Gabriel Valdés, *Pinochet's Economists: The Chicago School in Chile* (Cambridge: Cambridge University Press, 1995); Naomi Klein, *The Shock Doctrine: The Rise of Disaster Capitalism* (New York: Picador, 2007); Víctor Osorio and Iván Cabezas, *Los hijos de Pinochet* (Santiago: Planeta, 1995); and Pamela Constable and Arturo Valenzuela, *A Nation of Enemies: Chile under Pinochet* (New York: W. W. Norton, 1991).

70. See Constable and Valenzuela, *A Nation of Enemies*, 187.

71. Constable and Valenzuela note: "To these men [the Chicago Boys], the only kind of freedom that mattered was individual economic freedom, which de Castro argued was best guaranteed by an 'authoritarian government' with its 'impersonal' method of exercising power. Yet their definition of economic freedom was highly selective: businessmen were 'free' to move capital and raise prices, but workers were not 'free' to present collective demands or strike for better working conditions. Indeed, Chileans could be imprisoned or exiled for protesting policies aimed at making them economically 'free.'" Ibid., 188.

72. See Osorio and Cabezas, *Los hijos de Pinochet*, 40.

73. Ibid., 46.

74. Kathya Araujo and Danilo Martucelli, *Desafíos comunes: Retrato de la sociedad chilena y sus individuos*, vol. 1 (Santiago: LOM, 2012), 33. Araujo and Martucelli's *homo neoliberal* stands in stark contrast to Ernesto "Che" Guevara's famous idea of the "new man" (*hombre nuevo*)—socialist, anti-imperialist, community oriented—who would be at once the motor for and outcome of revolutionary change.

75. Joaquín Lavín, *Chile: Revolución silenciosa* (Santiago: Zig-zag, 1987), 11.

76. Here I paraphrase Araujo and Martiucelli's definition of *homo neoliberal*. See Araujo and Martucelli, *Desafíos comunes*, 33–34.

77. On the idea of the citizen-consumer, see also Tomás Moulian, *Chile actual: Anatomía de un mito* (Santiago: LOM, 1997), 81–123.

78. See Jorge Luis Borges, "Theme of the Traitor and the Hero," in *Labyrinths: Selected Stories and Other Writings*, ed. Donald A. Yates and James E. Irby (New York: New Directions, 1962), 72–75.

79. Ignacio Santa Cruz's "humanized" view of his uncle, the accomplice, dialogues interestingly with the filmmaker Marcela Said's "humanized" portrayal of Jorgelino Vergara, "El Mocito," a different kind of accomplice figure that I examine at length in chapter 5. Taken together, the two films may be hinting toward a tendency in some cultural production to lighten the moral and ethical burden that accomplices carry.

80. For commentary on the secretive nature of Guzmán's alleged homosexuality, see Alejandra Carmona, "La homosexualidad de Jaime Guzmán era un secreto a voces: Entrevista a Luis Larraín, presidente de Fundación Iguales," *El Mostrador*, August 27, 2013, http://www.elmostrador.cl/noticias/pais/2013/08/27/la-homosexuali dad-de-jaime-guzman-era-un-secreto-a-voces/.

81. Franco Fasola, "Ignacio Santa Cruz: 'La muerte de Guzmán se cocinó entre Pinochet y Contreras,'" *Caras*, October 18, 2013, http://www.caras.cl/cine/ignacio-san ta-cruz-la-muerte-de-guzman-se-cocino-entre-pinochet-y-contreras/.

82. Ibid.

83. Fernando A. Blanco, *Neoliberal Bonds: Undoing Memory in Chilean Art and Literature* (Columbus: Ohio State University Press, 2015), 55.

84. Fundación Jaime Guzmán, "Ante una película infamante," *El Mercurio*, October 17, 2013, Política section, C4.

85. Ignacio Santa Cruz, personal interview, September 3, 2015.

86. Ibid.

87. Avery F. Gordon, *Ghostly Matters: Haunting and the Sociological Imagination* (Minneapolis: University of Minnesota Press, 1997), 23.

88. Ibid., 19.

89. Ibid.

90. Rosario Guzmán Errázuriz, "Carta abierta a mi hermano Jaime," *La Tercera*, March 27, 2016, http://www.latercera.com/noticia/politica/2016/03/674-673995-9-car ta-abierta-a-mi-hermano-jaime.shtml. All subsequent quotations from the open letter can be found here.

91. Pablo Longueira, "Lenguaje odioso, retroceso de convivencia," *Diario Financiero*, May 9, 2016, https://www.df.cl/noticias/opinion/columnistas/lenguaje-odi oso-retroceso-de-convivencia/2016-05-06/212307.html.

92. Rosario Guzmán, *Mi hermano Jaime*, 96. "Just as the Gospel distinguishes between the sin and the sinner, [Jaime] distinguished between the person and the ideas that that person espoused."

93. Other open letters include Marco Antonio de la Parra, *Carta abierta a Pinochet:*

Monólogo de la clase media chilena con su padre (Santiago: Planeta, 1998); Armando Uribe Arce, *Carta abierta a Patricio Aylwin* (Santiago: Planeta, 1998); José Bengoa, *Carta abierta a Eduardo Frei Ruíz-Tagle* (Santiago: Planeta, 1999); and Armando Uribe Arce, *Carta abierta a Agustín Edwards* (Santiago: LOM, 2002).

94. Rosario Guzmán does not refer to Bellolio by name but calls him "ese tocayo tuyo" (your namesake). Bellolio is a young rising star in UDI who is currently taking steps to resuscitate the party's public image. Bellolio studied at the University of Chicago and has served on the board of the Jaime Guzmán Foundation. His genealogical links to Pinochet and Guzmán are therefore clear. In an opinion piece titled "La cruzada civilizatoria de Jaime Bellolio," Bellolio's brother Cristóbal notes that his brother's biggest political challenge is to "sacrifice Pinochet." He continues: "Can a collective that was born under the dictator's wing and with the expressed purpose of protecting the dictator's work renounce the dictator? It won't be easy, but the effort would be worth it. RN has already modified its 'Declaration of Principles' in that regard. Contrarian rantings by pinochetista deputies like Ignacio Urrutia or Jorge Ulloa should be reason for reproach within the new UDI-version-Jaime Bellolio. Also, the condemnation of human rights violations committed during the dictatorship should be unrestricted and without attenuation. That is the basic moral ground on which the political community of the twenty-first century must be established, and UDI has to decide if it is up to the task." Cristóbal Bellolio, "La cruzada civilizatoria de Jaime Bellolio," *El Mostrador*, January 26, 2016, http://www.elmostrador.cl/noticias/opinion /2016/01/26/la-cruzada-civilizatoria-de-jaime-bellolio/.

95. Recall that chapter 4 of Rosario Guzmán's book *Mi hermano Jaime* is titled "Sus ángeles y demonios" (His Angels and Demons).

96. The *boinazo* was a show of military power that took place on May 28, 1993. Just three years into the transition to democracy, then–Commander in Chief Augusto Pinochet wanted to show the citizenry and Patricio Aylwin's government that the military remained on the scene and could intervene at any moment. A group of soldiers wearing black berets (*boinas*) assembled in front of La Moneda palace that day to send that coercive message.

97. Akram notes that certain younger members of the right have publicly supported Piñera's "pyramid thesis" (see note 41) to rejuvenate the right's electoral strength. He cites the emergence of a new liberal right party called Evópoli (Evolución Política, Political Evolution Party) that stands as a challenge to UDI. Akram adds that Hernán Larraín Matte, son of the UDI hard-liner and president Hernán Larraín, has defected to Evópoli. Others, like Jaime Bellolio, have remained loyal to UDI but are working to renovate the party from within.

Chapter 3. Boundedness and Vulnerability

1. The noted Holocaust scholar Raul Hilberg discusses these categories in chapter 19 of his book *Perpetrators, Victims Bystanders: The Jewish Catastrophe, 1933–1945* (New York: Harper Perennial, 1992), 212–16.

2. Victoria J. Barnett, *Bystanders: Conscience and Complicity during the Holocaust* (Westport, CT: Praeger, 1999), 171.

3. Barnett writes: "Bystanders are confronted by a wide range of behavioral options, and they bear some responsibility for what happens. They may intervene to change the course of events. They may be apathetic, feeling that what is occurring has nothing to do with them. Or their emotions may be in turmoil: they may feel torn with anxiety, caught between a strong desire to become involved and the sense that they should do something. Other factors may influence their failure or readiness to help: the presence and behavior of people around them; feelings of powerlessness or fear; and a sense of identification with the victim or, conversely, indifference or active prejudice against the victim." Barnett, *Bystanders*, 10.

4. Diamela Eltit, *Puño y letra: Juicio oral* (Santiago: Planeta, 2005).

5. I discuss this case at some length in chapter 1.

6. Daniel Noemí uses the terms *author* and *documentarian* to describe Eltit's authorial function. See Daniel Noemí, "De *Puño y letra*: Justicia, documento y ética," in *Diamela Eltit: Redes locales, redes globales*, ed. Rubí Carreño Bolívar (Frankfurt: Iberoamericana, 2009), 201–13.

7. Barnett, *Bystanders*, 11.

8. Judith Butler, *Precarious Life: The Powers of Mourning and Violence* (New York: Verso, 2004), 134.

9. Ibid., 29.

10. Ibid.

11. Ibid., 135.

12. Adriana Cavarero, *Horrorism: Naming Contemporary Violence*, trans. William McCuaig (New York: Columbia University Press), 21.

13. Ibid.

14. Butler, *Precarious Life*, 29.

15. Ibid., 28.

16. For a thorough analysis of the memory script of Pinochet as savior, see Steve J. Stern, *Remembering Pinochet's Chile: On the Eve of London 1998* (Durham, NC: Duke University Press, 2004).

17. For deep analysis of the transnational dimensions of postdictatorial justice, see especially Naomi Roht-Arriaza, *The Pinochet Effect: Transnational Justice in the Age of Human Rights* (Philadelphia: University of Pennsylvania Press, 2005), and Kathryn Sikkink, *The Justice Cascade: How Human Rights Prosecutions Are Changing World Politics* (New York: W. W. Norton, 2011).

18. Cath Collins, *Post-Transitional Justice: Human Rights Trials in Chile and El Salvador* (University Park: Pennsylvania State University Press, 2010), 147.

19. Ibid.

20. A case in point: in July 2010 the Chilean Catholic Church caused widespread concern by issuing a call for presidential pardons (*indultos*) that would have had potential effects on the situations of some human rights violators serving prison sentences for crimes against humanity. The bill, which was eventually rejected by President

Sebastián Piñera, came to be known as the *indulto bicentenario* and risked instrumental-izing the bicentennial moment by turning it into an opportunity for reflection and generosity of heart toward human rights violators. The Church offered the bill to Congress in a spirit of clemency toward those it felt were too old or too ill to serve out their sentences. We recall, too, that similar arguments from the political right surfaced in the aftermath of Pinochet's detention in London (1998). The right has also maneuvered in other moments to mitigate sentences or improve prison conditions for perpetrators.

21. See especially Giorgio Agamben, *Remnants of Auschwitz: The Witness and the Archive*, trans. Daniel Heller-Roazen (New York: Zone Books, 1999), 18–20.

22. Nancy L. Rosenblum, "Justice and the Experience of Injustice" in *Breaking the Cycles of Hatred: Memory, Law, and Repair*, ed. Martha Minow (Princeton, NJ: Princeton University Press, 2002), 82.

23. Ibid., 78.

24. Cath Collins also acknowledges the imperfections of transitional justice, despite its vital importance. She writes that one possible remainder of justice, in the Chilean case, is precisely the ability to prosecute civilian accomplices: "Criminal cases lend themselves to [a] kind of reductionism and are inherently poorly suited to addressing questions of civilian complicity or enrichment." They tend to focus on defendants whose culpability is easier to prove. See Cath Collins, "Human Rights Defense in and through the Courts in (Post) Pinochet Chile," *Radical History Review* 124 (January 2016): 137.

25. Idelber Avelar, *The Untimely Present: Postdictatorial Fiction and the Task of Mourning* (Durham, NC: Duke University Press, 1999), 5.

26. Ibid.

27. Shoshana Felman, *The Juridical Unconscious: Trials and Traumas in the Twentieth Century* (Cambridge, MA: Harvard University Press, 2002), 54–55.

28. The Beagle Channel conflict was a notorious dispute over a major waterway. It drove the Chilean and Argentine dictatorships to the brink of armed conflict. In 1978 papal intervention was sought as a means of arbitration.

29. Those DINA agents were Manuel Contreras, Pedro Espinoza Bravo, Armando Fernández Larios, José Zara Holger, Raúl Eduardo Iturriaga Neumann, and Jorge Iturriaga Neumann.

30. The attempt to "modernize" the army's public image dates from General Juan Emilio Cheyre's well-known speech "Ejército de Chile: El fin de una visión," originally published in *La Tercera* newspaper on November 5, 2004. The full text is available at http://www.dawson2000.com/cheyre1.htm.

31. Zalaquett is quoted in Roht-Arriaza, *The Pinochet Effect*, 80.

32. In 2000 Chile revamped its criminal justice system. Trials are now oral, public, and adversarial in nature, and prosecutors rather than judges take the lead in investigations. Under the old system, which was used for many early human rights cases, judges served as the main investigators and arbiters, and all testimony occurred in writing. Witnesses' answers were recorded in documents from which the court's questions were ultimately excluded. Such documents gave the impression that they were uninterrupted,

spontaneously produced testimonies. In reality, the nature of those testimonies was wholly determined by the questions the court had asked. Witnesses were not allowed to stray from the proposed line of questioning. Often this resulted in documents that left out important details or emotional content that the court considered to be beyond the scope of the desired legal finality. I mention this to reinforce the idea that courts *require* a certain kind of testimony based primarily on the accrual of certain "facts." Court archives thus reflect those desired ends.

33. Eltit, *Puño y letra*, 160–61, emphasis mine.

34. Ibid., 154–55, emphasis mine.

35. Zambelli's highly illogical discourse reminds readers of the crisis of truth and memory evidenced in the voice of another of Eltit's *locos* (madmen), "El Padre Mío." Readers will recall that madness as a mechanism for questioning and exploring the contours of the testimonial act has been a repeated concern in Eltit's literary projects, not only in *El padre mío* but also in *El infarto del alma*. See Diamela Eltit, *El padre mío* (Santiago: Francisco Zegers Editor, 1989), and Diamela Eltit and Paz Errázuriz, *El infarto del alma* (Santiago: Francisco Zegers Editor, 1994). In both of these texts, the figure of madness, just as in *Puño y letra*, challenges us to look for alternative, metaphorical, and symbolic levels of truth-telling. The testimony of the *loco*, with its alternative logic, speaks, we might say, a different kind of truth. For a more developed discussion of how Eltit deploys and challenges the testimonial genre, see chapter 1 of my *Chile in Transition: The Poetics and Politics of Memory* (Gainesville: University Press of Florida, 2006).

36. Eltit, *Puño y letra*, 39.

37. Ibid., 83.

38. Ibid., 89.

39. Ibid., 127.

40. Derrida writes: "Perjury . . . presupposes this sworn word, which it betrays. Perjury does indeed threaten all bearing witness, but this threat is irreducible in the scene of the sworn word and attestation. This structural threat is at once distinct and inseparable from the finitude that any testimony also presupposes, for any witness can make a mistake in good faith; he can have a limited, false perception, one that in any number of ways is misleading about what he is speaking about; this finitude, which is just as irreducible and without which there would be no place for bearing witness, is nonetheless other, in its effects, than the kind that obliges us to believe and makes lying or perjury always possible. There are thus two heterogeneous effects of the same finitude here, or two essentially different approaches to finitude: one that goes by way of error or hallucination in good faith, and one that goes by way of deceit, perjury, bad faith." Jacques Derrida, "Poetics and Politics of Witnessing," in Derrida, *Sovereignties in Question: The Poetics of Paul Celan*, ed. Thomas Dutoit and Outi Pasanen (New York: Fordham University Press, 2005), 78.

41. Eltit, *Puño y letra*, 81, 104.

42. Ibid., 91.

43. Eltit, *Puño y letra*, 30. The latter quote comes from Erinn C. Gilson, *The Ethics*

of Vulnerability: A Feminist Analysis of Social Life and Practice (New York: Routledge, 2014), 77.

44. Gilson, *The Ethics of Vulnerability*, 77.

45. Elizabeth Jelin, *State Repression and the Labors of Memory*, trans. Judy Rein and Marcial Godoy-Anativia (Minneapolis: University of Minnesota Press, 2003), 33–34.

46. Gilson, *The Ethics of Vulnerability*, 75.

47. Ibid., 116.

48. On the subject of human failure to see another's pain, see Susan Sontag, *Regarding the Pain of Others* (New York: Farrar, Straus & Giroux, 2003).

49. Eltit, *Puño y letra*, 27.

50. Ibid., 26.

51. Jorge Escalante, Nancy Guzmán, Javier Rebolledo, and Pedro Vega capture these images in *Los crímenes que estremecieron a Chile: Las memorias de* La Nación *para no olvidar* (Santiago: Ceibo Ediciones, 2013), 192–93.

52. Ibid., 13.

53. Ibid., 187.

54. Ibid., 185.

55. Ibid., 189.

56. For an excellent study of CADA's "art actions," see Robert Neustadt, *CADA DÍA: La creación de un arte social* (Santiago: Cuarto Propio, 2001).

57. Eltit, *Puño y letra*, 189.

58. Diamela Eltit, "La memoria pantalla (acerca de las imágenes públicas como políticas de desmemoria)," *Revista de crítica cultural* 32 (November 2005): 33.

59. I say this scenario is rare because normally the underlings do not pay a judicial price when justice gets meted out symbolically. Trials tend to focus on top-ranking perpetrators. The case of Jorgelinc Vergara, "El Mocito," which I study in chapter 4, provides a good example of an accomplice who may have participated in crimes but is ultimately left unscathed in exchange for providing key information that helps bring the military's upper echelons to justice.

60. Raúl Eduardo Iturriaga Neumann's video statement was published by a group of his supporters in 2012: "Libertad para el General Eduardo Iturriaga Preso Político," YouTube, 3:58, July 21, 2012, https://www.youtube.com/watch?v=sT2yJuaXKUc.

61. Eltit, *Puño y letra*, 21.

62. See Amartya Sen, *The Idea of Justice* (Cambridge, MA: Belknap Press, 2009).

63. See Tomás Moulian, *Chile actual: Anatomía de un mito* (Santiago: LOM/ARCIS, 1997).

Chapter 4. Framing the Accomplice

1. Steve J. Stern uses the term *memory season* to refer to the unique presence that memories of the dictatorship have every September in the Chilean public sphere. According to Stern, commemorative dates function as "[memory] sites in time":

"Particular events and dates, whether spectacular scandals such as car bomb murders of former Chilean dignitaries on foreign soil, or culturally charged anniversary dates such as 11 September or May Day, concentrat[e] the symbolic power to 'convene' or project memory." The September memory season includes not only the anniversary date of the coup but also the September 18 celebration of Chilean Independence Day. The confluence of these symbolic dates makes September particularly disposed to memory battles. Although every September since 1973 has been important, major anniversaries of the coup such as the tenth, twentieth, thirtieth, and fortieth have proved to have even more intense convening power for memory battles, both public and private. See Steve J. Stern, *Remembering Pinochet's Chile: On the Eve of London 1998* (Durham, NC: Duke University Press, 2004), 122.

2. Primo Levi, *The Drowned and the Saved*, trans. Raymond Rosenthal (New York: Vintage International, 1988), 36–69. Levi is particularly interested in "the network of human relationships inside the Lagers . . . [that] could not be reduced to the two blocs of victims and perpetrators" (37).

3. "Los cien rostros de la dictadura," *The Clinic Online*, September 3, 2013, http://www.theclinic.cl/2013/09/03/los-100-rostros-de-la-dictadura/.

4. Osvaldo Romo Mena was one of Chile's most notorious civilian torturers. The journalist Nancy Guzmán studies his life and perspectives in *Romo: Confesiones de un torturador* (Santiago de Chile: Planeta, 2000). General Manuel Contreras was the head of DINA.

5. See Horacio Verbitsky, *El vuelo* (Buenos Aires: Planeta, 1995).

6. Claudia Feld, "Entre la visibilidad y la justicia: Los testimonios televisivos de represores en la Argentina," *Encuentros uruguayos* 2, no. 2 (2009): 52.

7. Ibid., 42–57.

8. Following the 1999–2000 Mesa de Diálogo (Dialogue Roundtable), the Chilean military recognized that some bodies of the disappeared had been thrown into the sea. However, no individual military official ever spoke publicly about how such missions were carried out. This changed on July 7, 2003, when a retired soldier, Subofficial Juan Carlos Molina H., testified on National Television's (TVN) nightly news program, *24 Horas*, that he had participated in two missions in 1979 to dispose of the bodies of nine *desaparecidos*. In his interview with a reporter, Claudio Fariña, Molina admitted to having witnessed the dumping of bodies from Puma helicopters into waters off the coast of Quintero. This type of disposal of bodies, which according to Molina continued to occur until at least 1981, was a reaction by the military to the 1978 discovery of (and subsequent publicity surrounding) a common grave located at Lonquén, outside Santiago. The military's fear of future discoveries caused them to dig up victims' remains and dispose of them in undisclosed locations. Molina, a mechanic who was asked to provide technical support for helicopters, told Fariña that the bodies were placed in sacks and bound to railroad ties so that they would sink more easily in the ocean. Though for years he could not admit to what he had witnessed, the death of his child, in 2003, prompted him to come forward and voice his shame publicly. TVN's report was an important public revelation of the official silences that had surrounded such

missions for thirty years. Unlike the case of Scilingo in Argentina, however, Molina's confession did not prompt other military officials to come forward.

9. Cath Collins provides a fair assessment of Piñera's shocking declaration of a "discursive war on diehard Pinochet supporters supposedly from his own side" via his reference to the dictatorship's *passive accomplices*: "Piñera's sudden conversion seemed a little surprising to those whose memories stretch back to 1999, as [General Manuel] Contreras could not resist pointing out in an open letter from prison. In the heady days shortly after Pinochet's arrest in the United Kingdom [in 1998], a fervent Piñera whipped up a storm at a right-wing rally in Santiago, proposing a commando raid on London's Bow Street magistrates' court to bring 'el Capitán General' home. As recently as 2009, Piñera's presidential campaign contained scarcely veiled promises to 'see the old soldiers right,' were he elected, by ensuring a 'correct'—that is, expansive—application of the 1978 self-amnesty law. However, times changed, and Piñera clearly planned to change with them, or even to get ahead of the game. His pronouncement may have had as much to do with internal turf wars as with principled conversion: Piñera employed the anniversary to attempt to draw a line in the sand. The 'bad' Right—dinosaurs who still defend the regime—were placed in contradistinction to a 'good,' modernizing, democratic Right to which Piñera wished to lay claim. Although Piñera's broader longevity is seriously in question, it may yet prove correct that this modernizing versus backward-looking rift is about to become the definitive feature of the political Right. If so, the undoubtedly potent issue of the dictatorship and attitudes to it is likely to continue to be a touchstone." Cath Collins, "Human Rights Defense in and through the Courts in (Post) Pinochet Chile," *Radical History Review* 124 (January 2016): 137.

10. Nelly Richard, *Crítica de la memoria (1990–2010)* (Santiago de Chile: Ediciones Universidad Diego Portales, 2010).

11. Alexander Wilde, "Irruptions of Memory: Expressive Politics in Chile's Transition to Democracy," *Journal of Latin American Studies* 31, no. 2 (1999): 473–500. The noun *irruption*, intentionally spelled with an *i*, derives from the Spanish verb *irrumpir* and refers to the manner in which traumatic memories appear on the political and cultural scene in ways that are often sudden and unanticipated.

12. DINA (Dirección de Inteligencia Nacional) was the Pinochet regime's first secret police organization. It functioned from November 1973 until 1977, when it was replaced by CNI (Central Nacional de Informaciones). Because the sole survivor of the Simón Bolívar detention center wishes to remain anonymous, he is not named in this chapter.

13. The four men whose remains were found are Ángel Guerrero (Movimiento de Izquierda Revolucionaria, Leftist Revolutionary Movement, MIR), Lincoyán Berríos (Partido Comunista, Communist Party, PC), Horacio Cepeda (PC), and Fernando Ortiz (PC).

14. Javier Rebolledo, *La danza de los cuervos* (Santiago de Chile: Ceibo Ediciones, 2012).

15. Both television programs can be accessed online. See *Mentiras verdaderas*,

YouTube, 1:54:45, September 9, 2013, https://www.youtube.com/watch?v=ZJGDwvYn VoA; and *Foreign Correspondent*, "Facing the Past," *ABC News Australia*, 27:47, March 25, 2014, http://www.abc.net.au/foreign/content/2014/s3971320.htm.

16. Richard, *Crítica de la memoria (1990–2010)*, 117.

17. Michael J. Lazzara, "Radiografía del pinochetismo: Una conversación con la documentalista Marcela Said," *Chasqui: Revista de literatura latinoamericana* 42, no. 1 (2013): 254.

18. Ibid., 252.

19. See Marina Loreto Donoso Rivas et al., *El Mocito: Un documental de Marcela Said y Jean de Certeau*, Serie Recordar y Conversar para un Nunca Más, Documentales para la memoria histórica de violaciones masivas y sistemáticas de Derechos Humanos, Santiago de Chile, Instituto Nacional de Derechos Humanos, no date, http://www.indh .cl/descarga-de-material.

20. Laub writes: "The absence of an empathic listener, or more radically, the absence of an *addressable other*, an other who can hear the anguish of one's memories and thus affirm and recognize their realness, annihilates the story." Dori Laub, M.D., "Bearing Witness or the Vicissitudes of Listening," in *Testimony: Crises of Witnessing in Literature, Psychoanalysis, and History*, ed. Shoshana Felman and Dori Laub, M.D. (New York: Routledge, 1992), 68.

21. This idea echoes, to some extent, the logic of the South African Truth and Reconciliation Commission, whose final report was published in 1998.

22. The Mesa de Diálogo (Dialogue Roundtable, 1999–2000) brought together representatives of the armed forces, the Catholic Church, the government, and other sectors of society with the purpose of discovering the whereabouts of the detained and disappeared. The initiative began during the presidency of Eduardo Frei Ruíz-Tagle and ended during the first year of Ricardo Lagos's presidency. At the roundtable's conclusion, the military gave the family members a list containing information about two hundred disappeared people. It was later discovered that much of that information was false. The "Mesa" therefore left many family members infuriated and mistrustful of both the military and the government. They felt that the military's response was an affront both to their pain and to their decades-long search for truth and justice.

23. Marcela Said, personal interview, Santiago de Chile, September 2013.

24. Ana Amado, *La imagen justa: Cine argentino y política (1980–2007)* (Buenos Aires: Colihue, 2009), 165.

25. Marcela Said turns Juan Morales Salgado into a fictional character in her film *Los perros* (Chile: Cinéma Defacto; France: Jirafa Films, 2017).

26. As examples of this tendency, we can mention the projects of novelists like Alejandro Zambra and Nona Fernández or the films of Bettina Perut and Iván Osnovikoff, among others.

27. In an article on the Nazi sympathies of the Chilean writer Miguel Serrano, Diamela Eltit defines "popular fascism" as follows: "Oppressed social groups . . . internalize all of the exclusionary tenets that emanate from society's dominant voices. They appropriate those discriminatory voices and use them against their peers and,

consequently, they reproduce in their own social spheres identical hierarchies to the ones that impact them in their own lives. That is what popular fascism is." Diamela Eltit, "Hagamos memoria: Cretinos filonazis," *The Clinic Online*, April 10, 2012, http://www.theclinic.cl/2012/04/10/hagamos-memoria-cretinos-filonazis/. In another text, Eltit coins the phrase "nomadic bodies" to describe subjects who adapt and mutate ideologically to conform to dominant power structures. See Diamela Eltit, "Cuerpos nómadas," in *Emergencias: Escritos sobre literatura, arte y política* (Santiago de Chile: Planeta/Ariel, 2000), 61–77.

28. Javier Rebolledo, *La danza del los cuervos*, 58, 175.

29. Ibid., 216.

30. Ibid., 12.

31. "Before Hannah Arendt, Martin Heidegger, Arendt's teacher in Freiburg in the mid-twenties, had already used the expression 'fabrication of corpses' to define the extermination camps. And, curiously enough, for Heidegger the 'fabrication of corpses' implied, just as for Levi, that it is not possible to speak of death in the case of extermination victims, that they did not truly die, but were rather only pieces produced in the process of an assembly line production." Giorgio Agamben, *Remnants of Auschwitz: The Witness and the Archive*, trans. Daniel Heller-Roazen (New York: Zone Books, 1999), 73. There is, of course, a certain irony that lurks behind Agamben's evocation of Heidegger in this context given that Heidegger collaborated with and was a member of the Nazi Party for twelve years (1933–45).

32. Javier Rebolledo invited Mosciatti to serve as a presenter at the launch of Rebolledo's third book, *A la sombra de los cuervos: Los cómplices civiles de la dictadura*, at Club Providencia, Santiago de Chile, in August 2015. Mosciatti's reading of the phenomenon of civilian complicity with the Chilean dictatorship was well informed and boldly honest.

33. Leonor Arfuch, *El espacio biográfico: Dilemas de la subjetividad contemporánea* (Buenos Aires: Fondo de Cultura Económica, 2002), 124.

34. Leigh A. Payne, *Unsettling Accounts: Neither Truth nor Reconciliation in Confessions of State Violence* (Durham, NC: Duke University Press), 23.

35. Nelly Richard, "Las confesiones de un torturador y su (abusivo) montaje periodístico," *Revista de crítica cultural* 22 (2001): 14–19.

36. Rebolledo, *La danza de los cuervos*, 275.

37. Leonor Arfuch, *Crítica cultural entre política y poética* (Buenos Aires: Fondo de Cultura Económica, 2008), 36.

38. Cherie Zalaquett, "Pinochet nos dejó absolutamente solos: Entrevista a Manuel Contreras," *El Mercurio*, September 11, 2004, https://es.groups.yahoo.com/neo/groups/testimonios-chile/conversations/messages/3262.

39. Arendt, Hannah. *Responsibility and Judgment* (New York: Schocken Books, 2003), 48.

40. Ibid.

41. Ibid.

42. "Before discussing separately the motives that impelled some prisoners to

collaborate to some extent with the Lager authorities, however, it is necessary to declare the imprudence of issuing hasty moral judgment on such human cases. Certainly the greatest responsibility lies with the system, the very structure of the totalitarian state; the concurrent guilt on the part of individual big and small collaborators (never likeable, never transparent!) is always difficult to evaluate." Levi, *The Drowned and the Saved*, 44.

43. "Nelson Caucoto: Protagonista de *El Mocito* también es una víctima," *Radio Cooperativa*, March 30, 2014, http://www.cooperativa.cl/noticias/pais/dd-hh/nelson-cau coto-protagonista-de-el-mocito-tambien-es-una-victima/2011-12-12/132259.html.

44. On the subject of military conscripts' memories, see Leith Passmore, *The Wars inside Chile's Barracks: Remembering Military Service under Pinochet* (Madison: University of Wisconsin Press, 2017).

45. Adriana Rivas's niece made a film that explores Rivas's lack of candor and the sordid details of her history. See Lissette Orozco, *El pacto de Adriana* (Chile: Salmón Producciones/ Storyboard Media, 2017).

46. There are inevitably moments in which Vergara, despite his will, loses control of his discourse. One of these moments comes when he talks about playing tennis with Lieutenant Armando Fernández Larios, a notorious DINA agent. When Cretton asks Vergara how he felt about the tennis matches, Vergara responds: "I really felt nothing. I didn't relate one thing [the violence] to another [the tennis match]. I was just living in the moment." Vergara clearly wants to compartmentalize these uncomfortable "grays" in his experience. Interestingly, the example of the tennis match brings to mind Primo Levi's well-known story of the soccer game between the SS and the Sonderkommando, symbolic of the very idea of the gray zone. Like the soccer game, the tennis match between Vergara and Fernández Larios seems to say, with Levi, "We have embraced you, corrupted you, dragged you to the bottom with us." At the same time, however, we must recognize a key difference between the case of Vergara and that of the Sonderkommando, Jews who were forced to labor in the camps and clear bodies from the gas chambers. While the Sonderkommando is squarely situated within the gray zone because its members were forced to collaborate with the Nazis, Vergara, though still an inhabitant of the gray zone, is arguably much less gray because it was his *will* to join DINA. I compare the tennis match and the soccer game simply to observe similarities in the dynamics at play, not to equate the Sonderkommando to Jorgelino Vergara. See Levi, *The Drowned and the Saved*, 55.

47. I have loosely paraphrased these quotes based on Vergara's logic throughout the interview.

48. In a way, they remind us of the Prats daughters. (See chapter 3.)

49. Prosecutions of "economic accomplices" such as Pablo Longueira (chapter 2) and many others may eventually come, but these people will be tried for financial crimes committed during the transition to democracy, not for their specific involvements with the Pinochet regime. In short, while the country is starting to demand accountability from the economic accomplices *of the transition*, it does not seem as interested in seeking judicial prosecutions of lower-ranking accomplices *of the dictatorship*.

Chapter 5. Complacent Subjects

1. Nicolás Casullo, *Las cuestiones* (Buenos Aires: Fondo de Cultura Económica, 2007), 240–41.

2. See, in particular, Nelly Richard, "El mercado de las confesiones: Lo público y lo privado en los testimonios de Mónica Madariaga, Gladys Marín y Clara Szczaranski," in *El salto de Minerva: Intelectuales, género y Estado en América Latina*, ed. Mabel Moraña and María Rosa Olivera-Williams (Frankfurt/Madrid: Iberoamericana, 2005), 299–313; Leonor Arfuch, *Memoria y autobiografía: Exploraciones en los límites* (Buenos Aires: Fondo de Cultura Económica, 2003); and Fernando A. Blanco, *Desmemoria y perversión: Privatizar lo público, mediatizar lo íntimo, administrar lo privado* (Santiago: Cuarto Propio, 2010).

3. See Leonor Arfuch, *El espacio biográfico: Dilemas de la subjetividad contemporánea* (Buenos Aires: Fondo de Cultura Económica, 2002).

4. Richard, "El mercado de las confesiones," 300.

5. Arfuch, *Memoria y autobiografía*, 47.

6. Blanco, *Desmemoria y perversión*, 52.

7. Arfuch, *Memoria y autobiografía*, 29.

8. Mónica Echeverría Yáñez, *¡Háganme callar!* (Santiago: Ceibo Ediciones, 2016), 16.

9. Two major scandals erupted in 2015 that demonstrated clear illicit ties between Chilean political elites and powerful financial and business interests. The first case, known as "Penta-gate," came to light when it was discovered that the Penta Investment Bank had been illegally funding the campaigns of political actors of *both* the right and the left. In addition to politicians from the right-wing Unión Democrática Independiente (Independent Democratic Union, UDI) and Renovación Nacional (National Renovation, RN) parties, certain politicians from Nueva Mayoría (New Majority) and the progressive left were also implicated, including Marco Enríquez-Ominami, whom I study in a later part of this chapter. As Penta-gate unfolded, it subsequently came to light that Sociedad Química y Minera de Chile (The Chilean Chemical and Mining Company, Soquimich) had also been crafting false invoices (*boletas ideológicamente falsas*) to cover up the funneling of money to politicians.

10. Ibid., 192.

11. Katherine Hite, *When the Romance Ended: Leaders of the Chilean Left, 1968–1998* (New York: Columbia University Press, 2000), 185. Chapter 2 of Hite's book, titled "Chile's Revolutionary Generation," provides a useful overview of the structural and ideological composition of the Chilean left in the early 1970s. By 1973, MAPU found itself engaged in a hotly contentious debate over the role of armed struggle. One faction, MAPU-Obrero Campesino, led by Jaime Gazmuri and Enrique Correa, supported Allende's position on revolution through peaceful means; the other faction, MAPU-Garretón, led by Óscar Guillermo Garretón and Eduardo Aquevedo, radicalized and advocated for armed struggle.

12. Cristina Moyano Barahona notes that, "according to the Rettig Report, only

twenty-four MAPU militants were direct victims of repression. Of these, only two belonged to the party's elite sector, Juan Mayno and Eugenio Ruíz-Tagle; the rest were mostly farmers who had previously been affiliated, in the 1960s, with the agricultural sector of the Christian Democratic Party and later joined MAPU." Cristina Moyano Barahona, *El MAPU durante la dictadura: Saberes y prácticas políticas para una micro-historia de la renovación socialista en Chile, 1973–1989* (Santiago: Ediciones Universidad Alberto Hurtado, 2010), 500.

13. For a convincing outline of this transformation, see Esteban Valenzuela Van Treek, "El MAPU y el rol transformador de las élites iluministas: Revolución, pragmatismo y disidencia," *Revista de ciencia política* 31, no. 2 (2011): 187–206. Van Treek identifies four phases in the evolution of MAPU: "messianic," "ideological," "skeptical," and "pragmatic."

14. Hite, *When the Romance Ended*, 194.

15. Ibid. In tandem with Hite's observation, the historian Alfredo Jocelyn-Holt Letelier adds the following about Chile's transition to democracy: "In the final assessment, what has been imposed [on the country] is an intoxicating, always unsatisfied desire for modernization and not one or another political tendency. Politicians have been defeated although, we must admit, they still survive. They have set a project in motion [modernization] that now escapes their control." Alfredo Jocelyn-Holt Letelier, *El Chile perplejo: Del avanzar sin transar al transar sin parar* (Santiago: Planeta/Ariel, 1998), 226.

16. Wendy Brown, *Undoing the Demos: Neoliberalism's Stealth Revolution* (New York: Zone Books, 2015), 222.

17. Ibid.

18. Moyano Barahona, *El MAPU durante la dictadura*, 502–3.

19. Patricio Navia, *Las grandes alamedas: El Chile post Pinochet* (Santiago: La Tercera-Mondadori, 2004), 236. Navia pinpoints the origin of this debate in two documents that appeared in 1998: "Renovar la concertación: La fuerza de nuestras ideas" (*El Mercurio*, June 17, 1998), representative of the autocomplaciente perspective, and "La gente tiene razón" (*La Tercera*, June 14, 1998), representative of the autoflagelante perspective.

20. An early philosophical study on complacency by Robert Bruce Raup argues that the human organism gravitates toward complacency and equilibrium as its most comfortable state of being. While meaningful change comes about through periods of "disturbance" to complacency, the human organism always tends back toward a complacent state, particularly in the wake of "adventure." Robert Bruce Raup, *Complacency: The Foundation of Human Behavior* (New York: Macmillan, 1925).

21. Steve J. Stern, *Remembering Pinochet's Chile: On the Eve of London 1998* (Durham, NC: Duke University Press, 2004), xxvii.

22. Jocelyn-Holt Letelier, *El Chile perplejo*, 275, 276.

23. Echeverría Yánez, ¡Háganme callar!, 23.

24. Ibid., 192.

25. See Tomás Moulian, *Chile actual: Anatomía de un mito* (Santiago: LOM-ARCIS, 1997), 81–123.

26. As evidence of his pro-Concertación stance, Navia writes: "As long as the Concertación can manage to carry out its intellectual debates, symbolically speaking, 'west' of Plaza Italia, that is, from within the heart of the new middle class, the most important governing coalition in Chilean history will also have a future as bright as the one that awaits the 1990s in the country's history books." Navia, *Las grandes alamedas*, 245. Navia's critique is not so much of the Concertación and its modernizing prowess as it is of the fact that the coalition, in his opinion, had not done a good enough job responding to the needs of the ample and emerging middle class that neoliberalism created.

27. Eugenio Tironi, *Sin miedo, sin odio, sin violencia: Una historia personal del NO* (Santiago: Planeta/Ariel, 2013), 13, 21.

28. Ibid., 29. Goffman's work has been influential in my own thinking throughout this book (see especially chapter 1). I was surprised to find that Tironi was also thinking about how Goffman's reasoning might apply to himself.

29. Tironi, *Sin miedo, sin odio, sin violencia*, 17. The original reference can be found in Daniel Kahneman, *Thinking, Fast and Slow* (New York: Farrar, Straus & Giroux, 2013), 204.

30. Tironi, *Sin miedo, sin odio, sin violencia*, 17.

31. Moyano Barahona, *El MAPU durante la dictadura*, 501.

32. Ibid.

33. Mónica Echeverría Yánez traces Marambio's fortune back to 1993. In 1993, in the midst of the economic crisis generated by the fall of the Soviet Union, Marambio and Carlos Cardoen created a milk and fruit juice production plant called Río Zaza. Simultaneously, Marambio started a real estate investment company, which originated in Panama, as well as a construction company. After amassing a multimillion-dollar fortune, he continued to do business in Cuba while also managing massive real estate interests in Chile. By 2008, Cuba, facing a shortage of foreign currency, prohibited foreign investors from withdrawing large sums of money. Marambio therefore became furious when Raúl Castro froze almost $30 million of Río Zaza's assets. Marambio's protests sparked an investigation by Cuba's Central Bank that resulted in accusations of bribery, embezzlement, and falsification of documents. In 2012 the International Court of Arbitration (Paris) cleared Marambio of charges, nonetheless solidifying his rift with Cuba. Today Marambio continues to do business in Chile, holds interests in the leftist Universidad Arcis (mired in scandal and on the verge of closing its doors as of this writing), and was the major financier for Marco Enríquez-Ominami's 2009 presidential run. See Echeverría Yánez, *¡Háganme callar!*, 192. See also "Potbelly and Rumbling Stomachs," *The Economist*, August 26, 2010, http://www.economist.com /node/16886803.

34. Marambio, *Las armas de ayer* (Santiago: *La Tercera*-Debate, 2007), 51.

35. Joseph Campbell, *The Hero with a Thousand Faces* (Princeton, NJ: Princeton University Press, 1949).

36. Ibid., 16.

37. Ibid., 22, 24.

38. Ibid., 38, 41.

39. Ibid., 49.

40. Ibid., 52.

41. Ibid., 97.

42. Ibid., 114–15.

43. Ibid., 171.

44. MIR gave the name "Operation Return" (Operación Retorno) to its plan to infiltrate Chile during the Pinochet regime. Invented in exile, the plan sent clandestine groups of militants back to the country between 1977 and 1979 with the goal of carrying out armed actions and mobilizing popular support.

45. Ibid., 181.

46. Ibid., 179.

47. Ibid., 22.

48. For more on this, see Eugenia Paleraki, "Max Marambio: *Las armas de ayer*," 2008. Paleraki's review of Marambio's book is no longer available on the internet.

49. Marambio, *Las armas de ayer*, 181. My reference here is to the book's final sentence.

50. John Beverley, *Latinamericanism after 9/11* (Durham, NC: Duke University Press, 2011), 99.

51. Eugenio Tironi, *Crónica de viaje: Chile y la ruta a la felicidad* (Santiago: Aguilar-El Mercurio, 2006), 16.

52. For more on this, see Rafael Gumucio, "Chile entre dos centenarios: Historia de una democracia frustrada," *Polis: Revista latinoamericana* 10 (2005), https://polis.revues.org/7463#text.

53. See Eduardo Aquevedo, "Eugenio Tironi: ¿Neoliberal desde los 70 o nuevo caso de 'transformismo'?," *Ciencias sociales hoy-Weblog*, September 3, 2012, https://aquevedo.wordpress.com/2012/09/03/eugenio-tironi-neoliberal-desde-los-70-o-nuevo-caso-de-transformismo/.

54. See Claudia Farfán and Gloria Faúndez, "MAPU: Asalto al poder," *Qué pasa*, May 27, 2001, http://www.archivochile.com/Izquierda_chilena/mapus/sobre_mapus/ICHsobremapus0005.pdf.

55. Héctor A. Hermosilla, "Jóvenes rebeldes y armados: Teoría, identidad y praxis del MAPU-Lautaro" (undergraduate thesis, University of Chile, 2007).

56. Moyano Barahona, *El MAPU durante la dictadura*, 391–420.

57. Tironi, *Crónica*, 114.

58. Ibid., 145.

59. Ibid., 129.

60. Ibid., 163.

61. Ibid., 200.

62. Ibid., 187.

63. Ibid.

64. Ibid., 189.

65. Ibid., 190.

66. See "Eugenio Tironi: Soy un capitalista reformador," *La Tercera online*, August

11, 2012, http://diario.latercera.com/2012/08/11/01/contenido/reportajes/25-115872-9-eugenio-tironi-soy-un-capitalista-reformador.shtml.

67. Ibid.

68. "Eugenio Tironi: La muerte del MAPU," *Emprende futuro*, January 17, 2006. The website is no longer available.

69. "Eugenio Tironi: Soy un capitalista reformador."

70. Patricio Navia, *El díscolo: Conversaciones con Marco Enríquez-Ominami* (Santiago: Random House Mondadori, 2009), 66.

71. Tomás Moulian, a Chilean sociologist and former MAPU member who still maintains a Marxist vision that is critical of the paths chosen by former comrades like Garretón and Tironi, defines *transformismo* (transformism) in the following way: "I use the term 'transformism' to refer to the long process that took place during the dictatorship to find a pathway out of dictatorship that would permit the continuation of basic structures hidden behind other political clothing: democratic clothing. The objective of this process is *gatopardismo*, change without [real] change. Furthermore, transformism refers to the operations that occur in Chile today to ensure that the 'infrastructure' created under dictatorship is reproduced but divested of its bothersome form, of the brutal and naked 'superstructures' of the past." Moulian, *Chile actual*, 145.

72. Marco Enríquez-Ominami and Carlos Ominami, *Animales políticos: Diálogos filiales*, prologue by Rafael Gumucio (Santiago: Planeta, 2004), 176.

73. Ibid., 141.

74. Ibid., 138.

75. Ibid., 139.

76. Hite, *When the Romance Ended*, 20–22.

77. Pilar Calveiro, *Política y/o violencia: Una aproximación a la guerrilla de los años 70* (Buenos Aires: Editorial Norma, 2005), 11.

Epilogue

1. All references to this film are taken from *The Act of Killing*, directed by Joshua Oppenheimer (2013; San Antonio, TX: Drafthouse Films, 2014), DVD.

2. Indonesia's National Commission on Human Rights (2012) recommended legal investigations and eventual prosecutions of perpetrators, but the government in power at the time, that of Susilo Bambang Yudhoyono, ignored the charge. Current president Joko Widodo (2014–) has finally expressed the government's "remorse" for the genocide but still has proved reluctant to open the flood gates to justice. Impunity for the 1965–66 genocide continues to reign in the country.

3. The quoted phrases are taken from an interview with Oppenheimer. See Reihan Salam, "Joshua Oppenheimer on 'The Act of Killing,'" podcast 034, *The Vice*, February 28, 2014, https://www.youtube.com/watch?v=9ibGiP_9Jd8.

4. Judith Butler, *Precarious Life: The Powers of Mourning and Violence* (New York: Verso, 2004), 144.

5. Oppenheimer uses the term *moral vacuum* in his conversation with Reihan Salam. See Salam, "Joshua Oppenheimer on 'The Act of Killing.'"

6. Ibid.

7. Judith Butler, *Giving an Account of Oneself* (New York: Fordham University Press, 2005), 82.

8. Ibid., 136.

9. Horacio Verbitsky and Juan Pablo Bohoslavsky, "Introduction: State Terrorism and the Economy: From Nuremberg to Buenos Aires," in *The Economic Accomplices to the Argentine Dictatorship: Outstanding Debts*, ed. Horacio Verbitsky and Juan Pablo Bohoslavsky, trans. Laura Pérez Carrara (New York: Cambridge University Press, 2016), 2.

10. Kate Connolly, "Trial of Auschwitz Medic Hubert Zafke Suspended in Germany," *The Guardian*, February 29, 2016, https://www.theguardian.com/world/2016/feb/29/auschwitz-medic-hubert-zafke-trial-germany.

11. Ibid.

12. Verbitsky and Bohoslavsky, "Introduction: State Terrorism and the Economy," 15.

13. It is worth repeating here, as I mentioned in the prologue to this book, that the Chilean courts handed down the first landmark conviction of a civilian accomplice with a dictatorship-era crime in November 2017. Although compelling evidence does not yet exist to speak of a new chapter of Chilean transitional justice centered on civilian prosecutions, I remain hopeful that such a chapter will eventually open.

14. The full name of the 1948 Genocide Convention is the United Nations Convention on the Prevention and Punishment of the Crime of Genocide.

15. See Daniel M. Greenfield, "The Crime of Complicity in Genocide: How the International Criminal Tribunals for Rwanda and Yugoslavia Got It Wrong, and Why It Matters," *Journal of Criminal Law and Criminology* 98, no. 3 (2008): 924.

16. Ibid., 946–47.

17. Martin Meredith, *Coming to Terms: South Africa's Search for Truth*, foreword by Tina Rosenberg (New York: Public Affairs, 1999), 287.

18. Naomi Roht-Arriaza, "Why Was the Economic Dimension Missing for So Long in Transitional Justice? An Exploratory Essay," in *The Economic Accomplices to the Argentine Dictatorship: Outstanding Debts*, ed. Horacio Verbitsky and Juan Pablo Bohoslavsky, trans. Laura Pérez Carrara (Oxford: Oxford University Press, 2016), 25–26.

19. Ibid., 25.

20. Kathryn Sikkink uses the term *justice cascade* to refer to the ever-increasing number of prosecutions of human rights violators in both national and international courts. She makes compelling arguments about how, since Nuremberg, ideas and practice of postviolence accountability have spread around the globe. See Kathryn Sikkink, *The Justice Cascade: How Human Rights Prosecutions Are Changing World Politics* (New York: W. W. Norton, 2011). As evidence of this cascade in the case of Chile, Cath Collins notes: "By late 2014, over eight hundred individuals were or had

been under investigation or charges. Of these, about 290 had been finally convicted of at least one offense. However, due to relatively lenient sentencing, and the fact that short term prison terms are frequently commuted to noncustodial sentences, less than a third of those convicted of homicide or kidnapping actually served prison time." Cath Collins, "Human Rights Defense in and through the Courts in (Post) Pinochet Chile," *Radical History Review* 124 (January 2016): 135.

21. Steve J. Stern, *Reckoning with Pinochet: The Memory Question in Democratic Chile: 1989–2006* (Durham, NC: Duke University Press, 2010), 200.

22. Ibid.

23. Ibid., 344.

24. Ibid., 335.

25. María Olivia Mönckeberg, *La máquina para defraudar: Los casos Penta y Soquimich* (Santiago: Penguin Random House Grupo Editorial S.A., 2015), 14.

26. Ibid.

27. Stern names a series of actors who, in the Pinochet regime's final round of privatizations (1987), sought to ensure the long-lasting impact of neoliberal reforms: "In part, the final round of privatizations had an ideological purpose, in addition to reflecting policy beliefs. By targeting 'natural monopolies' such as energy and utilities, and establishing a program to create some worker-owned shares in companies, the new phase took a last step toward inscribing the neoliberal idea that private property and market-driven decisions by investors and consumers constituted the key to good economic management in *every* sector of life. The privatizations also served to expand material interest in and political protection for the new economic order and the Pinochet legacy. They rewarded regime allies with wealth and market opportunities, enhanced by bargain prices and technical subsidies, such as debt-and-share swaps that transferred US $500 million of foreign debt from the giant electric generating company ENDESA and its subsidiaries to the state. Economic favor and opportunity went not only to traditional private investors, such as the powerful and regime-friendly Cruzat-Larraín clan, but also to former high officials and their relatives and friends. Consider but a few examples. Between 1987 and 1990, the former minister of economics and minister of finance Sergio de Castro emerged as director of Soquimich, the newly privatized nitrate-iodine-lithium company; the former minister of labor and minister of mining José Piñera Echeñique turned up as president of Chilmetro and president of the Directorate of Chilectra, the privatized electric utility companies; the former executive secretary of the National Commission on Energy Bruno Philippi Yrarrázaval took over as president of the electric generating company Chilgener (also known as Gener). Meanwhile, Richard Büchi, brother of the former minister of finance and 1989 presidential candidate Hernán Büchi, took on the general manager position in Chilquinta, another privatized utility company, and Julio Ponce Lerou, at the time the son-in-law of Pinochet and very well connected to military circles, emerged as president of Soquimich." Stern, *Reckoning with Pinochet*, 27.

28. Mönckeberg, *La máquina para defraudar*, 436.

29. Ibid., 441.

30. Peter Kornbluh, "The Declassified Pinochet File: Delivering the Verdict of History," *Radical History Review* 124 (January 2016): 214.

31. Ibid., 214–15.

32. See Diana Taylor, *Disappearing Acts: Spectacles of Gender and Nationalism in Argentina's "Dirty War"* (Durham, NC: Duke University Press, 1997), 119–38, 255–65. On the issue of "percepticide," chapters 5 and 9 are particularly relevant.

33. For an eloquent reflection on this phenomenon, see Susan Sontag, *Regarding the Pain of Others* (New York: Farrar, Straus & Giroux, 1999).

34. Taylor, *Disappearing Acts*, 264–65, 259.

Index

Page numbers in italics refer to illustrations.

Beverley, John, 148, 164–65
Bisama, Álvaro, 192n5
Blanco, Fernando A., 84, 149–50
Bolaño, Roberto, 26; *Nocturno de Chile* (By Night in Chile), 51–52, 202n85
Bolívar, Simón. *See* Simón Bolívar 8800 detention center
Bombal, Carlos, 67
Borges, Jorge Luis: "Theme of the Traitor and the Hero," 79
boundedness, 21, 66, 94–97, 102, 107, 109–11, 113, 118–20, 151, 178, 187
Brodsky, Roberto, 26
Brown, Wendy, 193n8, 193n11, 206n54, 220n16
Brunner, José Joaquín, 155, 170–71
Büchi, Hernán, xiv, 225
Büchi, Richard, 225
Bussi, Hortensia, 29
Butler, Judith, 10, 16, 178–79, 194, 194n29; on accounting for oneself, 8, 17–18, 20, 34, 36, 40, 66; on boundedness, 96; on Levinas, 199n34; on vulnerability, 95–96
bystanders, 6, 10, 21, 116; behavioral options for, 109, 210n3; boundedness and, 97, 107, 119; complicity and, 92–94, 97; justice and, 92–94, 112; narratives and testimonies of, 94, 109, 118, 151; political learning and, 117–18; theatricality and, 94, 97; truth and, 94, 109, 111; vulnerability and, 95, 97

Cabezas, Iván, 4
cadavers, 66, 86, 113, 134–35
Callejas, Mariana, 11, *28*, *39*, 60, 72, 87, 120, 143, 151, 185, 196, 201n83; "Atajo" (Shortcut), 42–43; "¿Conoció usted a Bobby Ackerman?" (Did You Know Bobby Ackerman?), 29; conviction and sentencing of, 29, 50; death of, 29; diaries of, 33, 37–38, 198–99n29; DINA, 11, 19, 26–29, 32–35, 37, 40–41, 43, 49; double life of, 27, 43–44; early years of, 26–27; escapism and, 42, 47–48; first marriage of, 26–27; "Heil, Peter," 48–49; justice and, 48–52; *La larga noche* (The Long Night), 19, 29–30, 41–43, 45, 48, 197n15; Letelier crime and, 19, 27, 34–35, 37–38,

40–41, 45–46; literary career of, 29; Lo Curro mansion of, 27, 29, 35, 40, 51, 52, 197n14; marriage to Townley, 26; "Mediodía del lunes" (Monday at Noon), 42–43; Prats-Cuthbert crime and, 11, 19, 21, 26–27, 29–30, 34, 39–40, 45–47, 49–50, 94, 103–4, 196n9, 197n17; "Reflejo" (Reflection), 44–45; release from prison of, 29; secret shame and, 19, 29, 31, 49; shame and, 19, 24–26, 29–37, 40–44, 47–52, 201n77; *Siembra vientos* (You Reap What You Sow), 19, 29–30, 35–41, 45, 48, 197n17, 197–98n18; "Sobre Meyer" (About Meyer), 48; "¿Te acuerdas, Angélica?" (Do You Remember, Angélica?), 47–48; "Un parque pequeño y alegre" (A Small and Happy Park), 45–47
Calveiro, Pilar, 174
Campbell, Joseph, 161
capitalism, 7, 54, 74, 76, 110, 149, 151, 158–59, 167–69, 171
car bombings, 11, 45–46, 94, 196n9, 214n1
Castillo, Carmen, 158
Castillo, Jaime, 190–91n10
Castillo Velasco, Fernando, 64
Castro, Fidel, 27, 161
Casullo, Nicolás, 148–50
Catholic University (Pontificia Universidad Católica de Chile), xiv, 56, 74–75, 158; Campus Oriente (Eastern Campus), 85; *gremialista* (guild-based) movement, xiv–xv, 60, 74–75, 203n21; Law School, 60, 154; television network, 200n58. *See also* Chicago Boys
Caucoto, Nelson, 129, 139
Celedón, Roberto, 62
Central Intelligence Agency (CIA), 27, 41, 99, 106, 176
Central Nacional de Informaciones (National Information Center, CNI), 124–27, 134, 136–37, 142, 201n74, 215n12
Chadwick, Andrés, 84
Chicago Boys, xiv–xv, 20, 39, 57–58, 65, 74–78, 121, 166, 200n51, 207n71; authoritarianism and, xiv–xv, 207n71; *El ladrillo* (The Brick), xiv–xv, 74, 76

Chicago Boys (documentary), 4, 20, 57, 75-78
Chilean Communist Youth, 26, 37
Christian Democratic Party, 23, 27, 29, 54, 154, 189n3, 219-20n12
civil obedience, 6
civilians, role of in dictatorships, xiv-xvii, 4, 6, 12-14, 27, 59-60, 65, 93, 103-4, 111-12, 121-23, 138, 147
Clinic, The (satirical weekly), 4, 72, 121-22
Clinton, Bill, 185-86
cognitive dissonance, 24, 172
Cold War, 13, 26-27, 61, 78, 87, 91, 119, 149, 166, 176, 185, 190n9
Colectivo de Acciones de Arte (Art Action Collective, CADA), 114
complacency, 6-10, 13, 16, 23, 150-59, 168, 174, 185-86; defining, 156-57; etymology, 7
complicit autobiography, 40
complicity: chain-of-command situations and, 12; contributory agency and, 11-12; defining, 7, 10-11; defining wrongdoing and, 13-15; direct involvement and, 7; historical conceptions of, 12; "I" of first-person accounts and, 15-18; joint project of Pinochet regime and, 13-14; legality and, 12; memories of, 15-18; moral responsibility and, 13-15; spectrum of, 10-15. *See also* accomplices; bystanders; fictions of mastery; justice
Concertación de Partidos por la Democracia (Coalition of Parties for Democracy), xiv-xv, 4, 67, 71, 73, 83, 98, 117, 152, 155-56, 158-59, 167-71, 189n3; human rights and, 204n24; neoliberalism and, 202n85, 221n26. *See also* Nueva Mayoría (New Majority)
confession, 36, 38, 51, 66, 80, 123, 137, 149, 159-60, 184, 196n5, 199-200n49; ethics and, 35; pseudo-confessions, 18, 58; remorse and, 25; of Scilingo, 122, 215n8
conspiracy, 10, 88
conspirators, 11, 21
constitution (1833), 189n4
constitution (1980), xv, 14, 53, 59, 64, 83, 86
Contesse, Patricio, 72-73
Contreras, Gonzalo, 29

Contreras, Manuel, 21, 35, 56, 64, 83-84, 88, 104, 122, 124-25, 127, 133, 135, 138, 141, 214n4, 215n9
Correa, Enrique, 155, 170-71, 219n11
coup d'état (September 11, 1973), xiv, xvii, 11, 23, 26, 38, 55, 58, 60, 62, 74, 84, 98; fortieth anniversary of, xvii, 65, 87, 120-24, 126, 140-41, 147, 205n41; memory and, xix; thirtieth anniversary of, 70, 72
Cretton, Jean-Philippe: interview with Vergara, 22, 141-43, 218n46
Cristi, Renato, 56
Crónica de la transición (Chronicle of the Transition; Otano), 4
Cuba, 27, 154, 160-64, 221n33
Cuthbert, Sofía, 11, 21, 26-27, 46, 94-95, 104, 112-13, 115-16, 196n9

Dalí, Salvador: *The Hour of the Crackled Visage*, 36
de Castro Spikula, Sergio, xiv, 20, 58, 73-79, 85, 87, 94, 120, 151, 185, 207n71, 225n27
de Certeau, Jean: *El Mocito*, 21, 125-32, 142
Delle Chiaie, Stefano, 27, 197n17
de Man, Paul, 16, 36, 195n1
Demjanjuk, John, 179-80
denial, 18, 25, 32, 40, 143, 157, 198n27
Derrida, Jacques, 49, 54, 57, 212n40; *Specters of Marx*, 54
Díaz López, Víctor, 21, 124, 139, 144-45
DINA. *See* Dirección de Inteligencia Nacional (National Intelligence Directorate, DINA)
Dinges, John, 27, 37, 40, 197nn11-12, 198-99n29
Dirección de Inteligencia Nacional (National Intelligence Directorate, DINA), xvi-xvii, 11, 19, 26-29, 32-35, 37, 40-41, 43, 49, 82, 93-95, 103-6, 116, 124-33, 142-44, 147, 154; Lautaro Brigade, 131, 144
Dirty War (Argentina, 1976-83), 175, 180
disappeared, 3, 53, 98, 122, 125, 130, 146, 189n1, 216n22; bodies of, 214n8; families of, 6, 20, 58, 112, 207n64
disavowal, 19, 54, 58, 86, 110, 150, 174, 185. *See also* avowal
diversionary schemas, 16, 25, 194n33, 196n3

Echeverría Yáñez, Mónica, 151–52, 158, 221n33
economic freedom, xv, 75, 207n71
Eichmann, Adolf, 21, 63
Eichmann in Jerusalem (Arendt), 21, 93
El ladrillo (The Brick), xiv–xv, 74, 76
El Mercurio (newspaper), xvii, 23, 29, 84, 194–95n40, 197n15, 200n58, 202n86
El régimen de Pinochet (The Pinochet Regime; Huneeus), 4, 203n17
Eltit, Diamela: *El infarto del alma* (Soul's Infarct), 113, 212n35; *El padre mío* (My Father), 113, 212n35; *Puño y letra: Juicio oral* (In My Own Handwriting: An Oral Trial), 21, 93–119, 212n35
empathic listener, 129, 216n20
Enríquez, Miguel, 22–23, 153, 162, 169–70, 172
Enríquez-Ominami, Marco (ME-O), 22, 168–74, 184, 219n9, 221n33; *Animales políticos: Diálogos filiales* (Political Animals: Conversations between a Father and a Son), 22–23, 153, 172, 174; *Chile, los héroes están fatigados* (Chile, the Heroes Are Worn Out), 22, 153, 170–73
Ernest, Allen, 26–27
Errázuriz, Carmen, 81
Escalante, Jorge, 46, 133
escapism, 42, 47–48, 177
Espinoza Bravo, Pedro, 27, 49, 104, 197n12

Felman, Shoshana, 8, 36, 102
Fernández, Nona, 192n5, 216n25: *El taller* (The Workshop), 26; *Space Invaders*, 93
Fernández, Patricio, 72
Fernández Larios, Armando, 218n46
Ffrench-Davis, Ricardo, 75
fictions of mastery, 5, 19–20, 24–25, 36, 41, 51, 58, 65, 77, 95–96, 117, 176, 179, 186–88, 196n5
Fish, Stanley, 16
Flores, Nicolás, 115–16
Fontaine, Ernesto, 75–76
Foucault, Michel, 8, 16, 66–67
Franco, Francisco, xiv, 56, 59, 189n4
Franz, Carlos, 29
Frei Montalva, Eduardo, 19, 53
Fresno, Anita, 27
Freud, Sigmund, 17, 32, 101, 198n27

Friedman, Milton, xiv, 56–57, 69, 74, 200n51
Fuentes, Carola, 4, 20, 57, 75, 78. See also *Chicago Boys* (documentary)
FUNA-Chile, xv, 189n1

García Lorca, Federico: *La casa de Bernarda Alba* (The House of Bernarda Alba), 112–13
Garretón, Guillermo Óscar, 155, 166, 170–71, 219n11, 223n71
Gazmuri, Cristián, 56, 62
genocide, xvii, 3, 176–81
Genocide Convention, 180
ghosts, 19–20, 48, 53–58, 66, 79–80, 83, 85–91, 96–97, 202n85
Gilson, Erinn C., 110
Giving an Account of Oneself (Butler), 17, 194n29
Goffman, Erving, 159, 200n55, 221n28
Gómez Leyton, Juan Carlos, 70
Goodin, Robert E., 10–11, 13
Gordon, Avery, 86
gremialista (guild-based) movement, xiv–xv, 60, 74–75, 203n21
Gröning, Oskar, 180
Guevara, Ernesto "Che," 148, 161–62, 207n74
Guzmán, Jorge, 81
Guzmán, Nancy, 46, 122
Guzmán, Rosario, 83, 87–89, 205n41, 209n94; *Mi hermano Jaime* (My Brother Jaime), 88, 205n41; open letter of, 87–88
Guzmán Errázuriz, Jaime, xiv, 19, 59–62; assassination of, 56, 83–85, 87–88; at Catholic University Law School, 56, 60, 75; *Chicago Boys* (documentary) and, 57, 75–78; constitution (1980) and, 53, 59, 64, 83, 86; de Castro and, 20, 58, 73–79, 85, 87; "Declaration of Principles" (1974) and, 59; early years of, 59–60; *El tío* (film) and, 20, 58, 79–91; *Escritos personales* (Personal Writings), 61; Fiducia and, 59; *gremialismo* and, 60, 91, 203n21; on hierarchy of rights, 61–62; *homo neoliberal* and, 57–58, 73–79; human rights and, 55–57, 60–62, 64–65, 70–72, 75, 78, 82–83, 86, 91; ideology of, 59–65; influence of, 59–61; Longueira's hagiography of

privatization, 225n27; on truth commission, 190–91n10; on Vial's influence, 190n9

subjectivity: compartmentalization of, 25, 39–40, 44–47, 49, 51, 72, 86, 88, 165, 171, 174–75, 218n46; depoliticizing of, 20, 50–51, 58, 77, 115, 163, 177

sublimation, 32, 83

Suharto, 176–77

Supreme Court (Chile), xvii, 29, 50, 103–4, 116, 123, 170

Taylor, Diana, 186–87

technologies of the self (Foucault), 16

Teitelboim, Volodia, 28

theatricality, 21, 94, 97, 104, 107, 109, 112, 117, 177

Tironi, Eugenio, 22, 153–56, 158–60, 170–71, 173–74, 185, 221n28, 223n71; *Crónica de viaje: Chile y la ruta a la felicidad* (Chronicle of a Journey: Chile and the Road to Happiness), 153, 164–68; "Soy un capitalista reformador" (I Am a Capitalist Reformer), 168

Townley, Michael, 19, 26–27, 28, 33, 35, 37, 39, 40–41, 47, 60, 103, 143, 196n9, 197n14; DINA recruitment of, 27, 197n12; in Federal Witness Protection Program, 49; Lo Curro mansion of, 27, 29, 35, 40, 51, 52, 197n14; marriage to Callejas, 27; trial of, 197n17

transitional justice, 12–13, 181–82, 191n11, 191n13, 211n24, 224n13

transparency, 8, 19, 69, 73, 131, 137, 217–18n42

trauma, 3, 100–102, 105, 113, 115, 121, 128–29, 149, 167, 173–74, 198n27, 215n11

truth, justice and, 104–12; limits of, 97–101

Truth and Reconciliation Commission (TRC; South Africa), 13, 72, 181, 191n11

truth commissions, 13, 72, 136, 142, 176, 179, 181–82, 190–91n10, 191n11

Unión Democrática Independiente (Independent Democratic Union, UDI), 15–20,

23, 54, 57, 63–64, 67–73, 75, 77, 72–85, 87–88, 90–91, 183, 209n94, 209n97, 219n9; "La Paz Ahora" (Peace Now), 70, 72, 207n64; Spiniak Case, 67

University of Chicago, 60, 91, 209n94; and Chicago Boys, xiv–xv, 20, 39, 57–58, 65, 74–78, 121, 166, 200n51, 207n71

utopianism, 8, 34, 77, 155, 158, 161–62, 169, 185

Valdeavellano, Rafael, 4, 20, 57, 75. See also *Chicago Boys* (documentary)

Valdés, Reginaldo, 104

Vega, Pedro, 46–47

Velasco Letelier, Eugenio, 64

Vergara, Jorgelino ("El Mocito" [The Little Butler]), 21, 120–47, 130, 151, 185, 208n79, 213n59, 218n46; Cretton's interview with, 22, 141–43, 218n46; *El Mocito* (film) and, 21, 125–32, 142; Mosciatti's interview with, 22, 126, 134–38, 143, 147; normalizing of, 140–46

Vial, Gonzalo, 190n9

vulnerability, 8, 10, 26, 34–35, 87, 128–29, 132, 137, 179, 186–87; bystanders and, 95–97, 102, 109–10, 112–13, 117–19; invulnerability, 6, 18–19, 96, 109–10, 112, 118, 177; linguistically vulnerable, 96; self-referential discourse and, 17–19, 21–23

Watson, Julia, 15–16

Welz, Claudia, 32

Willikie Flöl, Christoph, 104

Zafke, Hubert, 180

Zalaquett, José, 105–6, 190–91n10

Zambelli, Hugo Alberto, 11–12, 21, 94–97, 102, 104–13, 116–20, 151, 185, 212n35

Zambra, Alejandro, 192n5, 216n26; *Formas de volver a casa* (Ways of Going Home), 93

Zara Holger, José, 104

Zerán, Faride, 171

Zionism, 27

Critical Human Rights